The SECRET to RAISING STRONG, and COMPASSIONATE GIRLS

A Guide for Parents of Girls Ages 3 to 13

No More Mean Girls

KATIE HURLEY, LCSW

author of *The Happy Kid Handbook*

Foreword by Michele Borba, EdD, bestselling author of *UnSelfie*

Advance Praise for *No More Mean Girls*

❖

"Katie Hurley's *No More Mean Girls* will be an oft-referenced book on my shelf because Hurley's expertise goes beyond the academic. She has real, practical experience working with girls, and their words are one of the most valuable parts of this book. Hurley's practical advice is a boon to any parent who hopes to ease a daughter through the challenging terrain of childhood and adolescence, particularly when that childhood is lived in the harsh spotlight of social media. This book will definitely be on my list of most recommended books for parents and teachers."

— Jessica Lahey, *New York Times* bestselling author of *The Gift of Failure*

"Katie Hurley does the impossible—she takes the mystery and angst out of parenting a teen girl by thoughtfully illuminating her thoughts and experiences. *No More Mean Girls* is not just a guide to raising healthy, independent, and capable women, it's a light toward a brighter future for us all. I hope this book reaches the hands of every parent, teacher, coach, mentor, and individual who plays a role in helping girls grow and thrive in today's world."

— Rachel Macy Stafford, *New York Times* bestselling author of *Hands Free Mama*, *Hands Free Life*, and *Only Love Today*

"The landscape of girlhood is constantly changing, and even the youngest girls are tasked with learning how to navigate tricky social situations and emotional upheaval. *No More Mean Girls* provides practical, research-based tips for raising strong, confident, and compassionate girls. A must-read for parents and educators!"

— Amy McCready, author of *The Me, Me, Me Epidemic*

"An essential handbook for parents, teachers, counselors, and anyone who is fortunate enough to contribute to the raising of our precious daughters. I can't recommend *No More Mean Girls* enough."
—Susan Stiffelman, MFT, author of
Parenting with Presence and *Parenting Without Power Struggles*

"Katie beautifully intertwines two decades of working with girls, the experience of raising a daughter, her own kind and compassionate heart, and practical solutions to effect positive change and produce one of the most important books of our time. This is a must-read for anyone raising, influencing, teaching, or coaching girls."
—Rebecca Eanes, author of *Positive Parenting*

"As a parenting author, mother of a daughter, and survivor of the mean girl scene myself, I found this book so insightful, helpful, and enlightening. Based on many years of Katie's professional experience, along with extensive proven research, she gives practical examples of how parents can work together with their daughters to help them navigate their life's journey through this challenging time. I can't recommend this book enough. I only wish it had been around sooner!"
—Jessica Joelle Alexander, coauthor of
The Danish Way of Parenting

"I highly recommend Katie's book. Now more than ever, young girls need to learn to stand tall and stick together. Katie Hurley's *No More Mean Girls* provides a blueprint for parents and educators to raise confident and compassionate leaders in a modern world. The key insight Katie provides is that we all share a responsibility to ourselves and to our girls to live by example and be the change we wish to see."
—Idina Menzel, Tony Award–winning actress and singer

NO MORE
MEAN GIRLS

NO MORE MEAN GIRLS

The Secret to Raising Strong,

Confident, and Compassionate Girls

KATIE HURLEY, LCSW

A TarcherPerigee Book

tarcherperigee

An imprint of Penguin Random House LLC
375 Hudson Street
New York, New York 10014

TarcherPerigee with tp colophon is a registered trademark of Penguin Random House LLC.

Most TarcherPerigee books are available at special quantity discounts for
bulk purchase for sales promotions, premiums, fund-raising, and educational needs.
Special books or book excerpts also can be created to fit specific needs.
For details, write: SpecialMarkets@penguinrandomhouse.com.

Library of Congress Cataloging-in-Publication Data

Names: Hurley, Katie, author.
Title: No more mean girls : the secret to raising strong, confident,
and compassionate girls / Katie Hurley, LCSW.
Description: New York : TarcherPerigee, [2018] | Includes
bibliographical references and index.
Identifiers: LCCN 2017031973 (print) | LCCN 2017042115 (ebook) |
ISBN 9781524704674 (E-book) | ISBN 9780143130864 (pbk.)
Subjects: LCSH: Daughters. | Parenting. | Girls—Psychology. |
Compassion. | Self-confidence.
Classification: LCC HQ777 (ebook) | LCC HQ777 .H87 2018 (print) |
DDC 306.874—dc23
LC record available at https://lccn.loc.gov/2017031973

Printed in the United States of America
5 7 9 10 8 6

Book design by Elke Sigal

For my brother, John Godbout,
and for my oldest friend, Sarah Tonetti (the dream team)

❁

To every girl who ever wonders, "Am I good enough?"
You are (and then some).

Words can break someone into a million pieces, but they can also put them back together. I hope you use yours for good, because the only words you'll regret more than the ones left unsaid are the ones you use to intentionally hurt someone.

—TAYLOR SWIFT

Contents

Foreword

"I don't want to go to school," Jenna told me. "All the girls hate me, so I'll just sit by myself again while they laugh at me. I can't take it anymore!" Peer cruelty is heartbreaking at any age, but Jenna was only seven years old.

Today's childhood reveals a troubling portrait for too many of our daughters—it can best be described as "mean, calculating, and back-stabbing." Whether rural or urban, rich or poor, the "New American Girl" seems crueler and more aggressive. Parents know it, and they worry for their daughters.

A Harris survey of 1,144 parents nationwide found that almost 70 percent of parents of three- to seven-year-olds worry that their children will be bullied.[1] What's more, parents of preschoolers and grade-school-age children are significantly more likely to worry than parents of teenagers. And our qualms are justified. Girl cruelty seems to be starting at younger ages.

Mean girl behavior is commonly referred to by professionals as relational or social aggression, but by worried parents as bullying. The mean girl's goal is to damage the victim's social standing by intentionally manipulating how others view her. And her methods are cold and calculated—they can include deliberately isolating or excluding the victim, spreading vicious rumors or posting scandalous lies online, and creating situations to publicly humiliate her. And humiliate is what the mean girl does.

Loss of friendships and social standing is psychologically damaging, and the isolation and harassment can be unbearable. Being taunted and shunned, or hearing cruel words or malicious gossip about yourself, are emotionally traumatizing and can be every bit as damaging as physical abuse. Those slights in childhood are devastating, but their emotional scars can last a lifetime.

Childhood should be a precious time to forge friendships, develop a strong identity, acquire resilience, and learn to care about others. Instead, too many young girls hate school; experience stress, social anxiety, and depression; dial down empathy; and fear forging friendships.

As much as we'd like to just will this problem away, the harsh girl scene is flourishing, and must be taken seriously. To *not* address the mean girl scene is far too damaging for our daughters' well-being. So, what's a parent to do? Well, you can stop wondering, because the answer to how to make "no more mean girls" a reality lies in your hands.

Katie Hurley has given us a gift: practical solutions that are culled from research to stop girl cruelty and help us raise emotionally healthy, compassionate, strong daughters. I know Katie and value her work. She cares deeply about children. Katie is a leading parenting expert who has spent most of her adult life studying child development; she has extensive experience working with children who have learning differences and struggle with anxiety and low self-esteem. And she has real credentials: Katie is a child and adolescent psychotherapist, researcher, and writer who has worked with girls as individuals, in groups, and with their families. She even has a young daughter. If anyone can transform queen hornets into caring bees, it's Katie Hurley.

No More Mean Girls is a veritable treasure chest of ways to help you help girls learn to love themselves, realize their talents, get along and empathize with others, find their inner courage, and lead more successful and fulfilled lives. Her ideas are based on sound child development theory and proven research, and designed to be used *with* your daughter. The fact is, this may well be the only book you will need to raise great girls. Katie shows you how to empower young girls to work together for a brighter, better future. She guides you each step of the way as you help your daughter:

- Develop the resilience, integrity, and empathy she'll need to lead a good life.
- Learn friendship-making strategies and skills to get along with others and build healthy relationships.
- Cultivate social-emotional skills and find the courage to stand up for herself and others.
- Stop aggression if she crosses the line to meanness and hurts those she cares about.
- Acquire healthy self-esteem and strong integrity from the inside out.
- Learn self-regulation, manage stress, and release negative energy and negative thoughts.
- Develop assertive communication skills and a strong voice, and learn to say no without guilt.
- Find her passion, recognize her talents, and realize her power to make a difference in the world.

But that's not all, Katie includes engaging stories about girls from her many years of practice who suffered from the mean girl scene, along with the solutions she offered their parents to turn their children's lives around. And she provides a wealth of fun activities to do with your daughter, like making courage cards if she needs a little courage on the go, challenge sticks to encourage her to take healthy risks, confidence sheets to help her remember that she is capable of overcoming obstacles, coping cards to use when challenges are overwhelming, as well as so much more. She even provides "Parent-Teacher Conference" boxes to help you pause and reflect on how to apply the strategies with your child.

But don't stop when you're done reading this book. Get on board with other moms. Hold discussions at your school. Bring in speakers. Suggest that parents read *No More Mean Girls*. Do whatever it takes, but start talking about the mean girl scene and how to stop it together.

"Today's girls have what they need to change the course of girlhood for generations to come," Katie points out. "They can be the generation of girls that finally stands together as one and shouts, 'Together, girls can!'"

Katie has given us the parenting road map to do just that. Let's stand tall, speak out together, and help our girls become all they can be. Consistently using Katie's ideas will help our daughters proceed through life with confidence and resilience—not only now but for the rest of their lives.

What a difference you will make!

—Michele Borba, EdD

Author's Note

I was the third of four children in my family. Nineteen months behind my brother and sandwiched between two sisters, I was always labeled "the quiet one." An introvert before "introversion" became a household word, I spent most of my time daydreaming and engaged in quiet play. I also struggled to find my voice.

I was fortunate in that my parents understood my quiet nature from day one. They supported me as I gradually worked my way out of my carefully constructed safety net and followed my own dreams. They cheered when I took big risks ("I want to play ice hockey with the boys!") and encouraged me when I met obstacles. Always, they walked by my side with guidance and unconditional love at the ready.

I always thought of my father as an accidental feminist. Together with my mother, he brought three girls into this world, and my parents seemed determined to make sure that we all had strong voices, an excellent education, and what is now popularly referred to as grit. Tons of grit.

At some point during my childhood, I became focused on the fact that women still didn't have the same opportunities as men. "Can girls do that?" was a question I asked over and over again (as only young children can do). If my incessant questioning bothered my father, he never let on. "Girls can!" he would reply, with equal enthusiasm each time. It became my battle cry as I grew, and it's a phrase that I repeat often to my own daughter today. The only catch is that I add one word: *Together*, girls can! It's time to empower our girls to work together for a better future. They don't have to compete . . . because together they win.

This book is written in memory of my dad, Jim Godbout, who taught me (in no particular order and among other things) that it's important to stand up for your beliefs, if you can count your friends on one hand you're doing just fine, at the end of the line all we really have is who we choose to be on any given day, and every girl can throw a perfect spiral ("Beat 'em at their own game, Kate!"). Girls can!

✿

Introduction

It takes a great deal of bravery to stand up to our
enemies, but just as much to stand up to our friends.
—*J. K. Rowling*

Remember when mean girls only existed in high school or
middle school? Remember when the queen bee narrative you saw on
TV seemed just a tad dramatic and exaggerated? Believe me, I know, I
miss those days too. Having worked with kids for many, many years,
I've seen the pushing down of mean girls (where mean girls once ruled
the middle school, we now see similar behaviors among much younger
girls) and the rise of unnecessary competition among young girls. I've
seen first-grade girls exclude others on purpose and third-grade girls go
to great lengths to publicly humiliate their peers. I haven't given up
hope just yet, though. I've seen those same girls learn to relate to their
peers and empathize with them. I've seen them transform from queen
bees to benevolent bees right before my eyes. We can help these girls,
I'm sure of it. The thing is, we have to start *right now*.

You have to get really good grades so that you don't get in
trouble and because everything counts now. But you can't brag
about your grades because that's rude to your friends, and you
don't want to be the girl who always brags. It's better to pretend

your grades are just okay. It's the same with sports. Obviously, you have to be the best one on the team, but you should never talk about being the best or brag about a really great game because the other girls will get hurt feelings and stop talking to you if you do that too much. You have to pretend sometimes, but it's fine. Everyone does it.

—A third-grade girl

Some groups dress the same. One group always dresses exactly alike: black leggings, white T-shirts, high ponytails, and Adidas. Sometimes they change their shirts and stuff, but they always dress the same. There's another group that wears Converse, and the sporty girls wear mostly yoga pants, but not always the same colors. My friends just wear whatever, but a lot of groups like to dress alike. I guess it's fun, but I'm glad I don't have to do that.

—A fifth-grade girl

The thing that bugs me the most is you can never have a bad day because someone else always has a worse day. If I say something about why I'm in a bad mood, three other girls start telling their stories so everyone has to listen to them. It's like the person with the worst story wins the lunch table. So I just don't tell anyone because what's the point?

—A sixth-grade girl

I don't know how to get a group because I'm new and everyone has a group. I had a group at my old school. Groups are good because you know you have friends.

—A first-grade girl

I don't exactly like to be a group "leader" because then you have to tell the group what to do, and kids don't like to be told what to do or if their ideas don't work. I like to be in the middle of the group and listen a lot and just do my part of the project.

—*A fourth-grade girl*

The popular girls are pretty, and the boys laugh at all their jokes. They aren't always mean, but they don't like to make new friends.

—*A third-grade girl*

On my first day of graduate school at the University of Pennsylvania, I sat in a crowded auditorium with a large group of strangers, wondering how to start over again. Nervous chitchat filled the room until a professor stood before us and asked us to take out a paper and a pen and answer one simple question: Who are you? We were asked to write down the many roles we played in life, but we only had one minute to do it. I quickly scribbled a list of roles: daughter, sister, granddaughter, friend, nanny, student, and a few others I can't recall. At the very end, with a few seconds left on the clock, I wrote, "I AM ME," in bold letters. Years later I would stumble across that list in my old bedroom and wonder why I didn't just write that simple phrase and leave it at that. Why is it that being "me" never felt like enough?

In over 18 years of working with children and adolescents, I've witnessed a few common themes in girl world. One is that, despite living in a time when women are making great leaps in many fields, young girls are still conditioned to question themselves at every turn. Another is that girl world is infected with competition right now, and not the healthy kind that leads to risk taking and limit pushing. Finally, low self-esteem, which has a direct impact on things like assertiveness and self-confidence, is a significant roadblock for many young girls. In fact, the quotes you just read span those 18 years (and that's a very small sample). Bottom line: Growing up girl has never been easy, and it's time to help our youngest girls and hopefully get ahead of some of the negativity.

In 2008, the Dove Self-Esteem Fund released the findings of a survey they commissioned titled "Real Girls, Real Pressure: A National Report on the State of Self-Esteem," and the results were startling.[1] Results of the survey (which included input from more than 4,000 girls between the ages of 8 and 17) indicated that there is a self-esteem crisis for young girls that affects everything from family relationships to academic performance to peer relationships to how they look. The survey showed that 7 in 10 girls feel that they are not good enough or do not measure up in some way. It also showed that 62 percent of all girls feel insecure or unsure of themselves, and 75 percent of girls with low self-esteem reported engaging in negative activities (examples include disordered eating, bullying, and cutting, to name a few) when feeling bad about themselves.

A 2006 study conducted by Girls, Inc., a nonprofit organization that inspires girls to be "strong, smart, and bold," sheds even more light on the silent struggles that girls endure.[2] Fifty-six percent of girls responding to the survey agreed that girls are expected to speak softly and not cause trouble, 44 percent agreed that the smartest girls in school are not popular, 60 percent reported that they often feel stressed, and 69 percent of girls reported being concerned about their appearance. Two more numbers of note from this study: 74 percent of girls said they were under a lot of pressure to please everyone, and 45 percent said girls are told not to brag about things they do well. As it turns out, that third-grade girl who warned me about the dangers of showcasing your talents was simply responding to societal pressure that girls internalize every single day.

While some of these numbers probably triggered a feeling of

complete and utter panic in some of you (I know I broke into a cold sweat when I first read them), I'm here to tell you that there is good news in all of this. First things first: The Dove Self-Esteem Fund reports that the top wish among all girls is for their parents to communicate better with them. We can do that! Second, their numbers show that 91 percent of girls ages 8 to 12 turn to their mothers as a resource when they feel bad about themselves, and 54 percent (in that same age group) turn to their fathers.[3] This, right here, is the coveted silver lining in all of this. Yes, girls are struggling. Yes, relational aggression remains a problem, and it's happening at younger ages (more on that in chapter 1). Yes, very young girls are conflicted and internalizing mixed messages about growing up girl. But they are seeking help from Mom and Dad.

There are a lot of wonderful resources out there to help parents help their girls navigate the often tricky middle and high school years, but the fact is that young girls (think preschoolers on up) are struggling with these sophisticated "big girl" problems without the necessary skills to cope. My office sometimes feels like a revolving door of girl-world problems, and the parents are often shocked and confused by the issues their early elementary (even kindergarten) girls face on any given day.

That's where *No More Mean Girls* comes in. I've worked with girls as individuals, in groups, and with their families. One thing I've seen many times over is that the earlier girls work through these confusing and sometimes messy social and emotional conundrums, the better off they are at navigating tricky situations in middle school, high school, and beyond. *No More Mean Girls* is written with younger girls in mind. You'll find information and strategies to help your girls from preschool through middle school with developing friendships; dealing with relational aggression and other forms of bullying; and developing self-esteem, assertiveness skills, resiliency, and more. This isn't just another parenting book meant to guide parents through the storm; this is a book to use *with* your daughter. This is a journey you can take together.

No More Mean Girls is a call to action to empower young girls to work through their obstacles, work together, and build each other up. Girls have the power to flip the script on the "queen bee" narrative and reach for the high bar as a collective group. They don't have to push each other down in an effort to succeed, and they don't have to fight for social status. They can be kind, confident, and resilient while supporting one another through the ups and downs of childhood and adolescence.

The therapist in me wants to share every piece of interesting research on growing up girl to help you see the bigger picture, but the parent in me knows that time is always a commodity. With that in mind, *No More Mean Girls* highlights some interesting research findings, but it's balanced with anecdotes that bring these issues to life and with actionable steps your daughter can take to work through her own struggles. While you certainly can read this book chapter by chapter, you can also skip around and read about the subject matter that applies to your daughter right now. One thing I know about girls is that they shift and change almost overnight. I've seen highly confident girls suddenly question every thought they have and girls with low self-esteem morph into assertive girls. You might find that friendship building is the pressing issue right now, but peer pressure becomes the new problem to tackle in just a few months.

When you see "Parent-Teacher Conference" boxes along the way, that's your cue to stop and digest some key points that will help you process the information before you work through it with your daughter. You might find a list of symptoms of low self-esteem, for example, followed by some talking points to help start some of these difficult parent-child conversations. I call these boxes the "Parent-Teacher Conference" because as much as parents tend to seek resources when their kids are struggling, teachers spend the majority of the day with our girls. They are in the trenches. It is my greatest hope that both parents and teachers will utilize this book as a resource.

The "Girls Can!" sections provide activities and strategies to use *with* your daughter. That "with" is actually super important. When I ask girls what they want most from their parents, I hear a lot of "to spend time with me," "to just listen," and "to help me without telling me what to do." Make no mistake, our girls want our help (despite the eye rolls, feet stomping, and door slamming that sometimes occur), but they want us to work *with* them. They don't want the same tired advice ("Just don't let it get to you") or the one story they've heard 70 billion times. They want us to connect, to listen, and to get through this complicated stuff together.

Here's the deal: I would love for you to read some of this book *with* your daughter. Or at least read the "Girls Can!" parts of it to her. As a mom, I know all too well the pull to protect my daughter from the bad stuff, but as a therapist I know that when I talk about stuff like relational aggression, self-esteem, media (including social media, TV, movies, and music), and cyberbullying (in all its many forms) with my daughter, I empower her. I guide her through it and give her the information she needs to make positively navigating murky territory like Snapchat (or whatever the next big thing is) a little easier. Do this together. Resist the urge to read and lecture, and instead talk openly about this stuff.

Here's what I don't want you to do: feel guilty about the choices you've made so far or worry that you're doing it all wrong. You're not. I hear this from parents more than you might think. They read my writing (or sit and listen in my office) and instead of seeing the possibilities, they see the so-called failures. There's a reason #momfail is a popular hashtag. We all feel it at times. This time, as you read this book, look for the possibilities. Look for the course corrections that will help your daughters thrive as they grow.

As you read *No More Mean Girls*, you might find that you feel overwhelmed at times. This is difficult subject matter, especially given that we're talking about very young girls. We all want to protect our girls from things like relational aggression, cyberbullying, and social exclusion, and sometimes it might even feel like avoidance of these topics works to some degree. But if we don't deal with what's happening around us, we never truly learn to cope.

There's also the issue of parental guilt. Believe me, you're not alone on that front. If you read something about how sarcasm affects our girls and your gut check leaves you feeling guilty on that one, give yourself permission to shed that guilt. Parenting is trial and error most of the time. It's messy, complicated, and downright overwhelming, but it's also heartwarming, fulfilling, and beautiful. You can't beat yourself up about what you *might* have done. What you can do is meet your daughter where she is and start there today. You can move forward in a new light and make positive changes that help your daughter thrive.

Girls are growing up in a rapidly changing world, and girlhood is full of obstacles. *No More Mean Girls* is here to help you navigate those obstacles and raise strong, confident, and compassionate young girls. Now get to it!

NO MORE
MEAN GIRLS

CHAPTER 1

What's in a Friend?

The way we will survive is by being kind.
—*Amy Poehler*

My mom says [my classmate] is a mean girl. You know? Like the queen bee? The one who tells everyone else what to do and who to talk to?
—*A third-grade girl*

Mean girls and queen bees certainly aren't a new phenomenon, and these popular labels have been around for quite some time now, but hearing those words out of the mouth of an eight-year-old girl was a bit jarring. I didn't know the "mean girl" in question, so my frame of reference was limited. What I did know was the girl in front of me had her mind made up: That other girl was labeled and placed in the "Do not friend" file.

The "mean girl" narrative is so old that it even pops up in literature I read as a child. In fact, when I began reading a well-loved copy of *Little Women* to my daughter not long ago, I found (two pages in) that "mean girls" have a long history in the life of girls:

"I don't believe any of you suffer as I do," cried Amy, "for you don't have to go to school with impertinent girls, who plague you if you don't know your lessons, and laugh at your dresses, and label your father if he isn't rich, and insult you when your nose isn't nice."[1]

For reference, Louisa May Alcott first published *Little Women* in two installments in 1868 and 1869. Yes, mean girls come with the territory of girlhood, it seems. What's different is that those queen bees are getting younger and younger.

I was working as a school-based therapist in Los Angeles in early 2001 when I first noticed a subtle shift in the way elementary school girls related to one another. It was a small school, and the kids generally got along, but the tides turned for one particular group of girls in fourth grade. Together since first or second grade, they knew each other well and always sat in the same spots for lunch every day. Until they didn't. One day, three girls broke off and left the others devastated.

Molly was the first to come to me, a look of pure outrage across her face. In fairness, Molly was often outraged about something—homework, lessons she found boring, not enough to do at recess. She was the kind of kid who had advocacy running through her blood. On this particular day, the outrage was more personal. She was the first out to lunch and secured the usual table. Two of her daily lunch mates sat down within minutes, but three others never showed. After scanning the playground, Molly caught sight of them sitting under some trees.

In Molly's version of events, she walked over to the girls and politely inquired about why they weren't with the group. I knew her well enough to know that she likely marched over, fists clenched at her sides, demanding answers. Either way, the answer was a blow to Molly. "We just want to be alone today."

Had this been a one-time occurrence, it wouldn't have mattered much. But day after day for nearly a month, the three girls took off without inviting the others. They moved their seats in the classroom. They stopped playing with the other girls during recess. It was as if they formed a completely separate group. And the ones left behind felt hurt, confused, and abandoned.

At the time, I struggled to make sense of *how* the group reached that point. Sure, friends argue and kids often make new friends and move on from friendships that aren't working. But this felt different. It was as if someone took a giant Sharpie and drew a clear line down the middle of the group. Was it media influence? Older siblings? Did something catastrophic happen within the group? In reality, it wasn't any of those things. It was a powerful combination of frustration and poor communication skills.

After what felt like thousands of grievances and explanations coming in from both sides of the issue, I decided to offer a new solution. I created a girls' lunch group that met once a week during the lunch/recess period. It was open to any girl who wanted to join, and it was often packed. As it turned out, the girls were fairly bored at recess, and this negatively affected their relationships. They were high on complaints but low on solutions.

The larger problem, however, was that they were growing up and growing apart and needing some space some of the time, but they weren't communicating those feelings. Instead of talking to each other, they split off. Issues that annoyed them but went unsaid in an effort to avoid being "mean" came out in those lunch groups. It was slow at first, but a few weeks in they were sharing and communicating and yelling and apologizing. They talked about behaviors that bugged them (like one girl who always took over every conversation) and what they really wanted from a friend. It wasn't always perfect, but they were learning to work through the stuff that bothered them and caused them to pull away from one another.

If I'm being honest, there were weeks when I was convinced that this plan to reunite friends and teach social skills wasn't even making a dent in the problem. I didn't use a curriculum because I wanted to meet these girls where they were and go from there. It was complicated by the fact that the group was large and the lunch/recess period was short. But the day that I asked each of them to write a friendship compliment (a kind thought about one of their friends) on a balloon and toss it in the air was the day that everything changed. The girls laughed together as they tossed balloons around the room. They jumped around, joked, and acted like kids again. They let go of their insecurities and got lost in the moment. After that, they began to find their way again. Little by little, they chipped away at the negativity and worked through their friendship struggles. They also learned an important lesson: They could be friends and support one another without sitting in the same seats each day and following each other around.

In recent years, I've seen this behavior in girls as young as kindergarten. Behavior that was once considered middle school-ish in nature has trickled down to the early elementary years. By middle school, many girls have more complex social relationships. When they exclude others, spread gossip, or take to social media to air their grievances about other girls, they do it with intent to hurt. Young children, on the other hand, don't yet have the advanced social skills to understand this behavior, but they do engage in it. When a group decides to exclude one girl, for example, many of the girls in the group are likely to know that it's wrong and even feel uncomfortable about it, but they won't necessarily have the language to express it or the assertiveness skills to put a stop to it. Bystanders are everywhere.

A young girl midway through kindergarten came to me wringing her hands and staring at her feet. Silenced by guilt, she struggled to get a word out. A few rounds of Uno later, she finally met my eyes and started to cry. She had made a "huge" mistake that day. Two girls told

Parent-Teacher Conference

Young children tend to engage in black-and-white (all-or-nothing) thinking and other cognitive distortions. Watch for these kinds of thought patterns when it comes to friendship troubles:

- ✿ **Overgeneralizing**—Making a broad conclusion based on a single incident (e.g., I left her out one time, and she was upset, so now she'll never want to hang out with me).

- ✿ **Catastrophizing**—Putting more weight on the worst possible outcome than makes sense given the circumstances (e.g., She'll never be my friend because I don't play soccer).

- ✿ **Magnifying or minimizing**—These are the "mountains out of molehills" kids.

- ✿ **Mind reading**—These kids tend to infer (incorrectly) another child's thoughts based on behavior or facial expressions.

- ✿ **Blaming**—Some kids can always find a way to blame the other child.

- ✿ **Discounting the positive**—Some kids will see a positive communication as a mistake and focus on the perceived negatives instead (e.g., She only said "hi" because I was with her other friend; she really doesn't like me).

- ✿ **Predicting outcomes**—These are the fortune-tellers (e.g., I know that group won't want me to sit with them, so I won't try).

- ✿ **All-or-nothing thinking**—I see this one a lot with young girls (e.g., She didn't sit at my table, so obviously we aren't friends anymore).

her that to play house with them she had to leave her closest friend behind. She really wanted to play house at recess that day, but it came at a price. The price was that it wasn't any fun. She spent the whole recess looking over at her friend, who was alone in the yard, wishing that she could go back in time and change her mind. Instead of breaking away to apologize, she watched and stood silent. She didn't think she could fix the problem, so instead she worked herself into a stomachache and worried that her best friend was lost forever. She made a big assumption that day, and that assumption (which was, in fact, incorrect) caused emotional upset for her friend and for her.

One thing I have found over and over again in my practice is that young girls struggle with the art of friendship making. Years ago, preschools and kindergarten classrooms spent a fair amount of time working on things like social skills and character development. These days, childhood is on fast-forward, and kids are cruising through the early years without learning essential life skills. They don't have the time to practice friendship skills, and they don't get the necessary feedback to learn better ways to relate.

When I was in fourth grade, I started a girls' club with my best friend and one other friend. It was an impulse club, most likely started to keep meddling brothers away. We spent one Saturday afternoon in my best friend's basement making signs for our nonexistent clubhouse. We called ourselves the Smelly Sneakers. Pretty catchy, don't you think? And we made the colossal mistake of discussing the club the following Monday morning at school. By lunch, word had spread, and the teacher called us in to talk about what it feels like to be left out. Despite the fact that the club was nothing but a poster and a funny name (it wasn't our intention to be "exclusive"; we just happened to play together that day), clubs were outlawed and the Smelly Sneakers came to a quick demise. The three of us learned an important lesson: Even when you think something is just funny, you might hurt someone else's feelings. Think twice.

In hindsight, that was an early peek into what could have become relational aggression. Our teacher took the time to teach us about the potential impact of a secret club. She might not have used words like "empathy" and "compassion," but she did get us thinking about what it would feel like to be the one on the outside. When we went back out to play, we joined the larger group, and that was the end of clubs. From that point on, we all played in groups during recess based on what we wanted to play. That was then; this is now.

With young girls living fairly scripted lives—playdates are planned on their behalf, afternoons are full of structured activities (coached or taught by adults), weekends are jam-packed with games and parties (overseen by adults)—they don't have the opportunities to practice these necessary friendship skills. The Smelly Sneakers might have been a friendship fail, but three girls learned some very important lessons from it, and that translated to better social skills down the line. Unfortunately, girls don't always have the time or opportunities to learn these important social skills on their own because their days are heavily supervised.

What Is Relational Aggression?

Relational aggression plays a significant role in girl world right now. I can't tell you how many messages I field about this very topic. Part of the problem is that it's confusing at best. It's difficult for girls, parents, and teachers to determine when an act of unkindness is a social misstep due to lack of sophisticated social skills versus when it's a deliberate act to harm another girl. Relational aggression is also very difficult to spot. Things like alliance building and gossip can be carried out in whispers (or under the cover of technology), making it hard for teachers to "see" the behavior in real time.

The Ophelia Project, a national nonprofit organization with expertise in relational aggression, defines relational aggression as "behavior that is intended to harm someone by damaging or manipulating his or her relationships with others."[2] A few fast facts shared by the Ophelia Project paint a fairly grim picture. According to their statistics, 48 percent of students are regularly exposed to relational aggression.[3] Another study shows that students ages 11–15 reported that they were exposed to 33 acts of relational aggression during a typical week.[4]

Being the victim of relational aggression can come with some long-term consequences. In fact, relational aggression is said to be as painful and devastating as physical blows, and the negative effects of these behaviors can last even longer.[5] Part of this is no doubt due to the fact that relational aggression is hard to spot, and that makes it difficult to address. When girls do come forward, it's often viewed as "girl drama" (my least favorite word combination ever), or it quickly becomes a "she said—she said" debate. It's a lose-lose for the victim (and the aggressor, if we're being honest, because she doesn't learn how to be a better friend or how to stop hurting other girls).

Relational aggression comes in many forms these days, and advances in technology mean that very young girls are dealing with some very mature issues, whether or not they're developmentally prepared to do so. The average age that a child gets a smartphone is 10.3 years. That's roughly fourth grade. But what it really means is that there are some younger girls walking around with technology in their pockets. Once upon a time, relational aggression was restricted to note passing and rumor spreading, but these days a group text can take down a child in an instant. Is sheltering our daughters from technology the answer? No. Understanding what's happening, familiarizing ourselves with the communication patterns of the modern girl, and educating our girls is a much better approach.

To that end, it helps to know a bit about relational aggression. Gossip, rumor spreading, public embarrassment, social exclusion, and alliance building are all considered forms of relational aggression. Not

Parent-Teacher Conference

Relational aggression has been observed in kids as young as preschool and comes with big consequences:

- ❀ School absences
- ❀ Mental health issues (depression, anxiety, suicidal thoughts)
- ❀ Headaches and stomachaches
- ❀ Poor academic performance
- ❀ Behavioral problems (at school and at home)
- ❀ Eating disorders
- ❀ Substance abuse

sure what that means or where to draw the line between, say, wanting to sit with another kid and exclusion? You're not alone. This stuff is difficult to deal with because so much of it flies under the radar. And while an act of relational aggression might seem purposeful and intended to harm, it can also be a sign of poor social skills. That's why it's vital that we teach girls about the whole arc of friendship making early on. We can't sit around and wait for social blunders to morph into relational aggression; we have to be proactive. We owe it to our girls to help them understand how their actions can negatively affect others and what to do instead.

Seven-year-old Sophia had a best friend. She always spent lunch and recess with her, and they played together after school a few days a week. In second grade, however, the girls landed in different classrooms. Sophia quickly made three new friends and invited them to join her and her best friend for lunch. Later that day, her best friend issued a threat: Stop hanging out with those girls or I won't be your friend anymore. Sophia was torn. She liked her new friends, but she didn't want to lose her *best* friend. She did what many girls in her position would do: She gave the new friends the silent treatment and stuck with her best friend. Within a few weeks, the so-called "best" friend found her own new friends and left Sophia in the dust. Sophia's mom blamed Sophia for making poor choices. Her teacher chalked it up to "growing pains." But Sophia was devastated.

Sophia's case is a tricky one, as many of these instances are with young girls, because she played the parts of both victim and aggressor. When her best friend threatened to abandon her, she felt scared and upset. She didn't want to lose a friendship that dated back to kindergarten. Instead of seeking help, standing up to her best friend, or taking turns sitting with her best friend and her new friends, however, she turned around and silenced the new friendships without a second thought. She didn't do it to act mean; she genuinely liked those girls and wanted to make new friends, but the fear of losing the "best" friend was too much to process. She ended up alone and anxious as a result.

Maggie was in third grade when the trouble began. A very highly social girl by nature, she had a large group of friends that formed in kindergarten and stayed together despite different teachers and teams in the years to come. Midway through third grade, however, the tides turned. The girls she knew and trusted began to tease and taunt her. At first, it was whispers and giggles each time she left her seat. It escalated to dropping tiny balls of tissue on her seat that stuck to her black leggings when she stood up. Before long, there were subtle threats. "Do you think it would hurt if she sat on tacks?" All of this went unnoticed by the teacher, as it all happened in whispers behind notebooks and textbooks.

As bad as the classroom taunting felt, it was the lunch table antics that caused the most public humiliation. While experts often caution educators to look for the child who has no one to sit with, I would

Parent-Teacher Conference

Be on the lookout for these signs that a young girl might be the victim of relational aggression:

❀ Anxious or nervous behaviors (nail biting, hair twirling, clinging)

❀ Psychosomatic complaints such as headaches or stomachaches, particularly before school or social events

❀ Often alone during lunch and appears to lack friends

❀ Appears withdrawn or depressed

❀ Avoids recess or sits alone at recess

❀ Change in academic performance

❀ Acts out in class or at home; might even turn the tables and bully others

❀ Talks about having no friends or being "hated"

❀ Talks about death or engages in self-harm behaviors such as cutting

❀ Sleep disturbance

❀ Changes in eating habits

caution that we should also look for the child who appears visibly upset while the rest of the table laughs.

One day, Maggie and her closest friend sat at their usual table. They attempted to trade snacks without getting caught while discussing Dork Diaries, as they did most days. Until the former friends arrived. Three girls sat down directly across from Maggie and her friend. Maggie, being the more social of the two, said hello and smiled before getting back to her conversation. The leader of the pack, described by Maggie as "tall and perfect looking," looked directly at Maggie and said (in a booming voice for all to hear), "This table *smells*. Let's get out of here." The leader's two sidekicks shrugged their shoulders at Maggie and her friend as they grabbed their lunches and moved on. Laughter from nearby tables echoed through Maggie's ears as she sat there in a stunned silence.

You might think that was the worst of it. It wasn't. When the girl who seemed to dislike her the most found out that Maggie saw a therapist, she pounced. She waited ever so patiently for the teacher to step one foot into the hallway one morning and announced, "My mom said that Maggie has so many troubles that she has to see a therapist." Nervous giggles filled the air while Maggie put her head down on her desk. She was done.

Gossip and Rumors

I once asked Maggie if she had ever experienced the power position—if she was ever considered the leader of the pack. Without hesitation she replied, "No way. I'm not pretty enough or perfect enough to be the one they all like. You have to be *really* pretty for that." My heart sank as the words left her mouth. She didn't cry. She didn't appear angry. In fact, she didn't seem to have any emotional response to this at all. In Maggie's world, this was simply a matter of fact.

I could tell you that Maggie was incredibly bright. She taught herself to read before kindergarten, and she was always above grade level in math. I could tell you that she spent her weekends riding horses, training for equestrian competitions. I could tell you that she was kind, empathic beyond what you would expect from an eight-year-old, and loyal to a fault. I could tell you that she never gave up on those friends, even when they were at their worst. I could give you a long list of her positive traits. Sadly, none of that mattered in third-grade girl world.

What mattered most, evidently, were the rumors and gossip spread by one other girl in the social hierarchy.

Gossip and rumors are difficult to address with young children, partially because it's difficult to understand the impact of these things

Parent-Teacher Conference

It's important to talk about the words "gossip" and "rumors" early and often. We can't protect young girls from gossip and rumors, but we can empower them to rise above them.

Gossip: Noun. 1. Information about the behavior and personal lives of other people. 2. Information about the lives of famous people. 3. A person who often talks about the private details of other people's lives.[6]

Rumor: Noun. Information or a story that has been passed from person to person but has not proven to be true.[7]

Try some of these questions to get girls thinking about gossip and rumors:

- ✿ Is gossip always mean?
- ✿ How does it feel when you tell a friend a secret but your friend tells another person?
- ✿ How does it feel to be the one spreading those secrets?
- ✿ What's the difference between gossip and rumors?
- ✿ When does sharing stories become gossip?
- ✿ Is it ever okay to share information about others? When?
- ✿ How is gossip spread? (word of mouth, notes, technology)
- ✿ What can you do to repair the damage if you are the one spreading gossip?

unless you've experienced it (either on your own or through a best friend) and partially because we live in a world that runs on gossip. Taking a "sneak peek" into the lives of others has become a national pastime, so much so that people take sides when it comes to topics like celebrity divorce (remember those "Team Jen" hats?) and post heartfelt (and almost heartbreaking) RIP messages on social media when an icon passes away unexpectedly (simply because that icon once wrote a song or book that moved them). People engage in heated debates about politicians and actively seek out what would otherwise be classified as "personal information" in an effort to prove their point: "See! I was right about that one!"

In our need to understand celebrity culture and normalize just about everything (Alert! Ben Affleck ate an ice cream cone!), the lines have become irreparably blurred. We think we know these people (sorry to be the bearer of bad news here, but we don't), and somehow that gives us the right to watch and criticize their every move. But does it? And is *this* how we treat people we know and respect? What message are we trying to send?

You might think that you can protect your daughter from the worldwide rumor mill by avoiding it, but I find that difficult, at best. I'm not one for magazines full of lies and ill-timed photographs of "celebrities: they're just like us," but I find them difficult to avoid. Grocery stores, pharmacies, newsstands, salons, medical office waiting rooms, and countless other areas where kids sometimes have to sit and wait are full of them.

"She looks nice." I turned to see my daughter staring at a picture of Jennifer Aniston. She did, indeed, "look nice" in that photo, but the caption was anything but nice. I quickly scanned the other covers before breaking it down for her: "The truth is that most of these magazine stories aren't true. I'm not exactly sure why these stories are so popular, but I suspect that sometimes people just want to feel like we're all the same. But take a closer look. Three covers have pictures of her, and they all have different headlines. One says she's having a baby girl, another says she wants a baby, and the last one says she's getting a divorce. These are rumors, and they hurt people, even celebrities. They have feelings too." We left it at that for a while, but later that night we had a long discussion about how rumors start and why they spread. We also discussed ways to stop a rumor.

The fact is that gossip and rumor spreading are easy tools for targeting another child when it comes to relational aggression. While text messaging and social media (yes, even nine-year-olds have figured out that if you fudge your date of birth, you can get access) have certainly exacerbated the problem, my conversations with young girls continue to show that gossip and rumors are a huge problem at elementary and middle school campuses.

More often than not, when I talk to rumor spreaders, they fail to see the damage the rumors inflict on other girls. In fact, many girls

Parent-Teacher Conference

Instead of attempting to brush rumors and gossip under the rug (or "nip it in the bud"), take the opportunity to talk to young girls about ways to be an "upstander" (someone who stands up for others).

✿ Refute the rumor.
✿ Meet a negative with a positive.
✿ Say something kind to the victim of the rumor.
✿ Get help from an adult.

get so much positive feedback from rumor spreading that they don't think about the victims at all. I always ask girls (both aggressors and victims) about what they gain from gossip and rumors. The responses tend to sound like this:

- When I have the latest info on someone, other girls want to hear my story.
- Sharing stories about other girls helps me fit in.
- Gossiping is fun!
- Everyone gossips!
- Telling something bad about another girl makes me seem like I'm better than her.
- If I'm mad at my friend, I can share her secrets to get back at her.

A fourth-grade girl once told me that it's not the rumors and gossip that are so bad, it's getting caught. She explained a complicated system of gossip that occurred at her lunch table most days. It can't be the same person with the latest scoop each time or else everyone will know that that girl is just a gossip. The story has to be exciting and have some hook that keeps the other girls interested, but if it's too big, the other girls will know it's a complete lie. Also? You can't one-up another girl's story, especially if the other girl is in the leadership position. That's decidedly uncool in the elementary and middle school years.

While I hear parents chalk this stuff up to lack of knowledge (I don't think she even knows what she's talking about), the stories girls tell me paint a much different picture. In the above-mentioned case, for example, girls have to consider timing, content, and who else has a story to tell. That's a lot of pieces to consider before starting a rumor or spreading gossip. It sure doesn't seem like the work of the naïve at heart.

Building Alliances and Social Exclusion

Gossip and rumors aren't the only forms of relational aggression that negatively affect young girls. Carefully constructed (and often destructed without a moment's notice) alliances ensure that girls have support when they need it, but they also come at a cost. One wrong move and girls can be ousted from the alliance without care or warning. As humiliating as gossip and rumors can be, alliances are downright devastating for many young girls.

Nearing the end of her first-grade year, Annie thought she had a nice group of recess buddies. Though Annie was a floater and sometimes switched groups based on the nature of the play, she played with two girls at least three days a week. One day Annie decided to invite another girl to join them. Annie knew this girl to be silly and to enjoy playing pretend, and she thought it would be fun to have another person in the group. She thought wrong. The other two separated themselves from Annie and her friend. At lunch, they stayed away from her. It was after school that the two girls pulled Annie aside and issued a dire warning: "We don't like her. She's annoying. She's not in our group. If you're friends with her, you can't be friends with us." Annie was both heartbroken and utterly confused. What happened to "the more the merrier?" She genuinely enjoyed the other girl, and she knew that her two friends weren't being kind, but she didn't know what to do. She faked a stomachache (or she didn't—kids can and do "worry themselves sick"). On the third day of tummy troubles, her mom reached out for help.

In some ways, alliance building comes naturally to young girls. It feels good to know that you have people who will stick with you through thick and thin. Positive alliances exist when girls form close friendships that offer support, empathy, and understanding. The problem, however, is that alliance building among young girls often results in the social exclusion of other girls. Girls might build alliances to create social support, but they also build alliances to keep others out.

In Annie's case, the two friends used alliance building to force her to choose. Not only did they call the other friend "annoying" and state their intention to keep her out of the group, but they also tapped into Annie's insecurities to shame her into forcing that new girl out. They repeatedly reminded her of how much fun the three of them had without other girls around. Shame and guilt trigger powerful emotions in young children, and Annie felt it on both sides. She did enjoy her friendship with those two girls, but she didn't want to hurt her new friend. Annie felt the only thing she *could* do was stay home from school to avoid the whole situation.

Sadly, there is yet a third way that young girls use alliances: to seek revenge on a girl who has "wronged" them. Allie experienced this very problem. A fairly outgoing third-grade girl, Allie never had any trouble finding friends. In fact, Allie would later think that that might have even been the problem (it wasn't). Allie's mom promised her a sleepover party for her birthday. Allie could invite six people to the party. The only catch was that Allie already had three cousins around her age living nearby. That left just three friends to invite to the sleepover. After much debate, she decided the "fair" thing to do was to invite the three girls she had known the longest. As you might imagine, that didn't go over well.

Allie didn't want anyone to feel left out, so she sent the invitations in the mail and asked her friends not to talk about it at school. Truthfully, her mom coached her to do that. It almost worked. Unfortunately, as the date of the party approached, one of the girls slipped up during lunch and mentioned the party. She was excited, and it popped out of her mouth, a common communication style of young children. The table fell silent as all eyes stared at Allie. She quickly explained that she had to include her cousins and was only allowed three other girls. She also explained that she asked the others not to tell so that she wouldn't hurt anyone's feelings. "That didn't work," replied one girl. "Don't worry, Allie, it's fine that we're not good enough," remarked another. She apologized over and over and begged her mom to let her invite the others.

For a few days, the girls continued to hang out at school. One day, however, everything changed. The three girls who didn't get the party invitation distanced themselves. That's actually a nice way of saying that they ran a fairly heated campaign against Allie. They told the rest of their classmates about the social blunder. Naturally, the others were horrified (because that's the "natural" reaction when a girl in a power position gossips about the "mean" behavior of another girl). The class spent so much time discussing the issue, in fact, that the teacher caught wind of it and brought Allie in to discuss the "insensitive" choice to talk about her party at school.

Ultimately, the three who felt "shunned" tried to build alliances with as many classmates as possible, including the girls who were invited to the sleepover. The good news is that Allie's friends stood by her. They weren't able to stand up to the other girls, but they didn't abandon Allie. Sadly, Allie's first sleepover wasn't as exciting as originally anticipated. And the group never did rekindle the friendship. They went their separate ways. For Allie, the breakdown of the group left a lasting effect. She would question that decision over and over again, and she struggled to assert her needs from that point forward. She was so afraid of accidentally hurting others that she began to withdraw from social events altogether. She felt that if she could avoid big social gatherings, she wouldn't be in the position of hurting a friend.

Not all alliances are negatively charged or used to hurt others. In fact, having at least one very close friend can be a great source of social support for young girls. Talking to other girls to problem-solve a confusing social

Parent-Teacher Conference

Alliance building can be difficult to spot. It can also be hard to manage, as it includes a fair amount of manipulation. Check out these fast facts about alliance building:

✿ A minor grievance between two friends can be escalated by alliance building.

✿ Many problems between young girls are misunderstandings due to different levels of social sophistication.

✿ Using alliance building to exclude one group member can lead to social isolation, anxiety, and/or depression for the one who is excluded.

✿ It has become common practice for young girls to build and use alliances for the sole purpose of "punishing" a girl who "wronged" another girl.

✿ When girls struggle with conflict resolution, they are likely to engage in alliance building as a form of support.

✿ Sometimes girls invent conflicts or grievances to get one girl out of the group.

✿ Girls do switch roles at times—you might find that the "victim" is actually the aggressor attempting to garner adult support.

situation is actually a great strategy and a big step toward independence. The trouble is that sometimes that attempt to seek social support snowballs and morphs into an alliance fueled by negativity.

I once confronted a group of three girls about excluding and gossiping about another girl who was once in their group. Without missing a beat, these three girls fired off a laundry list of grievances presented as indisputable facts. They rallied around the friend they chose to support without stopping to consider that (1) they might be blowing things out of proportion and (2) there might actually be two sides to the story. The original conflict had occurred only one day earlier. That's a quick turn-around on that kind of negativity.

In an effort to help that group of girls learn to use social support to work *through* a problem (versus using it to work *against* another girl), I pulled the three of them and the girl they excluded into my office. First, I set some ground rules. I asked the girls to use "I feel" statements and to avoid blaming or making accusations. Second, I gave them each a turn to vent their feelings and frustrations. Third, I mediated the conversation. I repeated statements for clarification and asked a few questions. It wasn't an instant success, and there were some tears involved, but eventually the girls realized that miscommunication played a significant role in their on-going conflicts. By learning to work together and empathize with one another, they were able to repair their friendships.

Of course, it's never that simple, and I met with those girls many times to help them work on communicating clearly and helping each other instead of hurting each other. Those girls also knew me well and trusted me to help them. That's important. For many girls dealing with alliances and other forms of relational aggression, surviving the fallout is a long and lonely process. More often than not, these behaviors go unchecked in the school setting.

Public Humiliation

Teasing often begins in early childhood and it's sometimes difficult to determine the difference between "good-natured" teasing and teasing that is meant to hurt others. I find that many families use sarcasm and "teasing" at home as a form of humor. In an effort to teach children that not all teasing is bad and sarcasm can be funny, parents engage in these behaviors with their kids. While this can be fun if kids are socially savvy, the vast majority of young children can't actually process and understand sarcasm, and even "friendly" teasing can be difficult to understand. Most of the time, kids feel hurt or confused by teasing and sarcasm. Also? They have a tendency to try these behaviors out on their friends, and that can lead to conflict and hurt feelings . . . even if the child tacks on the compulsory "Just kidding!" after the joke is made. To add insult to injury, some socially sophisticated girls attach "Just kidding!" or "JK!" to cover up their unkind behavior. More on that later.

Caroline was a "Just kidding" kind of girl. She actually had a great sense of humor and a fairly sophisticated understanding of sarcasm for a 10-year-old. She never shied away from asking adults to explain their own use of sarcasm. In this way, she was an information gatherer. Though her sense of humor was mature for her age, her social skills were not. She struggled with entering groups, a common problem for kids her age. In an effort to get attention or make an entrance, she used teasing and sarcasm. This often backfired on her. The other girls didn't like her jokes and felt hurt when she made them. In fairness, her jokes sometimes missed the mark.

"Wow, that's, like, the ugliest shirt I've ever seen" was met with blank (and embarrassed) stares during an after-school class. "It's a joke! It's funny!" did nothing to lessen the blow. I watched from afar, wondering if Caroline would see her error and take the opportunity to apologize. She didn't. Her cheeks flushed as the other girls shook their heads and walked away, but she didn't make an effort to engage those girls for the remainder of the class. The whole scenario, which probably lasted less than one minute, happened when the teacher was in the hallway talking to a parent. By the time the teacher reentered the room, the girls had moved on without Caroline in their circle.

Teasing and taunting are two very different things. Have you ever watched a group of kids at play using teasing to add some humor to the play? In these cases, you'll observe the teaser and the person being teased switching roles and having fun. When the "teasing" is one-sided and the teaser refuses to stop, the child crosses the line into taunting.

Given that good-natured teasing is a fairly sophisticated skill to master, I find that many young girls honestly don't know when they've

Parent-Teacher Conference

It's important to understand the difference between good-natured teasing and mean-spirited taunting so that adults can handle reports of teasing with care.

TEASING

✿ Teasing is generally clever, lighthearted, and fun.

✿ Teaser and target switch roles often.

✿ Words are not hurtful in nature.

✿ Intended to make the other child laugh *with* the teaser.

✿ Teaser stops when someone objects to the teasing or asks the teaser to stop.

TAUNTING

✿ Teasing is one-sided, and the teaser is in a position of power.

✿ Teasing doesn't stop when the target objects.

✿ Can be humiliating and cruel.

✿ Intended to harm the target.

✿ Teaser wants to get others to laugh at (not with) the target.

crossed the line. In Caroline's case, she tried to emulate what she viewed as funny at home. Her parents engaged in good-natured teasing in the home, and she watched and practiced. The error for Caroline was that she used her parents' words to try to engage her peers. More often than not, those words were both completely out of context and not funny to her audience. Her intention was not to taunt her friends, but her poorly executed teasing hurt them just the same.

I find that young girls tend to face a "hurry up and grow up" mentality in the world today. From fashion trends to media input to hypercompetitive sports culture to parents who count their kids as friends to rigid school environments, young girls are forced to cope with behaviors and issues beyond their developmental level. Even the concept of "meetings" to work out issues with other girls and their

Parent-Teacher Conference

Girls use public humiliation to push down other girls on their way to the top of the social hierarchy. Watch for these behaviors that cross the line:

❂ Cruel comments about appearance (even when a girl adds "JK!").

❂ Using demeaning gestures behind another girl's back (examples might include imitating that girl, eye rolls, pretending to cry, dirty looks, etc.).

❂ Taunts or insults in public places (lunch room, recess yard, hallways).

❂ Making a joke of hiding personal property.

❂ Leaving notes or using technology to make cruel jokes and get other kids in on the joke.

moms is decidedly adult in nature. Sure, I might meet a friend for coffee to discuss difficult topics, but that's not appropriate for young girls. When girls are put on the spot to "resolve" an issue under the watchful eyes of the moms, it's difficult to engage in meaningful conversation and work through emotionally charged social scenarios. And yet I see this particular conflict-resolution strategy played out over and over again. The truth is that younger girls sometimes do need help working through their peer problems, but a "meeting" can feel like a lot of pressure, and older girls often need time and space to work through their feelings before they attempt to resolve the problem independently. Interfering, in that case, can do more harm than good.

The Fast-Tracking of Girlhood

Engaging in behavior beyond developmental capability goes hand in hand with the fast-tracking of girlhood. A mom once asked me, "Since when do third-graders act like middle schoolers?" The truth is that first-graders and even kindergarten students are engaging in some of these "mature" social behaviors. While it's easy to blame the media or other families (you know, because older siblings are a cause for concern—insert eye roll here), the truth is that we have to consider our own behaviors. Yes, girls learn things from their friends, but most of the time they look to us to figure out how to relate to others. If we are quick to blame others when things go wrong, our girls will grow into blamers. If we ditch friends the minute a better offer comes along, our girls will learn to be social climbers. If we rely on sarcasm to communicate passive-aggressive feelings instead of communicating clearly and honestly, our girls will do the same.

We can't talk about fast-tracking without keeping a close eye on some of the recent research into the socialization of young girls. For instance, a 2016 study by researchers at Kenyon College found that more

Parent-Teacher Conference

Sarcasm: Noun. The use of words that mean the opposite of what you really want to say, especially in order to insult someone, to show irritation, or to be funny.[8] By definition, sarcasm is intended to hurt others (in a "funny" sort of way), and yet we use it around young children regularly. Check out these reasons to avoid sarcasm with kids:

✿ Sarcasm is difficult to understand and often feels hurtful.

✿ Young girls don't always understand the context of the conversation, but they do understand voice tone, exasperated sighs, and eye rolls.

✿ It doesn't actually resolve the issue.

✿ It's embarrassing.

✿ It can lead to girls developing negative core beliefs (e.g., I'm bad, I'm unlikable, even my mom thinks I'm annoying).

✿ Many girls tell me that they avoid talking to their moms about personal issues because they are afraid they will either be dismissed or met with "mean jokes" (that's kid talk for sarcasm).

than half the female characters in children's Halloween costumes, action figures, and even Valentine's Day cards wear provocative or revealing clothing.[9] Yikes. Before we blame the local Hallmark store for the downfall of girlhood, however, consider this: A 2014 study published in the journal *Body Image* found that many four- to 10-year-old girls engage in "teen culture" by using the latest beauty products and following current fashion trends. This study included 815 mothers of four- to

10-year-old girls and found that girls do engage in "grown-up" and "potentially sexualized" behaviors that are not benign for their development.[10] Finally, according to a 2015 study published in *Child Development*, nearly three-fourths of 208 children ages six to 11 rated paper dolls wearing short, low-cut tops and miniskirts or short shorts as more popular than dolls dressed in loose, long-sleeved tops and jeans.[11] Gulp. They also rated those sexualized dolls as less intelligent, athletic, or nice.

What we can take away from these studies is twofold: Young girls are engaging in behavior (influenced by a variety of sources) that is beyond their developmental level, and they are learning to judge and assess themselves and other girls based on this input. I don't know about you, but unflattering jeans and oversize striped rugby shirts were all the rage when I was a young girl. While I'm not suggesting that we turn back the clock on girls' clothing, I am suggesting that we put the brakes on this new trend of dressing young girls like teens and exposing them to media and other content intended for much older audiences.

When we fast-track girls through developmental levels without considering the potential consequences, we set girls up for negative behaviors and friendship fails. When we gloss over the basics (as in how to be a good friend) to get to the more advanced stuff (as in having a defined "group"), we rob our girls of the opportunity to experience and understand the ebb and flow of friendships. Early friendships tend to form by way of class placement or family friends, but as girls grow, they learn to try on different friendships and find their own tribe. I find that girls aren't seeking out their own friendships as much as they once did.

While completing a "friendship map" with a young girl who recently found herself an outcast among her peers, it quickly became evident that *all* of her friendships were orchestrated by her mom. "I can't tell my mom what she said because my mom and her mom are best friends." She repeated this refrain over and over again, until I finally shifted her focus to what she believes friendship means. When I spoke to her mom about her friendship struggles, she admitted that it's easier for her when her daughter hangs out with daughters of her friends. She doesn't have to worry about much because she knows the other mom well and doesn't have to start from the beginning. "I just want her to have a group, and when the moms are all friends, it's easy to create a group for them." I hear this sentiment over and over again.

I believe that moms have the best intentions when they interfere with friendship making. Many moms confide in me that they don't want their daughters to have the same struggles they experienced as young girls, and in taking an active role in friendship making (or creating the friendships for their daughters), they hope to push them ahead to the good part—the part where they have friends they can trust. The problem is that, more often than not, our daughters are quite different from us. As parents, we are hardwired to look for similarities. We try to find hints of our own personalities hidden within our girls, but the truth is they have their own personalities. They have their own strengths, and they have their own quirks. They will have their own struggles, and they will experience their own triumphs. They will form their own friendships . . . if we let them.

We can't control what happens around us, but we can choose to slow down and let our girls learn and grow at their own pace. Girls need the opportunity to find their strengths and interests through unstructured play, free time, and long periods of boredom. They need to work through their differences, learn to resolve conflict, and figure out how to build each other up without tearing other girls down. When parents interfere and orchestrate friendships in an attempt to hit the fast-forward button and avoid the emotional pitfalls that naturally occur during the early years, girls miss vital opportunities to practice friendship making, kindness, and coping skills.

As hard as those "pitfall" moments might feel (for girls *and* their moms), they are important moments. Those early friendship successes and blunders are the foundation from which they will continue to build friendships as they grow. Support young girls through the highs and lows by listening and sharing your own stories, but don't take those moments from them.

Getting Back to Basics

There was a time when kids worked on social skills in school. It wasn't necessarily part of the curriculum, but teachers had the time and freedom to work on social issues as necessary. They front-loaded kids with coping skills and problem-solving strategies to help them deal with the various social-emotional stressors and pitfalls that are bound to crop up on any given day, instead of solely focusing on the extreme endpoint of the social-emotional arc: bullying.

Today, teachers face a packed curriculum, and many teachers tell me that they problem-solve to work through peer issues as they come up, but they don't have the time to break it down and create a lesson for the whole class. In short, kids are winging it when it comes to socializing and receive meaningful input only when things go wrong.

It's a shame that social-emotional learning doesn't have more of a presence in our schools (although the good news is that programs like MindUp and RULER are gaining steam), because research shows that teaching these "soft" skills actually improves both emotional stability in the classroom and academic achievement. A report published in *Child Development* showed that not only did student participation in social and emotional learning improve standardized test scores by 11 percentile points (compared to nonparticipating peers), but students also showed improved social skills, less emotional distress, better attitudes, fewer incidents of bullying, and more frequent positive behaviors (e.g., cooperation and helping others).[12] This makes perfect sense. Calm and stable kids make for a calm and stable teaching environment.

The input girls receive at home also plays into how they relate to one another outside the home. It's no big secret that our girls are running on busy these days. I'm an under-scheduler by nature, and I still can't seem to find balance! When the one-sport rule includes a sport that requires multiple practices each week, and then a sudden interest in literary theater (which is totally opposite her norm) crops up, it's hard to find that sweet spot that includes enough of each with a healthy side of downtime.

I see the same problem in my office. Parents want to empower their girls to take chances and try new things, but those things add up to very busy schedules, so downtime is nearly nonexistent and sleep suffers. This often results in behavioral changes and social-emotional struggles, and without adequate time to address them at home, girls learn to sweep things under the rug and move on.

In my practice, I find that insufficient sleep is a big problem among young girls. Late practices and after-school commitments, hours of

Parent-Teacher Conference

Our girls need more sleep! Check out these updated guidelines:

❀ Ages 3–5: 10–13 hours
❀ Ages 6–12: 9–12 hours
❀ Ages 13–18: 8–10 hours[13]

If you notice emotional and/or behavioral changes in your daughter, double-check her sleep schedule and aim for a consistent bedtime.

homework, and difficulty settling down at night are making it hard for girls to get enough sleep. In fact, lack of sleep is such a problem today that the American Academy of Sleep Medicine actually released updated sleep guidelines.

Data collected by the American Psychological Association for the Stress in America survey found a direct correlation between high stress levels and insufficient sleep in the teen population. In addition, survey results showed that highly stressed teens who are low on sleep are more likely to feel irritable and/or sad or depressed.[14] One thing I can say for certain is that it is very difficult for parents to connect with kids when they are low on sleep and high on stress. Irritability and negative emotions can result in power struggles and arguments between parents and their daughters, and repairing these intense parent-child interactions becomes the immediate focus in the home, leaving little time to help girls work through difficult social-emotional issues that crop up outside the home.

While sleeping, eating, and downtime are important "basics" when it comes to raising young girls, it's also important to focus on early friendship skills. I find that when we gloss over these important early social interaction skills, girls struggle to figure out how to relate to others. In fact, a study that surveyed 123 middle school students and their parents found that when parents used social coaching (advice about how to interact with peers and handle peer challenges), kids experienced stronger friendships and more peer acceptance.[15] Results of this study highlight the importance of listening and guiding to help girls improve their social interaction skills.

I recently tasked a second-grade girl with finding one new friend outside of school. We role-played simple conversation starters (e.g., "What's your favorite TV show?") so that she would know how to begin a conversation with a new peer in her Girl Scouts group. When she got there and stared at the sea of unknown faces, she panicked. She forgot the phrases we had practiced and reverted to primitive skills that had backfired in the past. Instead of opening a conversation by commenting on the present situation or asking a question about interests, she went from girl to girl asking, "Do you want to be my friend?" Caught off guard by this toddler-esque form of friendship making, the other girls moved away from her. She was devastated.

This young girl is not alone in her lack of social interaction skills. In our collective effort to make sure girls know they can do it all (which can lead to feelings of guilt if they don't do so) and in the current culture of "busy is better" (and a sign of success), girls are missing out on the basics of friendship making and social skills. Sure, they're becoming scientists, computer coders, athletes, musicians, and beyond, but all of this "doing" (or overdoing, really) comes at a cost.

Skipping over the development of crucial social-emotional skills in the name of creating a generation of supergirls doesn't actually empower our girls. In fact, it does the opposite: It creates a culture of cutthroat competition. She who rises to the top first wins (although what she wins remains to be seen). That's not girl power; that's a recipe for mean girl behavior. It fuels the fire of relational aggression, shifting alliances, and frenemies. In short, we can't skip the prosocial (positive friendship skills like empathy, compassion, and listening skills) stuff. In fact, we should front-load our girls with these skills to teach them what it really means to be empowered and to empower others (to feel and offer others "girl power").

To raise girls who understand the power of friendship and the importance of lifting one another up (instead of pushing one another down with bullying or negative behavior), we need to get back to basics. We need to talk openly and often about friendship skills, including how to work through tricky situations. I tell young girls over and over again: You don't have to forge close friendships with every girl you meet, but it never hurts to be kind. When we empower young girls to work together and build each other up, we teach them to find the positive in new people and situations and to keep their minds open to new possibilities in friendship and in life.

Girls Can!

Make a Friendship Tree

We often talk to young kids about their family trees; they might even make one as a school project at some point. When creating a family tree, we cover the branches with immediate relatives, followed by cousins, moving on up to distant relatives we might not know very well. The tree shows us that families are more than just the people living in our homes, that family support has deep roots.

I like to use the tree metaphor to help young girls consider friendships. Girls are often conditioned to find a best friend. Walk the aisles of any children's retailer and you'll find just about everything (necklaces! shoelaces! sunglasses!) branded with the three coveted letters that make some girls feel empowered and others left out: BFF. But friendship isn't quite as simple as one BFF who is always there. Do I have a best friend who has been there for me through thick and thin since we played in a sandbox in the late seventies? Yes. When was the last time we lived in the same city or even close enough to see each other on a regular basis? Many, many years ago.

A close friendship is a beautiful thing, but so is a not-so-close friendship. Girls meet countless other girls as they grow. Through school, sports, after-school activities, and just by showing up to the local playground, girls can build new friendships and fill their trees with endless limbs of support.

Help your daughter create a friendship tree so that she can stand back and appreciate the many amazing girls in her life. Add fun pictures or stickers to show where they met or what they have in common. Talk about ways to reconnect with friends she hasn't seen in a while (don't hold off on that e-mail address for too long) and encourage her to think of ways to bridge friendships. A friendship tree is a great tool for young girls because not only does it show them the many forms friendship can take; it also serves, when they're feeling alone, as a reminder of the friends they have.

Conversation Starters

My daughter and I are learning French together, and we are constantly talking about the formal versus the informal. "So I use the formal one with Mimi but the informal one with my friends?" When you practice a foreign language, you learn the different ways people use language. When you're lost in your day-to-day life, you forget that those lessons are actually quite important.

Remember the story of the girl who went around the Girl Scouts group asking each girl to be her friend? She lacked sophisticated conversation skills, and that affected her ability to make friends in new settings. In the end, I went back to the beginning with her. I taught her how to greet various people: a group of known friends, a group of new kids, an adult friend, an unknown adult, a grandparent, a teacher, etc. We went through basic greetings step-by-step. In all honesty, I find that a lot of kids can use this input.

Another skill to work on is slipping in and out of conversations. If a group is already in conversation, for example, it's rude and off-putting to interrupt in a loud voice. To teach girls how to slip into a group, I encourage them to make eye contact with at least one group member, smile, wait just outside the group for a break in the conversation, and then greet them appropriately.

A great place to practice this skill is at large gatherings (family parties or birthday parties) where people break off into small groups to chat.

While you're practicing, include some conversation starters. I find that some young girls become silent when they don't know how to join a conversation, while others blurt out the first thing they think of. Practice interesting conversation starters (e.g., "Have you been in the bounce house yet?") that apply to the present situation to help your daughter learn how to slide into a group. *Bonus tip: Keep a bunch of conversation starters written on small slips of paper in a Ziploc bag in your purse. This makes it easy to practice on the go before a party or other group event!*

Self Report Card

Sometimes girls get stuck in a certain pattern of behavior. For better or for worse, the mean girl thing feels like it works. They have friends, they're never alone, and other kids look up to them. When girls get stuck in a negative pattern of behavior, they don't necessarily see the repercussions of their choices.

Help your daughter create a weekly (or even daily) report card that focuses on soft skills she's employed, like empathy, kindness, helping others, and positive social skills. Keep it simple. Some examples might include:

- Complimented a friend
- Helped a friend in need
- Invited someone into my group
- Used kind words
- Listened to others

Ask your daughter to give herself a rating (use emoticons to make it fun) for each category and talk about why she gave herself that rating. Do your own self report card at the same time to illustrate your strengths and weaknesses when it comes to interpersonal skills.

The self report card can be eye-opening for girls. Sometimes the act of sitting down and talking about the subtle ways we relate to others helps them see how their behavior can affect other girls.

Define "Mean Girl" Behavior

I can't tell you how many parents hesitate to discuss this topic with young girls because they don't want to worry their daughters or are afraid that talking about it will somehow make it happen. First of all, your daughter is probably already worrying about this on her own because it's happening right before her very eyes, and second, teaching our kids about the hard stuff doesn't make the hard stuff happen. Another line I wish parents would stop using: "It's just something all girls go through." It doesn't have to be, but it will be if we don't address it.

Talk to your daughter about relational aggression. Define words like gossip, teasing, taunting, public humiliation, excluding, cliques or groups, and cyberbullying (yes, even if your child "never has screen time" and "has no chance of getting a phone anytime soon"). Avoiding these topics will only keep your daughter in the dark and render her powerless when she does confront them. Educating her and talking about positive alternatives empowers her and prepares her.

Social stories are a great way to help young girls put this information to the test. Give your daughter a scenario (e.g., a group won't let one girl sit with them at lunch because she doesn't like Shopkins or use Instagram) and ask her to create two cartoons: The first should be from the perspective of the unkind girls doing the excluding; the second should be from the perspective of a kind friend who wants to help. Practicing positive alternatives through social stories helps girls internalize good choices that can be made in the moment.

Upstanders and Supporters

One thing we can always do is model "upstander" and "supporter" behaviors. It's really hard to stand up to a bully, and some kids are stronger than others in these moments, but we can teach our kids to take on positive roles by modeling these behaviors in our own lives and role-playing at home.

- Upstanders: Stand up to bullies with words or actions. Practice upstander phrases at home (e.g., "Stop! I don't like it when you treat my friends that way").
- Supporters: You don't have to use your voice to lend your support. If standing up to a bully feels hard, something as simple as making eye contact with the victim or standing near the victim can show support and help the victim feel less alone.

Faces of Me

If you feel like your daughter is the perfect angel at school but show-cases an entirely different personality at home, you're not alone. This is a common concern among parents of young girls. If you're looking for the silver lining, this is it: Your daughter trusts you enough to show you the ugly emotions that she attempts to hide from the rest of the world. The anger, the tears, the hopelessness, and the door-slamming frustration are often saved for those they trust the most. She knows you will love her no matter how heated it gets. Go ahead and give yourself a pat on the back for years of unconditional love and support paying off (even if it doesn't feel like much of a prize at the moment).

It takes a lot of emotional energy to put on a brave face day after day, especially when girls are dealing with complicated emotions and friendship issues. It's no wonder they wear different faces in different situations. If you stop and think about it, you probably do the same (minus the door slamming, maybe).

"Faces of Me" is a great activity to do *with* your child. When you share your faces and experiences with your daughter, you send a powerful message of trust and empathy. You communicate that you get it, and you know she gets it too.

Get crafty and make some paper-plate masks or get tech savvy and create them on your tablet or computer (hint: tweens love technology). Either way, take some time to talk about how you and your daughter present yourselves in different situations. How are you different at home, for example, than you might be at a PTA meeting? How would you act at a family reunion versus at a barbecue with friends? What is the difference between "working mom" and "silly at-home mom" (or dad)? Use the masks to create visuals of the different faces you wear and encourage your daughter to do the same. Talk about why you might show different faces in different places.

You can also flip the script on this one and create faces for each other. In doing this, you and your daughter can discuss your own perceptions about how each acts. This can be very therapeutic. As one mom told me, "I had no idea how much time I spend looking down instead of looking her in the eyes and really listening." Understanding how we communicate, and why, helps girls consider what works and what doesn't. It's a great way to talk about how our behaviors affect others.

Friendship Troubles Dos and Don'ts

Be honest: How many times have you told your daughter to "Walk away" or "Let it go" when she complains of peer issues? If your answer is "At least once and probably more" (or something like that), you're one of many. In fact, many bully-prevention programs advise kids to "walk away from" or "ignore" a bully. Girls hear this message over and over again. Here's the thing: Not all peer problems are a form of bullying, and walking away and getting over it are not that easy to do (particularly for young girls who are likely still living in the stage of instant gratification).

Girls need guidance when it comes to coping with friendship troubles.

You know your daughter best, so you know what she's capable of doing in the moment, but try to come up with a list of dos and don'ts to navigate tricky situations. Try these:

DO

- Say that you need time to think. You don't have to solve every problem right away.
- Talk about how you're feeling.
- Use "I" statements to avoid the blame game (e.g., "I feel embarrassed when other people make jokes about me").
- Take responsibility for your role in a conflict.
- Use a calm but assertive voice to communicate your thoughts (see chapter 8 for more on building assertiveness skills).
- Be honest.
- Listen.
- Consider your friend's perspective.
- Work together: State the problem. Talk about feelings on both sides. Brainstorm possible solutions.
- Talk it out with a trusted adult if you don't know how to solve the problem.

DON'T

- Exaggerate or lie to make the situation seem bigger than it is.
- Gossip or build alliances to get other friends in on the conflict.
- Blame. It takes two to have a conflict.
- Use the silent treatment to retaliate. It never solves a problem and often makes the problem worse. If you need time alone to think, tell your friend.
- Pretend you have no feelings or keep your face devoid of emotions.

- Use phrases like "whatever" or "I don't care" to hide your true feelings.
- Talk over your friend.
- Taunt your friend to make onlookers laugh.
- Dismiss your friend's feelings.

Play "Tattle or Tell"

I find that most girls don't understand the difference between telling (seeking adult help because you can't resolve a problem but want to) and tattling (seeking adult help because you want to get the other person in trouble). When kids tell, they usually feel helpless and need input to resolve a conflict. When kids tattle, they often want to bring attention to the "problem." It can actually be used as a sneaky form of public humiliation.

Ask your daughter to help you come up with some scenarios for when a girl might need to tell an adult (e.g., a friend is doing something dangerous) or when a girl might want to tattle (e.g., her "usual" seat at lunch was taken) and make a game show of it. Talk about the details of each scenario to help your daughter understand the differences between telling and tattling. Award bonus points for alternate solutions to avoid tattling. We like to use jelly beans instead of points around here, but you do your own thing.

Solve the Maze

Sometimes dealing with peer conflict can feel like being trapped in one of those completely overwhelming corn mazes. Just when you think you've rounded the corner, you hit another dead end. Corn everywhere. No way out. Girls often tell me there's just no way to solve a problem once it gets too big. It's important to empower them to keep on trying.

Draw a maze on a sheet of paper. The only catch to the maze is that instead of avoiding the dead ends, your daughter has to work through an issue to get through each dead end. There is no "right" path to take, and the dead ends should occur incrementally along each path. The goal is to help your daughter get from start to finish while solving problems along the way.

Write the problem at the starting line (e.g., "I had a fight with my best friend"). At the first stop, write, "What caused the problem?" Pause here to talk about possible triggers of the conflict. At the next stop, write, "How did I contribute to the problem?" Help your daughter sort out her role in the conflict here. Next, create a stop that says, "How do I feel about the problem and how we handled it?" Encourage your daughter to verbalize her feelings about the conflict and how she and her friend interacted. At the next stop, write, "Think of three possible solutions." Take the time to brainstorm ideas and consider the possible outcomes. And just before she gets to the end of the maze, create one last stop, "Choose a solution."

In working through a problem-solving maze with your daughter, you teach her the importance of thinking about the problem, considering emotional reactions, and coming up with strategies to solve the problem.

Lifesavers!

Remember candy necklaces? I can remember sun-drenched summer days walking around with my friends, sharing each other's candy necklaces, and laughing about nothing and everything at the same time. Those were the early years, before I knew that girls could be mean and friendships might come to a grinding halt without warning. How I wish I could go back and reassure that younger version of me.

One way to help girls understand that they will get through the hard stuff (the fights, the embarrassing moments, the left-out feelings) is to encourage them to identify their support systems. I like to use one of my all-time favorite candies, Lifesavers, and string to illustrate this point (and, yes, to create delicious candy necklaces).

Most girls know that they can turn to Mom and Dad when things are hard—they are the obvious supports in place. But I like to challenge girls to think beyond their immediate family to find their "lifesavers." I describe lifesavers as people who will listen, support, and help no matter what. I give girls a pack of Lifesavers and a piece of string and ask them to talk about one lifesaver at a time. It might be a grandmother, an aunt, a friend, or a teacher. It might even be a neighbor or the town librarian. The catch is that before she adds the Lifesaver to the string, she has to describe why that person fits the description. What clues does that person provide that he or she will serve as a lifesaver?

I have some girls walk out of here with three or four Lifesavers on their necklaces, and some with more than ten. Either way, they feel relieved and a bit more confident after this exercise. Girls are often socialized to get through things—to just keep swimming—but that's a mistake. We all need support systems in place; we all need our very own lifesavers. Knowing whom they can rely on when the going gets tough helps young girls remain calm and confident in the face of adversity.

Friendship Cookie Recipe

I love to bake. It's my favorite way to relieve stress and reset my soul. Some of my favorite childhood memories involve baking with my mom and my siblings, particularly around holidays, so it makes good sense that my kitchen is my happy place. I was working with a group of girls when it occurred to me that my love of baking might actually lead to a useful discussion about friendship.

I gave the girls art supplies to create a cookie of their own imagination (though I would suggest actually baking with your daughter if you're doing this at home). We talked about recipes—specifically how some ingredients are sweet (sugar), some are boring (baking powder), and some even add a little excitement (chocolate chips), but that you need *all* of the ingredients in just the right amounts to bake the cookies. If you forget the boring stuff, like baking powder, your cookies might be flat. If you add too much excitement, like the whole bag of chocolate chips, your cookies might be overwhelmingly sweet. You have to mix it up and use a little bit of everything in the recipe.

As the girls crafted cookies and discussed recipe ideas, I challenged them to create a recipe for friendship to go with their cookie recipe. If the recipe called for one teaspoon of vanilla, for example, the corresponding friendship recipe might call for a teaspoon of kindness. It was a challenge at first, but we soon found ourselves lost in a discussion about what ingredients add up to friendship and whether or not our made-up cookie recipes would even work.

This activity is a great way to discuss an important topic while having a little fun together. And who knows? You might even invent an amazing new cookie recipe!

Celebrate Your Own Friendships

This might sound too simple to be effective, but our girls learn more from watching us relate to others than they do from hearing us drone on and on about doing the right thing and being a good friend. And yet, how often do you find yourself thinking about what's wrong instead of what's right? (Guilty as charged.)

Talk about the great friends you have. Share stories of friendships that have lasted a lifetime (my daughter loves to see pictures of me and my oldest friend in impossibly high knee socks) and talk about the people who fill your cup each and every day. Make time to actually be with your friends so that your daughter sees your friendship skills in action, and include her when you do kind things to lift your friend up during a difficult time. Bottom line: Be the friend you hope your daughter will become.

Keys to Friendship

When girls come to me with their friendship troubles, they want to vent about what they think others are doing wrong. They don't often come in aware of their own friendship fails. While I certainly let them vent and provide support, I also help them understand one simple mantra: It takes a friend to make a friend. Sure, sometimes people hurt and disappoint us, but we also have to think about our own roles in these friendships. What do we bring to the friendship? What do we need to work on?

This is a great activity to do with a group of girls because it tends to spark lively discussions, but it also works well one-on-one. Download and print a few copies of an illustration of a key. Talk about how keys open doors, start cars, unlock safes, and perform a variety of functions. Without keys, we wouldn't be able to lock things up when we want to keep them safe or open doors to new people or experiences if we want to let them in. Keys, though low tech in these modern times, continue to play an important role in our lives.

Now shift gears and talk about the keys to being a good friend. What does it mean to be a good friend? What kind of qualities does a good friend have? Together with your daughter, decorate your keys, adding one quality in a good friend to each, and talk about how you both can work on those qualities. Challenge each other to set a "good friend goal" and check back in a week to talk about what you've done to work toward that goal.

The level of some of these activities might seem a little too superficial. How can friendship-building activities possibly guard your girls against things like relational aggression and cyberbullying? The truth is that you can't protect your girls from everything bad in this world, but when you build them up and teach them how to be a friend, they are hardwired to turn away from mean girl behavior and stand up for their peers. As it turns out, empowering our girls to be the kind of friend they want to have is one of the best ways to help them through these tricky friendship moments.

CHAPTER 2

Like Versus Likable and the Pursuit of Popularity

Avoid popularity; it has many snares,
and no real benefit.
—*William Penn*

Sienna was a friend collector. Part of this could be attributed to her anxiety. She had a profound need to be liked by all, and she became anxious and uncomfortable when she felt like people didn't like her. By fourth grade, she had a long list of friends.

The problem with friend collecting is that it forced Sienna to act as a chameleon of sorts. She was forever trying to change her ways to attract new and different friendships, and this caused problems with her existing friendships. She wasn't being honest with anyone, and in time, this lack of honesty only increased her anxiety. She became fixated on pleasing her friends. She *needed* them to like her. And in the process of trying to be "liked" by all, she burned bridges with friends who had been there all along. By the end of fourth grade, she felt like she didn't have any "real" friends left. Tears spilled from her eyes one day as she expressed remorse and guilt (two fairly complicated emotions for a

10-year-old to process). She had traded a "best" friendship for a big group of superficial friendships, and she wished she could go back in time to fix what felt like a life-altering mistake.

We think of identity formation as a struggle for the tweens and teens of this world, but the truth is that kids start trying on new roles and thinking about who they are versus who they think they should be long before the hormones kick in. Middle childhood (between the ages of six and 10) marks a time of rapid social and emotional development for kids. Children strive to achieve autonomy, competence, and

Parent-Teacher Conference

Middle childhood is a significant time period in the development of a child's self-concept for a number of reasons:

- ❀ Kids spend more time away from the family unit and begin to figure out their role in society.
- ❀ They become less egocentric, and empathy grows.
- ❀ Skill acquisition soars as kids try new things (art, sports, clubs, etc.).
- ❀ Their social worlds take up more space in their lives, and they begin to consider how others view or judge them.
- ❀ Perspective taking improves, and they begin to assess social roles.
- ❀ Belonging becomes important, and kids work hard to figure out what they need to do to belong (to a team, a group of friends, a class, etc.).
- ❀ They attempt to manage both increased freedom and individuality and heightened demands from outside influences (teachers, coaches, etc.).

individuality. They also work on developing friendships and establishing relationships with adults outside of the family (teachers, coaches). This is the time when kids begin to build their own villages of support. It's a period of a lot of growth and development.

It is during middle childhood when girls first step outside the orbit of parental control and begin to manage their behaviors and relationships. Well, that's how it's supposed to work, anyway. Sometimes parents get in the way of this already complicated process. By clinging, hovering, and offering constant advice (all with great intentions, I know), parents can actually impede their daughter's ability to take control of her own choices and relationships. While I'm certainly guilty of sharing a long-winded story or two, and sometimes those stories are just what my girl needs, it is the job of the parent to step back and wait to be called upon for such advice. Parents are playing a strong offense these days (get in there and fix it before any emotional damage is done!), but it is important to allow girls the freedom to self-manage—even if that freedom comes at the cost of some tears, some struggles, and some heated emotions.

Stepping outside the carefully guarded parental safety zone gives girls the opportunity to figure out who they are and who they want to become. As girls spend time developing competencies (hooray for softball!) and coping with failures (dance is too hard!), they begin to individuate from their parents. They spend a lot of time trying to figure out both how they stand out and how they fit in.

Self-esteem can get wrapped up in achievement during this time as girls measure themselves against other girls and the perceived expectations of others, and lack of sophisticated social skills can lead to negative peer interactions. This can, in turn, affect self-esteem. In short, the need to please, to showcase competence, and to be liked can result in the perfect storm for young girls—one that can result in anxiety and depression if left unchecked.

Parents often ask me about the degree to which a dip in self-esteem can actually affect their girls. We all go through times when we feel like we don't measure up, right? Don't all girls struggle with body image, mean girls, and low self-worth? Isn't that just part of growing up? These were once the questions that parents of teen girls asked me during those infamously rocky years, but today I hear the same questions from parents of girls in early elementary school. When they dare to answer their own questions before I even offer up my advice, it often sounds something like this: "She just has to learn to deal with this stuff. It's part of being a girl."

I won't argue the point that girls deal with complicated issues at times, but a "Just deal with it" attitude doesn't actually teach girls how to deal with things like poor body image and queen bees. It also glosses over the big red flag: low self-esteem.

Low self-esteem isn't a feeling a girl has for a minute or two that will eventually dissipate and cease to bother her. It isn't a choice she's making (I mean, who would choose to think negative thoughts about themselves all day long?). And most of the time, girls don't even realize that they're stuck in a cycle of negative beliefs. Comments like "Kids don't really like me" and "I'm not smart" begin to roll off the tongue without much thought when you're lost in the vortex of low self-esteem. Low self-esteem is not just about "feeling bad"; it's a state of mind that can negatively affect every single part of a girl's life. It can affect school performance, social relationships, participation in sports, clubs, and other activities; it can even mar family relationships. Parents can't afford to gloss over low self-esteem because it just might be silently destroying the little girl who battles it.

While you're probably thinking that those potential risks seem like teen problems, it's important to remember that growing up girl is constantly changing. What happens in the elementary-school-age years directly affects what happens in the tween and teen years. It's

Parent-Teacher Conference

Girls with low self-esteem are at risk for:

✿ Anxiety disorders

✿ Depressive disorders

✿ Self-harm (e.g., cutting)

✿ Disordered eating

✿ Poor academic performance

✿ Early sexual behavior

✿ Alcohol and drug abuse

✿ Criminal behavior

✿ Dropping out of school

✿ Teen pregnancy

all connected. The research on young girls from all over the world shows that parents, educators, and mentors for girls need to take action right now.

Take the results of the latest Girls' Attitudes Survey (2016) by Girl-guiding in the United Kingdom. As a leading charity for girls in the UK, Girlguiding annually surveys more than 1,600 girls and young women between the ages of 7 and 21. Here's what young girls are saying:

- 36 percent of girls ages 7 to 10 say people make them think the most important thing about them is how they look.
- 69 percent of girls ages 7 to 21 feel like they are not good enough.
- 25 percent of girls ages 7 to 10 have experienced someone saying mean things about their bodies.
- 28 percent of girls ages 7 to 10 feel worried or anxious.

- 40 percent of girls ages 7 to 10 worry about not doing well in school.
- 31 percent of girls ages 7 to 21 worry about what other people think of them.
- 37 percent of girls ages 7 to 10 worry about bullying.[1]

Jessica was a perennial quitter. This upset her parents for a couple of reasons: The cost of the activities she chose to start and promptly quit was too much of a financial burden on the family (although when I asked her mother whether the cost would bother her as much if Jessica *didn't* quit everything, she said no), and Jessica didn't seem to have any "work ethic" or "direction." That was how her parents perceived the situation. Behind closed doors, Jessica told a much different story.

Jessica was 100 percent certain that she wasn't good at anything. She quit things not because they were hard, but because she felt that she didn't measure up. Quitting wasn't easy for her, by the way. She was the kind of kid who had a way of making it look like nothing bothered her, but each time she begged to quit an activity she experienced intense feelings of guilt and shame. These feelings fueled her secret belief that she was a giant disappointment to her parents, and her self-esteem dipped a little bit more with each failed attempt to "find her direction." For Jessica, it felt like a never-ending cycle of negative thoughts, but she couldn't find the strength to communicate this to her parents. Believe it or not, it was easier for her to continue to accept the criticism about her lack of personal drive and commitment than to confront her biggest fears about herself.

Jessica's story is one I hear from young girls over and over again. While I love that girls have so many opportunities these days (I would have loved a girls' lacrosse league at age 10 instead of proving myself to the boys just to get the ball once in a while), I also see it as a pressure cooker. With opportunity comes expectation, and young girls are expected to find their passions, their strengths, and their life goals at an impossibly young age. They're also expected to succeed right out of the gate.

Marlee *hates* soccer. Her mom tells me she's "really talented," but she doesn't like it at all. In fairness to soccer, it's not the sport she hates. It's the pressure. Marlee gets a lot of "positive" feedback about her soccer skills. In fact, she is even told that she's the "best" player on the team. While all of this is no doubt meant to inspire her, it has the opposite effect. Marlee feels like she's under a ton of pressure each week. In fact, she wants to quit the team so she can stop worrying about how well she plays on Saturday.

Sadly, the internal pressure isn't the only overwhelming part of this soccer experience for Marlee. The other girls see the attention she gets. They see the goals scored and the positive feedback from the parents and coaches. Some of them even have to hear their own parents compare them to Marlee (as in, "Why can't you play more like Marlee?"). Because of that, the girls begin to turn against her. They're tired of it. She's tired of it. What was supposed to be a fun and healthy after-school activity is now a highly competitive pressure cooker with relatively few friendly moments. Marlee is stressed out and done with it. She would much rather have friends and do nothing than be the big soccer star but have no friends. By the way, she's in fourth grade.

Marlee's parents were appropriately baffled by her request to quit the team. They couldn't understand how a girl with so much talent could have anything but high self-esteem. Therein lies the problem. Parents often view specific talents as fuel for high self-esteem. The belief is that if girls find their strengths, they will feel good about themselves. It's a simple equation that many parents use to help build up their girls. The problem is that it doesn't account for everything. Marlee, for example, spends about six hours per week engaged in soccer. On the field, she feels strong, capable, and unstoppable. But when she walks off that field, she feels lost. Although her parents place a heavy focus on soccer, the reality is that soccer is just one small part of Marlee's life. It's everything else that she struggles to manage.

Your daughter's self-esteem reflects how she feels about herself and how she approaches and contributes to the world around her. Although subtle daily shifts in self-esteem are to be expected, every girl has a general feeling about her self-worth. That's a good thing. Without a certain amount of self-valuing, girls wouldn't step outside their comfort zones and take chances.

When girls have high self-worth and judge themselves to be capable,

Parent-Teacher Conference

Watch for these sneaky signs of low self-esteem in young girls (even if you think your daughter is "fine"):

✿ Negative self-talk
✿ Overly critical of her skills or efforts
✿ Pessimistic statements
✿ Body language that lacks confidence (slumped shoulders, downcast eyes, sad facial expressions)
✿ Lack of effort or giving up easily
✿ Avoidance behaviors
✿ Puts other people down
✿ Blames others
✿ Overly apologetic
✿ Isolates from peers
✿ Overreacts to constructive criticism or feedback
✿ Behavioral changes (acting out, talking back, regressed behavior, bullying peers or siblings)
✿ Difficulty accepting praise

they try new things, establish new friendships, and take healthy risks. When girls struggle with low self-worth, on the other hand, they can get stuck in a cycle of devaluing themselves. This tends to manifest as discomfort with new situations, avoidance of healthy risks, and staying within the safety zone. This can actually be fairly tricky to spot, as girls with low self-esteem tend to be fairly adept at masking their feelings. They stick to the friends they know they have, engage in activities they know they're good at, and showcase a skill set they've already honed. In a sense, they often appear "just fine" on the outside while struggling on the inside.

A lack of self-esteem can hold girls back in a number of ways. It actually affects every aspect of their lives. When girls lack self-esteem, they are less likely to raise their hands in school and engage in meaningful class discussions. This negatively affects their academic performance. In a social setting, girls with low self-esteem are less likely to seek out new friendships or join new groups. They also struggle to speak up when something isn't right. In sports, girls who struggle with self-esteem take fewer healthy risks and tend to hang back and watch more than they engage. The same goes for art, theater, and music. When girls don't value their abilities, they stop trying, and this prevents them from moving forward.

One of the most difficult things about spotting low self-esteem in our girls is that we always see the best in them. Marlee's parents struggled to accept that she had low self-esteem because they viewed her as a strong, talented leader. I see this with parents of young girls over and over again. Questions like "How can she possibly feel that way?" aren't asked in anger or disappointment; they're asked because parents always focus on the highlight reel when it comes to self-esteem. When parents are frustrated with behavior or want to get to the source of a problem, they share the negatives. But when it comes to self-esteem (much more of a gray area),

I hear a lot of "Oh, she's great and happy!" or "If anything, she has *too* much self-esteem!" Behind closed doors, I hear a much different story.

Nellie was the master of self-esteem deception. She had a (secret) routine with her mom each day. The drive home from school was always full of questions. How was your test? How was lunch? Do you want to have anyone over this weekend? The list was never-ending, as if her mom had spent the entire school day thinking up questions to ask during the 10-minute drive. For a while, this bugged Nellie. She just wanted to sit and look out the window, not tell her mom every single thing. At some point, however, Nellie decided that the constant questions must serve some purpose. She figured that her mom just wanted to know that Nellie was doing well in school and super popular (or something along those lines). That's when she developed the secret routine: Tell her three great things that happened and one not-so-great thing for balance (and so her mom would have a problem to solve). With this plan in place, the questions stopped.

The truth is that Nellie struggled that year. In third grade, school suddenly seemed hard. She felt like she couldn't keep up with her friends. Also? Her friends weren't really her friends anymore. She never knew where to sit during lunch, so she often sat alone and pretended to read a book (that she actually struggled to read). It wasn't always bad. On the good days, she had friends to sit with, and she kept up in class. Sadly, there were more bad days than good, and more often than not, she felt left behind. She wasn't allowed to watch the same shows as her friends and felt left out of conversations. She didn't get invited to sleepovers or to hang out as much as she once did. Each day had some failure in it. But her mom needed her to be happy, so she put on her happiest face and said the right things. No sense in both of them feeling miserable.

Given that low self-esteem can be hard to spot (particularly if your daughter doesn't want you to spot it), it's important to be aware of the many things that can trigger low self-esteem for young girls. Adults have a tendency to look for the big things that might trigger a dip in self-esteem: not making the travel team, poor academic performance, or the loss of a close friendship (to name just a few). And those things can be devastating for young girls. But it's not necessarily the big things that affect their overall self-esteem; it's what I refer to as "micro-stressors" and "micro-rejections" that leave a mark.

When we take a closer look at Nellie's story, there isn't a clear "aha!" moment that sheds light on her steady decline in self-esteem. She felt like she was struggling in school, but she wasn't failing. She felt left out at times, but she managed to continue her friendships. There wasn't any big change that caused internal upheaval for Nellie; it was more of a slow decline in self-worth over time.

Nellie did confront a number of micro-stressors each day. Reading out loud was torture for her, but she had to do it sometimes. While she loved hands-on activities, she had difficulty speaking up in groups. This made group projects stressful for her. Homework was difficult on a light day. She also dealt with micro-rejections. Shifting peer relationships, heated interactions with her mom about homework, and teasing by her brother all added up to feel huge over time. While there was no big event that negatively affected Nellie, numerous small stressors and re-jections snowballed to cause the dip in self-esteem.

What Triggers Low Self-Esteem in Young Girls?

Wouldn't it be great if I could just give you a giant list to check off and you wouldn't have to worry about your daughter's self-esteem ever again? Believe me, I wish that too. Unfortunately, it's not that simple. While there are certainly some commonalities when it comes to low self-esteem in girls, we have to remember that every girl is different. I always tell young girls that we all view the world through our own lenses. While some girls might have a naturally rosy lens with an ability to seek out the silver lining in even the darkest moments, others might view the world through a murkier lens. That makes it difficult to give you a "do this; don't do this" kind of list. We can, however, look for the patterns.

The first step is to think about your daughter's baseline. What is her general outlook on any given day? What do you perceive as her strengths? What might she identify as her strengths? What are her hurdles? When we take the time to sit back and evaluate our daughters' baselines, we get in touch with who they are as individuals and what might contribute to changes in those baselines.

Parent-Teacher Conference

Consider these questions to determine your daughter's baseline self-esteem:

✿ Is she generally optimistic or pessimistic?

✿ Is she a worrier?

✿ How does she approach a problem?

✿ How does she cope with negative feedback?

✿ What does she do with her free time?

✿ What does she like to do with friends?

✿ How does she bounce back if things don't go her way?

✿ What are her strengths?

✿ Why are other kids drawn to her?

✿ What are her obstacles?

Once you've established your daughter's baseline self-esteem, you can begin to think about the outside factors that might contribute to spikes and dips. Positive feedback from a teacher after a report she worked hard on might cause a spike, for example, while negative feedback from a coach during lacrosse practice might trigger a dip. Take a look at the potential self-esteem dippers that can occur in the following areas and consider whether or not they might affect your daughter.

Relationships

Relationships with parents, siblings, teachers, coaches, and friends play an enormous role in the lives of school-age girls. Once girls begin elementary school, they work hard to individuate and develop meaningful relationships with positive influences outside of the immediate family. While reciprocal relationships (in which both girls put in the same effort) can positively affect self-esteem, relationships that don't work can trigger low self-esteem.

Frequent criticism from parents, consistent negative feedback from teachers or coaches, poor sibling relationships, and being left out or rejected by peers can all contribute to low self-esteem.

Appearance and Body Image

It doesn't matter how many young girls sit in my office and talk about what they wish they could change about their appearance or why the "pretty" girls have the most friends—my heart still drops each time it happens. This was once a conversation I had with middle school girls on a regular basis, but now I have second-graders looking me in the eyes and wondering about how fat they might be or what they look like to other people.

It's fine to rely on clichés like "It's what's on the inside that matters" when words elude you for a moment, but the truth is that girls confront body image issues early and often. If they are asking difficult questions that make you want to move to a deserted island until your daughter turns 21, it's because they are hearing this stuff out in the great big world, and they are trying to make sense of it. For many, these thoughts and feelings negatively affect their self-esteem.

In fact, the Dove Global Beauty and Confidence Report, which surveyed over 10,000 women and girls in 13 countries, showed a startling decline in the body confidence of women and girls.[2] Of note, 79 percent of girls say they opt out of important life activities—such as trying out for a team or club, and engaging with family or loved ones—when they don't feel good about the way they look. Additionally, seven in 10 girls with low "body-esteem" say they won't be assertive in their opinion or stick to their decision if they aren't happy with the way they look. While clichés (The grass is always greener . . .) might have a point, clearly our girls are still struggling.

Accomplishments

As previously mentioned, self-esteem can get wrapped up in achievement when it comes to young girls. Many experts point to overuse or inappropriate use of praise as a cause for concern on this front. Some might have us believe we're raising a generation of praise junkies who can't survive without constant positive input. While this extreme certainly does exist, I'm not convinced it's the only factor at play here.

When I ask young girls why success is so very important to them, they often tell me that success and friendship go together. Sure, they like the praise their parents bestow upon them when they do something great; but they also think that other kids will look up to them and want to be around them, and teachers will take notice; and they like the feeling they get when they score the winning goal, see an A on a paper, or receive that coveted trophy (and no, I don't mean participation trophies). Bottom line: Success feels good.

The issue, of course, is that life is complicated, and most kids experience a series of successes and failures along the way. The ones who know how to cope with failure (more on that in chapter 10) can work their way through the low moments. The ones who don't, on the other hand, take a hit to their self-esteem.

Unexpected Life Changes

Sometimes life throws us curveballs, and that can definitely affect self-esteem (positively or negatively). For young girls, big life changes can cause significant emotional upheaval. Be on the lookout for dips in self-esteem if you are dealing with any of the following:

- Moving
- Divorce
- New school
- Loss in the family

Academic Struggles

Academic struggles and low self-esteem tend to go hand in hand. It makes perfect sense. For years, I worked with kids with learning differences. By the time some of these kids got to us, they had been struggling in public or private school for years. It's difficult to feel good about yourself when you constantly feel like the one kid who doesn't understand what's going on in the classroom.

I once described it to a parent of a young girl as a deflated tire. When you run over a nail, you lose a bunch of air at once, but the tire can keep on going. If you keep on driving over nails, more and more air escapes until the tire is completely flat. For this mom's little girl, school felt like an endless path of nails. With each failed quiz, mixed-up words while reading out loud, or misunderstood assignment, she lost a little more air. Every. Single. Day.

If your girl struggles in school, even just a little bit, there's a solid chance that what she perceives as her lack of ability is chipping away at her overall self-esteem. Middle childhood is a developmental stage characterized by building competencies. If your girl struggles in the place where she spends most of her waking hours, she's likely to feel deflated as a result.

Watch Out for Negative Core Beliefs

Remember Sienna (the friend collector/people pleaser)? When we finally broke down her need to be liked by all, we found the root cause of her maladaptive behavior: negative core beliefs. Sienna, as it turned out, believed that she was actually fairly "unlikable." Her parents divorced when she was young, and her father traveled often, sometimes even canceling their weekends in favor of work. She fought with her mother almost daily. They fought about little things, like taking out the trash, and big things, like getting along with Dad. Sienna's home life involved a near constant state of negative input, and because of that, she developed negative core beliefs about herself.

Each time she fought with her mom, for example, she felt intense feelings of guilt afterward. From this, she developed the belief that she is unkind. Each time her dad canceled their plans in favor of work, she felt sad and hurt. From these feelings stemmed the belief that she is unlikable. So why did she put so much energy into being popular at school? She felt that the only way to counteract those negative core beliefs was to get out there and be better. Instead of dealing with the belief system and working through her feelings, she tried to get around the issue by putting on a different mask at school and acting a completely different part.

It's not just a matter of family stress that causes kids to do this. Jane always struggled to make friends in school. She had difficulty keeping up with conversations and was often on the outside looking in. The other girls were nice to her, but they didn't seek her out. She was just kind of there. She took to studying characters in TV shows to figure out how to fit in (I thought this was rather clever). To get attention, she acted out story lines from her favorite shows. It worked for a little while, until one of the other girls figured out what she was doing. That was when the girls stopped being so nice and starting avoiding her. When I helped Jane unpack her feelings, we uncovered the fact that her behavior was directly affected by one negative core belief: She was certain that she was incapable of making friends on her own. She *had* to become someone else.

Negative core beliefs are sneaky because they develop over time. When girls have the same negative experiences over and over again (such as Jane struggling to join the group), they develop a belief system in response to that negative input. They develop negative attitudes about themselves and feel helpless to change the way they feel. The good news is that they can change these belief systems.

It should come as no surprise that most girls have a longing to find where they fit in. Part of the challenge of middle childhood is figuring out where they belong (other than in their immediate family). Girls want to find their tribes. Parents often communicate fears that their girls will either be associated with a clique that leaves other girls out or be left out of the cool clique, but young girls don't necessarily think in terms of cliques. They look for groups of other girls with similar interests. They want to find their people. They want to belong.

A 10-year-old girl once described the recess yard at her school. She talked about the girls who play tag, the girls who walk and talk, the girls who play pretend, and the girls who play four square. When

I asked her if one group was preferential to another, she simply stated that the groups are formed based on interest. If I wanted to figure out who the "popular" kids were, she said, I should look at their clothes. The popular kids dress alike and don't do anything but sit and talk at recess. Otherwise, girls break off into groups based on what they like to do. In some ways, this group mentality felt refreshing at first. To hear this girl tell it, there was a group for every girl. The only problem is that once those groups are formed, they rarely change. And leaving the group to join another (even just for the day) is considered "mean girl-ish."

Girlhood involves a complicated hierarchy, it seems. If you're still wondering why self-esteem plays such a big role in the social development of young girls, the answer is this: Once you find your tribe (if you find your tribe), you can't ever leave it. You have to continue to work to please (and impress) the other tribe members or you might lose your place. It's not easy. Every positive interaction leads to self-esteem boosts, but every negative interaction chips away at the self-esteem. Girlhood isn't as simple as finding some other nice girls to hang out with; it's actually a never-ending game of "Do you *still* like me?"

Like Versus Likable

I spend a fair amount of time dissecting the word "like" with young girls. I hear a lot of "She doesn't like me," "I don't like her," and "Do you think people like me?" from my side of the couch. The pressure to fit in and find the right group is so very intense for young girls that they spend a lot of time wondering about whether or not other people actually like them. They even worry about whether or not their parents like them! As a second-grade girl once told me, "Your parents have to love you, but that doesn't mean they actually like you." Imagine that?

Part of shifting those core beliefs from negative to positive involves helping girls understand the difference between like and likable (see the chocolate bar experiment in the Girls Can! section below). Girls get so wrapped up in wondering how they're being judged by others that they forget that the judgment of a few doesn't accurately reflect who they are. Sometimes one simple question helps girls shift their thinking: Why are you likable?

How Does Popularity Contribute to Mean Girl Culture?

When girls become fixated on the number of friends they have instead of the quality of their friendships, relating to other girls becomes a numbers game. Someone has to have the most, and someone has to have the least. That's the simple math of the social hierarchy in mean girl culture. To be the one with the most friends, you might have to take down a few girls on your way to the top. This can become dangerous, for both the aggressor and her victims. This cycle of negative interactions affects the self-esteem of both the social climbers and the girls being pushed down. While it might be difficult to empathize with the aggressor (particularly if you are the mother of a victim), it is important to note that it's lonely at the top when your path to social success includes emotionally detaching yourself from every other girl along the way.

That's why it's essential to focus on positive friendship skills from the beginning. Instead of dismissing friendship problems as "drama" or reducing the aggressor to a "mean girl," we have to get in there and help girls learn how to relate to and support one another.

When girls are encouraged to approach early friendships from a positive mind-set, they learn to look for positive attributes that each girl brings to the group. Instead of worrying about how many other girls like them and what they have to do to be liked by other girls, they learn to look for the unique qualities of others and to rely on their own strengths as sources of likability. This positive mind-set helps girls learn to build each other up and support one another. It also decreases unhealthy competition among girls.

Self-esteem fluctuates as girls grow (that's natural), but it's important to focus on a positive sense of self during middle childhood. If a negative sense of self develops during this time, kids can get stuck in a rut and struggle to work through it. While it's perfectly natural to have bad days (and even terrible, horrible, no good, very bad weeks), helping girls recognize their strengths can boost their overall self-esteem.

Girls Can!

The Chocolate Bar Experiment

Have you ever asked your kids to organize their Halloween candy by favorites? I remember doing this as a child. First, we sorted the loot by brand. Next, we lined up the piles from most to least favorite. Then we traded. I think back on this Halloween ritual when I talk to kids about likability. In essence, the great candy bar trade of Halloween night all boiled down to likability. Each item had a different likability scale for each kid, and the trades were made accordingly.

I use mini chocolate bars (with parents' permission, of course) to help young girls think about the difference between like and likability. Though the candy bars each look appealing in their shiny wrappers, it's natural to like one more than another. When we take the time to break each bar down into what it makes it likable, we see the beauty beneath the surface. In describing the small details that make the bar so yummy, girls learn to look for the nuances. Also, who doesn't love a project that involves tasting candy?

Grab a bag of assorted mini chocolate bars (or a bunch of different fruits, if candy isn't your thing), and set up a tasting center. Use a blindfold to help your girl rely on her senses. Ask her to describe the details of each bar. Is it creamy or crunchy? Is it sweet or a little bitter? What makes it stand out from the others? What makes it likable? Once you've had your fill of taste testing, ask your daughter to think about what qualities she has hidden beneath the surface that make her likable. How does she stand out? Why is she a good person to be around? This exercise helps girls shift their thinking from "Do other girls like me?" to "I am likable because . . ."

Teach Cognitive Reframing

I can't tell you how many times I hear moms respond with "So much drama!" when girls communicate negative thoughts. It's as if young girls aren't allowed to verbalize the thoughts that bring them down, but we all have negative thoughts and feelings at times. A better (and far less publicly humiliating) strategy than reducing their feelings to "drama" is to teach young girls the power of cognitive reframing. When girls learn how to shift their negative thinking to positive thinking, they are empowered to work through difficult emotions independently.

First of all, allow your girl to vent. We all need to get our feelings out, even if those feelings are negatively charged and disproportionate to the situation. Venting emotions helps girls work through anger and frustration before moving forward with solutions. Next, encourage your daughter to restate her negative thoughts and reframe them with positive thoughts. Check out this example to see what I mean:

NEGATIVE THOUGHT	POSITIVE THOUGHT
I have no friends.	I have friends at school.
I'm not popular.	I have a small group of good friends.
I can't solve this problem.	I can keep trying until I figure it out.

When girls learn to reframe their negative thoughts, they are empowered to take control of a situation and create a positive outcome or outlook. Low self-esteem can get in the way of focusing on the positive attributes girls have. This subtle shift in thinking helps girls tap into their strengths instead of getting caught in a negative thought cycle.

Plant a Positive Thought Garden

There are mixed messages in the media when it comes to praise. Don't praise too much or your kids will be praise hungry. Praise only effort, not results. Praise sporadically. The list of tips on praise goes on and on. Here's the thing: It feels good to get a pat on the back. It feels even better when you know your strengths and can give *yourself* a pat on the back.

Plant a praise garden with your child (limited crafting skills necessary). Cut out several circles using construction paper. Next, cut some flower petals. Ask your daughter to write her name in the circles. On each petal, have your daughter write (or draw) something about herself. She might write "loves to dance," "good friend," or "enjoys math." It can be anything—big or small. Glue the petals to the circles, add some stems, and plant those flowers right on the bedroom wall! A praise garden reminds your daughter that she is likable. She might not befriend every kid in her grade, but that doesn't mean she isn't likable.

Good Friend Collage

Girls get so caught up in finding their tribes that they forget to consider what it actually means to be a good friend. It's important to help girls shift their thinking from "How can I be more popular?" to "What can I do to be a good friend?" To do that, it helps to encourage girls to think about what they consider good qualities in their existing friends.

This is a great activity for your daughter to do either on her own or with another girl. I find that young girls love collages for a few reasons. Searching for imagery to go with the theme of the collage is fun and sparks interesting conversation. It's easier to talk about difficult topics when engaged in a creative activity because it reduces the pressure of filling the silence. Finally, the finished product provides an appealing visual that can be revisited later.

Break out the old magazines and grab a small poster board. Encourage your daughter to search out words and images that represent what it means to be a good friend. Talk as you work and share your own thoughts about good friends. This activity helps girls open up while considering the importance of being a good friend.

Create a Friendship Word Cloud

Young girls are socialized to equate numbers of friends with popularity. If you have a ton of friends, more people want to be friends with you. But focusing on numbers doesn't account for the *quality* of the friendships.

Wordle is a fun Web site for creating free word clouds and a great tool for helping girls focus on positive friendship traits. If technology isn't your thing, you can help your daughter create a word cloud using markers and paper, but I do recommend exploring technology with your daughter. Ask your daughter to think of traits that make up a good friend. Examples might be loyal, caring, kind, funny, smart . . . you get the point. Type those words into the Wordle text box, push the "go" button, and watch her personal friendship word cloud appear. You can flip through to find the colors you like and print or save for later use.

Personal Rainbow

I find that young girls get so caught up in what they wish they could be that they forget to consider what they already are. We all have strengths and positive qualities, but overthinking the strengths of others can cause us to devalue ourselves. That's where the personal rainbow comes in.

I like to remind girls of the power of the rainbow. When the storm moves on and the sun begins to emerge, beautiful colors light up the sky for a moment. In that moment, the world feels like it stops. People stop what they're doing (driving, working, exercising) to look up and enjoy the brief vision in the sky. Girls can find their own inner rainbows by taking the time to discover and highlight their strengths and positive qualities.

Easy craft alert: All you need is a pile of construction paper in rainbow colors, markers, glue or tape, and a pair of scissors. Start by asking your daughter to cut out a cloud and write her name in the center. Next, ask her to cut a thick stripe for each color of the rainbow. This is when you stop to talk about those positive qualities. Ask your daughter a simple question: What makes you great? What makes you special? Have your daughter write one positive quality on each stripe and glue the stripes to the cloud. Voila! Your daughter has a personal rainbow to hang in her room and remind her that she is full of great qualities.

Good Stuff Calendar

It's no big secret that girls live busy lives these days, and sometimes our culture of busy makes it difficult to stop and smell the roses once in a while. Part of developing a healthy sense of self includes making time to do things that make us feel happy. When girls are always on the run, fulfilling obligations, they don't necessarily have the time to enjoy the simple pleasures of life that actually build them up by making them feel calm.

I encourage girls to create their own "good stuff" calendars to remember to enjoy the little things in life. Print out a calendar (including each month of the year). Ask your daughter to put one happy activity per day on each day of the week. These should be small things that remind your girl to slow down and appreciate life. Examples might include: go for a bike ride, water the flowers, draw a picture, swing, play outside, etc. It might take a while to fill in the whole calendar, and there will be some repeats, but once it's complete, your daughter will have a year of happy activities on her wall.

Like Button

Chances are you've used some form of social media in front of your daughter. If not, I'm hoping you've at least discussed social media with your daughter. She's hearing about it, that much I can promise. Either way, your daughter probably knows a thing or two about the "like button" on Facebook or that little heart on Instagram that shows how much you enjoy a post. I once overheard an eight-year-old girl ask her mom, "How many likes did my video get?" every five minutes while at the park.

The upside of social media is that it keeps us all connected. It makes it easy to share information and engage with friends and loved ones. The downside for young girls (and no, you shouldn't fudge her age to get your daughter an account just because another mom did it for her kid) is that they get caught up in likes and hearts, and they begin to judge their own worth based on how many positive reviews they get from others. It's an endless cycle of anticipation and disappointment for some.

I encourage parents to flip the switch on the like button by empowering girls to look for likes. First, talk about why it feels good to receive positive feedback from others. Second, discuss what it *actually* means when someone hits the like button. Does it make a person popular? Important? Confident? Break it down so that your girl can see the flawed nature of living in a society of likes. Last, encourage your daughter to be a "liker" and look for good things to like, both online (for older girls actively using social media) and in her daily life (for girls of all ages). By focusing on the good stuff and providing kind feedback (both online and in real life), we empower our girls to build healthy and positive relationships with others. I always tell young girls that it never hurts to give a "like," but it just might hurt if you don't.

Team Player

Not all girls want to play team sports, and that's okay. There are plenty of ways to be a team player without playing on an athletic team. Working together for a common goal with other girls helps girls practice friendship skills and learn about the power of building each other up. While there are formal groups designed to do just this (Girl Scouts of America is a wonderful resource, as is Girls on the Run), there are also art classes, theater groups, and various clubs for girls.

The best way to encourage your girl to join a group of some kind is to find one that inspires her. All too often, parents attempt to plug girls into teams because friends are on them or those activities are easy to access. The truth is that all girls have their own unique interests, and finding group activities that match those interests is the best way to get your girl involved in a group. Sometimes that means extra time in the car or looking a little harder to find the best fit, but the rewards are life-changing. Girls' groups empower girls to work together, empathize with each other, and lean on one another.

It's natural for young girls to struggle with trying to fit in and finding their place in girl world. But they shouldn't have to suffer in silence. When we help girls work through things like low self-esteem and friendship skills, we give them the tools to cope with these complicated issues as they grow.

CHAPTER 3

Risk Taking in the Name of Courage

If you obey all the rules, you miss all the fun.
—*Katharine Hepburn*

"I'm not allowed to climb trees anymore." Flynn says this without emotion. She doesn't seem upset about it, and she doesn't sound like she's longing to climb trees again. It's more of a statement of fact. I take the bait and ask why. "I fell out of a tree and broke my arm. Now trees are off-limits." I ask her if she climbs on monkey bars at the park. "Yes, but most parks are safe with the bouncy stuff if you fall." I ask her if she's ever tempted to climb a tree when she's out playing. "I learned my lesson about that. I don't want to break my arm again."

Flynn is a nine-year-old girl who plays soccer in the fall and enjoys riding her bike after school. She likes to ride around the park but not down the big hill (too dangerous) and only under the watchful eye of her mom. Before you scream, "helicopter parent!" I can actually tell you that Flynn craves the watchful eye. She feels safe when her mom is watching. That feeling of safety doesn't encourage her to take more chances, but she feels at home in her carefully constructed comfort zone (where arms don't break and moms are there for the rescue).

I see a lot of risk-averse young girls these days. Even when they know their strengths and have their goals, there is a pressure to play it safe. When you play it safe, you are likely to get it right. When you get it right, you succeed. The flip side of that, however, is that many young girls live with crippling self-doubt. Nudge them just outside their comfort zones and they fall apart.

Self-doubt can have long-term consequences. Negative emotions are closely tied to self-doubt. In fact, a study published in *Child Development* found that children who suffered from high levels of anxiety and depression were more likely to experience self-doubt.[1] The study, which evaluated more than 900 children between the ages of 9 and 13 during a 12-month period, found a clear link between emotional distress and negative beliefs about the self. This study sheds light on the fact that negative core beliefs, including feelings of self-doubt, can adversely affect how a child interacts with the world. What does this mean for our girls? It means that self-doubt makes them more likely to be risk-averse. It's difficult to take chances and step outside your comfort zone when you're convinced that any attempt to do so will likely result in failure.

It's natural for parents to worry about (or even just to consider) the safety of their kids at times. We say things like "Be careful!" because we don't want our kids to get hurt, and if we're being honest with ourselves, we really don't want to rush to the ER with broken bones and head injuries. In the mind of a parent, issuing warnings about potential safety hazards makes good sense. But it can backfire.

I actually learned this the hard way. I consider myself a laid-back mom. My kids have plenty of free time to play what they want when they want. I don't offer many restrictions, and when my daughter is

Parent-Teacher Conference

While all girls have their own stories to tell, there are some common themes that emerge when I talk to girls about their triggers for risk aversion. Keep these in mind if you sense that your daughter is always "playing it safe":

✿ **Fear of failure**—We've become such a success-driven society that many girls won't take risks so that they don't have to experience and own up to failure (see chapter 10 for more on failure and resilience).

✿ **Self-doubt**—Many girls talk about feeling like they don't have what it takes to succeed a lot of the time.

✿ **Unfair comparisons**—All girls have their own strengths, but sometimes girls get caught up in comparisons that leave them feeling deflated.

✿ **Safety concerns**—While "Look before you leap" is solid advice some of the time, girls hear this kind of advice so often that they feel like the world is a dangerous place.

✿ **Fear of embarrassment**—Many girls tell me they worry about the reactions of their peers.

✿ **Lack of free time**—Believe it or not, overscheduling can rob girls of the time they need to think about healthy risks (like climbing that tree) and to take action without adult supervision and instruction.

outside, she quite literally swings from vines. I issue a few silent prayers now and then when she takes a really big risk, but I don't stop her. There was a time, however, when I used a phrase (fairly regularly—she's been a climber since she learned to walk) that negatively affected her. The words I used were meant to encourage her to assess the situation first, but she interpreted that to mean "You don't think I'm capable." Fortunately, she had the guts to tell me about it. "When you say 'Be careful,' it makes me think you don't think I'm strong enough." I was stunned for a moment. My tree-climbing, vine-swinging, Irish dancing daughter has freakishly strong arms and legs and unnerving determination. I'm fairly certain she knows that I'm in awe of her most days. But my warnings to avoid falling off the staircase, for example, communicated a different (unintended) message. These days, I usually say, "Have fun!" when she makes a risky move (but I keep those silent prayers going, just in case).

What Causes Self-Doubt?

When I see a girl doing something really great and I don't think I can do it as well as her, I just walk away and say I'm not interested.

—*A fourth-grade girl*

Young girls struggle with self-doubt for a variety of reasons. Take Amanda, for example. A funny, bright, and playful third-grade student, Amanda enjoyed reading, art, and playing softball (but only if coached by her dad). She enjoyed the academic part of school (mostly) but struggled with the social hierarchy. She couldn't make sense of shifting friendships and lunch table groups that seemed to change almost daily. The big problem, though, was her relationship with her mom. While the social stuff caused mild discomfort and math wasn't her favorite subject, it was the interactions with her mom that left her crippled with self-doubt.

Amanda was the oldest of four kids, and also the "quiet" one. She didn't need a ton of attention in that she was generally fairly responsible for her age, but she craved it. Week after week, she talked about wanting one-on-one time with her mom that was "fun." Week after week, she didn't get it. Though her younger siblings were loud, fought often, and required near constant attention, Amanda's mom viewed her as the "demanding one." "She makes me feel guilty if I spend time with my friends," her mom explained. "I work hard and I need that time for myself." It was a constant battle between the two. Mom needed her time to decompress after a long workday, but Amanda needed time with her mom. What Mom considered an exercise in self-care felt like a huge rejection to Amanda. The more Mom chose her friends, the more Amanda doubted that her mom enjoyed spending time with her.

Unfortunately, rejection wasn't the only problem. Though Amanda excelled in nearly every subject in school, her reading grade was consistently average. Average. Not low. Not below grade level. Perfectly average—on grade level. Instead of celebrating Amanda's strengths, however, her mom chose to hyper-focus on what she perceived as her area of weakness. She hired a tutor. She quizzed Amanda about what she worked on in reading groups at school and corrected her homework each night. In short, she filled Amanda with self-doubt about her ability to learn to read proficiently.

Overinvolved parenting can trigger self-doubt in young girls. When parents micromanage everything that girls do and tell them how to do absolutely everything, girls feel like their parents think they're incapable of most things. While we all need to learn how to handle constructive feedback, if all you ever hear is that you can do things in a better way, you start to question your self-worth and your capabilities. When girls receive only negative or critical feedback from their parents, they feel like they aren't good enough (like they really don't measure up).

On the other end of the parenting spectrum, uninvolved parenting fills girls with self-doubt because they crave input, understanding, and connection. When parents are disengaged, girls feel rejected. They want their parents to appreciate them and take an interest in their interests. It's difficult to feel appreciated when even your greatest accomplishments seem to go unnoticed. Not all girls want to rehash their school days each night. Often, that feels like work. What they do want to do is share their hopes and dreams, seek advice on complicated issues, and even just spend time being together.

And then there's parental conflict. Whether parents live together or apart, parental conflict can trigger feelings of self-doubt and anxiety in young girls. In fact, one study found that marital discord (including verbal aggression, hostile conflict, and negative perceptions about the quality of the relationship) was associated with greater childhood insecurity, including both internalizing (such as heightened fears and anxiety, somatic complaints, and social withdrawal) and externalizing (commonly viewed as "acting out," which can include verbal and physical aggression) behaviors.[2]

When caregivers argue in front of or around young girls (try to remember that kids in this age group are excellent spies), they absorb both the negative emotions in the room and the communication patterns modeled for them. Young girls often tell me that it feels scary and overwhelming when they hear their parents (or other caregivers) argue, and they wonder what role they played in the argument. Many young girls engage in self-blame and feel like they are the source of the problem in the home. Because they generally don't know the specifics of the conflict, they attempt to fill in the blanks with the information they *do* have. If they hear a fight about finances, for example,

Parent-Teacher Conference

Conflict is inevitable, and it's important for girls to see that people can "fight fair" without hurting others. Consider your own conflict-resolution style and try some healthy tips to model adaptive conflict-resolution skills for your daughter (see chapter 9 for more on helping your girl learn to express her emotions):

❀ **Tune in:** Listen to your partner before responding.

❀ **Take breaks:** It's okay to "take five" to calm down. Tell your daughter what you will do to calm down (take a walk outside, deep breathing, exercise).

❀ **Use "I" statements:** Expressing your emotions is great; blaming isn't. Arguments grounded in blame rarely get anywhere. Use "I" statements to express your feelings and needs without blaming.

❀ **State the problem from both points of view:** Taking the time to clearly state the problem from each side can help people move from anger to problem solving.

❀ **Problem-solve together:** One of my favorite phrases to use in these situations is this: "We know what the problem is; how can we work together to solve it?" Make a list of potential strategies and talk them through.

❀ **Apologize and forgive:** We all say things we don't mean to say sometimes. Apologizing for our negative behaviors and accepting an apology from a partner shows our girls that mistakes can be undone and broken bridges can be repaired. Resist the urge to sweep an argument under the rug and make a point of repairing the damage instead.

they might worry that after-school sports cost too much money and triggered the argument.

Self-doubt isn't just about communication in the home, however. Remember those micro-rejections and micro-stressors we discussed earlier? Those play a significant role in both negative core beliefs and risk aversion. Many girls tell me that small rejections from authority figures like coaches, teachers, and other extended family members add up over time and leave them feeling worthless. That might sound like an exaggeration, but left unchecked (or unprocessed), these small rejections can snowball and trigger feelings of low self-worth.

One girl, who is a self-proclaimed "picky eater" ("I just like what I like. What's the big deal?"), shared how awful she feels at big family parties because one of her grandparents constantly criticizes her eating in passive-aggressive ways. She'll pass the mashed potatoes while declaring, "These look so amazing! Of course, you won't even try them. Your loss!" After years of this, this little girl has come to dread family parties. She knows the comments will come, even if she shovels food she hates down her throat without saying a word. The damage has been done.

Let's also discuss Kim. She's a 10-year-old softball star. That's what they tell her anyway. She tells me that she doesn't think she's the best player on the team, and she doesn't even like softball very much. "All they ever do is tell me what I'm doing wrong. I'm sick of it." On the one hand, at the end of a game or behind the scenes, she's referred to as a "star." That should be a good thing, right? On the other hand, her coaches have higher expectations for her and spend most of her practice time coming down on her for her "mistakes." That's how it feels to her, anyway. Without being on the field, there's no way to know the intent behind the words versus Kim's understanding of them. She feels like the other girls get more cheers than corrections, but she gets more corrections than cheers. She's burnt out on corrections.

For Kim, getting out of the game and avoiding the risk of what felt like constant negative feedback made sense. If she stopped trying, the criticism would also stop. She craved a break from the pressure that piled up each time her coaches called her out for her "mistakes," and avoiding the game altogether seemed the best (or only) option.

I hear a lot of complaints that girls are too "soft" and that we have to "toughen them up" to handle rejection from parents, coaches, teachers, and other adults in their lives. I've always had an issue with the "shake it off" style of raising kids that lurks beneath this sentiment. Yes, kids need to learn to hear and cope with constructive criticism. It's part of learning and growing. But "toughening girls up" isn't the same as empowering

Parent-Teacher Conference

Girls need to learn to accept constructive criticism and feedback from both adults and peers. A great way to help girls with this is to provide consistent feedback. Providing balanced feedback helps girls recognize that they have strengths and weaknesses (just like everybody else) and there are always things to work on. Try this:

"Something you do really well is . . ."

"Something I noticed you're having a hard time with is . . ."

"Do you have any goals you want to work on?"

We don't have to drill girls with negative feedback to help them see that they need to work on things. We simply have to focus on direct, honest, and balanced feedback. Pro tip: Share your own strengths, struggles, and goals to normalize it.

them to work through their struggles. And crying, feeling rejected, and expressing negative emotions are certainly not signs of "weakness" or being "soft." In fact, quite the opposite is true. When girls have the ability to get their internalized emotions to the surface, they are better able to hear and take on feedback and constructive criticism.

Do Peers Play a Role in Risk Avoidance?

> Sometimes I'm quiet because other kids don't get mad at you
> if you're quiet.
> —*A third-grade girl*

Peer conflict is yet another complication in the life of girls. While it's natural for friendships to change over time, and arguments can actually be quite healthy when girls are respectful, I find that most girls struggle to cope with the ebb and flow of friendships, and lack the skills to "fight fair"—not to mention the role that relational aggression plays.

Courtney spent three weeks dissecting a hot/cold friendship that had her running in circles. At first, the "cold" episodes seemed more lukewarm. Her friend sat somewhere else at lunch. Courtney was left out of a game at recess because she was "too slow eating." She wasn't in on a joke. Each time she told her mom, her mom encouraged her to move on. For the record, this *does* make sense. Sometimes there are miscommunications. Sometimes friends switch up their lunch spots. Sometimes a game begins long before you get there, and it's difficult to join. In isolation, any of these episodes wouldn't be a big deal. When you add them up, on the other hand, they feel enormous. Courtney felt unlikable.

Courtney had two theories on the matter: (1) She did something super horrible (though what she did was unclear), and her friend no longer liked her, and (2) she was not the kind of girl other girls liked. Both of those theories missed the mark, but because she never processed the events (she just kept "moving on"), she engaged in a pattern of negative thinking that resulted in significant cognitive distortions. "Other girls don't like me" is a tough pill to swallow at age 10. While her friend did leave her out some of the time, Courtney later confided that she gets jealous when her friend plays with other girls, and Courtney tries to keep her to herself. In this case, the relational aggression worked both ways.

Six months later, the girls were friends again, and the group expanded to include other girls. It took a lot of work, but Courtney learned to verbalize and cope with her feelings instead of internalizing negative emotions. She also learned to expand her social circle so that she wasn't tied to just one friend.

I find that unhealthy competition plays a fairly significant role in negative peer interactions these days. Girls are conditioned to look for flaws in other girls. Instead of celebrating one another's strengths, they attempt to spot the weaknesses. Instead of working together, they try to climb to the top. Instead of learning from one another, they make comparisons and build resentments. Does this happen all the time? Of course not. But it does, indeed, happen and not just on the playing field.

I was volunteering in a classroom one day, and a little girl confided in me that she's better at drawing horses than her best friend. "How great that you both love to draw horses," I responded, in an attempt to focus on the positive. "Yes, but I'm just *way* better at it than her. That's just true." I wasn't there to teach social skills, but I wanted to. I wanted to take a moment to talk about compliments versus comparisons. I wanted to discuss the fact that making comparisons is often useless and sometimes unfair. I also wanted to talk about feelings. It wasn't for me to discuss those things on that occasion, however, so instead I said, "Well, I think it's great that you and your best friend share that interest. It seems to me that if you help each other out, you can probably draw a whole book of horses together!" She smiled and walked away. I later heard her talk about making a "horse drawings book" with her friend.

The good news in the above scenario is that the young girl confided in me instead of putting her friend down. The bad news is that I can't be sure she hasn't put her friend down on another occasion. If her go-to feel-good strategy is to criticize her "best friend" to make herself look better, she probably does offer up peer-to-peer criticism at times. That can be very painful.

Young girls can trigger risk aversion in their friends when they criticize them a lot, make unfair comparisons, engage in highly competitive behavior (as in they always have to win *and* they always have to be the best), use put-downs when feeling jealous, and use relational aggression to remain in the power position. As one third-grade girl told me, "When other girls give me mean looks because I did something great, it makes me never want to do that thing again." No one likes to feel that other people are criticizing them or putting them down, and it hurts when others dismiss your achievements or react negatively out of jealousy.

What About Sibling Rivalry?

Andrea and her sister are polar opposites. Andrea loves to study; her sister loves to daydream. Andrea has her entire future mapped out; her sister doesn't know what she's doing five minutes from now. Andrea loves science and math; her sister loves drawing all over her notebooks. Andrea prefers to keep their bedroom neat and tidy; her sister doesn't. Andrea gets straight A's in school; her sister hardly turns in her homework. You might think that Andrea's sister is the one with the jealousy issues (it must be hard to live with perfection, after all), but it's actually Andrea who fuels the rivalry.

"She doesn't ever study, she can't be bothered to put her clothes in the laundry, she leaves stuff everywhere, and everyone thinks she's so great!" In Andrea's mind, she's doing all the right things, while her sister is lazy and disorganized. Andrea feels like she's the shining star of the family, yet her sister seems to get more attention. She's angry with her sister so often that she can't see the situation clearly. She can't see that maybe her sister struggles in school and that's why she's checked out. She can't see that maybe her sister leaves her stuff everywhere because that's how she finds things. She can't even see that her sister's strengths (art) aren't valued in their school so she doesn't have the opportunity to grow in that particular area. She can only see the problems. Andrea argues with her sister a lot. It doesn't get them anywhere, but she does it anyway. It's the only thing she can think to do.

Once Andrea works through her negativity, I help her consider what it must feel like to be her sister. Does Andrea really believe that her sister, who hates school and rarely does her work, receives positive feedback from her teachers each day? Does Andrea believe that it feels good to be criticized about everything from schoolwork to cleaning your room every day of the week by your own sister?

When anger and jealousy take center stage, empathy quickly dissolves. When family members get stuck on fair versus unfair or better versus worse, relationships suffer and self-doubt skyrockets. When your own family members lose faith in you and treat you poorly, how can you be expected to walk confidently into the world? I see this over and over again with young girls. Instead of empathizing with their siblings, they step all over them to rise to the top of the family.

When parents fail to intervene and teach siblings how to work through their emotions and conflicts, sibling rivalry can quickly snowball into sibling bullying, and that can come with significant consequences. In fact, research shows that sibling rivalry is often filled with psychological and physical aggression, which can result in higher rates of anxiety, anger, and depression later on in life.[3] Sibling relationships, as it turns out, can come at a cost (for years to come).

I always encourage parents to view sibling relationships as friendships first. Yes, they will argue sometimes. They will feel jealous, and they will hurt each other's feelings. When we help them work through these conflicts and emotions, however, we help them learn and grow. Nurturing the sibling bond not only gives kids a solid foundation of friendship and support; it also gives them a safe space to practice these difficult social skills that are essential out in the world.

Parent-Teacher Conference

You can't (and shouldn't) solve every argument for your kids, but you can teach them how to work things out. Practice these skills with your kids at home (or in the classroom):

❀ Show that you're listening by making eye contact and repeating back what you hear.

❀ Share your thoughts in a calm voice.

❀ Tell how *you* feel.

❀ Brainstorm solutions together. Take turns sharing ideas.

❀ Use rock, paper, scissors or pull from a hat to choose a solution.

❀ Try three solutions before you ask for help.

How Does Mean Girl Culture Increase Self-Doubt?

Girls are highly social beings, and no matter how many times you tell your daughter not to care about what other girls think, it's really hard to do that. It's natural for girls to compare themselves to other girls, and it's also natural for girls to wonder how other girls judge them.

When girls use social aggression to keep other girls down, they send a clear message: I'm on top. That leaves the victim feeling hopeless and questioning her own self-worth. It's very difficult to tap into and celebrate your strengths when other girls are putting you down. In fact, I find that victims often become hyper-focused on trying to get back in with the group, only to face further humiliation and embarrassment when the behavior continues.

One thing parents can do to help their daughters step out of this negative cycle is to enforce a friend vacation for a specified period of time. This should not be presented as a direct order to end the friendship forever. Instead, it should be viewed as an opportunity to explore new possibilities while letting go of the negative emotions tied up in the friendship that isn't working. During that time, encourage your daughter to take healthy risks like reaching out to a new friend or trying a new activity. I find that when I request that girls take a friend break for a certain period of time, it creates the emotional space they need to move in a different direction without the fear of losing that former friendship forever (even if it isn't a healthy friendship at the moment).

The Benefits of Being a Risk-Taking Girl

When girls take healthy risks, they push their own personal boundaries. When they push themselves, they become more confident and resilient. Taking risks is not just about pushing limits, though. When girls consider risks, they have to weigh the pros and cons of the situation, they have to tap into every ounce of courage they can muster, and they have to face down the fear that their risks might not pay off. When the risks fall short, they find a way around it. The more they do this, the more they learn to believe in themselves and to work through obstacles to achieve their goals. This is where resilience is born.

I hear a lot of complaints about "giving up." Lack of resilience is a common problem among young girls right now. When something feels difficult or just out of reach, the easy thing to do is to bail out. If you quit *before* you fail, you didn't really fail. I once had a little girl look me straight in the eyes and tell me that the reason she quits activities often is that she doesn't like it when she feels like everyone else is doing well and she's struggling. The truth is that she wasn't struggling with any particular activity, but her low self-esteem clouded her ability to see her own strengths. She bopped from activity to activity without ever finishing anything, but she never had to feel like a failure.

Risk-taking girls grow up feeling powerful and strong. They feel secure about themselves. They aren't afraid to fail because they know they can get back up and try again. They learn to take action and make positive choices, but they also learn to use critical-thinking skills to assess the risks and benefits of their choices. Risk-taking girls aren't afraid to express their emotions and seek help when they need it, and though they also have periods of self-doubt (as we all do), they aren't overwhelmed by it. Risk-taking girls know that working through difficult problems is hard but can be done, and they usually come out stronger for it. In short, risk-taking girls harness their power to act and solve their own problems, and that makes them self-confident and resilient.

Parents often ask me how their girls ended up with so much self-doubt. Why are they so afraid to try new things and put themselves out

Parent-Teacher Conference

There are endless possibilities when it comes to healthy risks for girls these days, but below are a few ideas to get you started:

✿ Climb a tree!

✿ Ride a bike down a steep hill.

✿ Sleep at a friend's or relative's house.

✿ Try a new sport.

✿ Join a theater group.

✿ Try a musical instrument.

✿ Run for student council.

✿ Climb a giant rock wall (one step at a time!).

✿ Learn to dive.

there? Which came first, the negative emotions or the paralyzing self-doubt? That may be impossible to answer, but the important thing to remember is that it's a cycle, and one that needs to be broken. The best way to curb self-doubt is to teach young girls to be courageous.

Girls Can!

Create a Power Thoughts Wall

One thing that really helps girls who get stuck in a loop of "I can't" or "I don't know" is to add some power thoughts to their bedrooms.

Kids internalize the messages they hear, so we might as well make them powerful ones. You know your daughter best, so try to choose phrases that will make sense to her. Ask for her input. What kinds of positive phrases would she want someone to say about her? Consider phrases like "I know that kindness matters" and "I can make my dreams come true." When your daughter is surrounded by positive messages, she will internalize them over time and replace negative self-talk with power thoughts. Side note: I surprised my own daughter with a power thoughts wall, and I find that she is drawn to it when she needs a little uplifting.

Courage Cards

Sometimes kids need a little courage on the go. Courage cards are a great way to provide gentle reminders when your girls are at school, off to a game, or sleeping out for the night.

Handwritten notes are a fun way to connect with your daughter while she's away from you. Take that concept one step further by adding notes of encouragement. Phrases like "I am creative," "I am brave," or "I am strong" remind your daughter that she can handle whatever comes her way, even when you're not right next to her. Write the words that will empower your daughter on index cards and stick them in her backpack, her lunch box, or her sleepover bag.

Challenge Sticks

Sometimes risk aversion develops because kids don't want to make mistakes; other times they don't want to break the rules. More often than not, they don't know what constitutes a healthy risk. Parents spend so much time cautioning kids about potential dangers that we forget to encourage them to go for it.

Instead of making resolutions on January 1, I like to ask my kids to come up with three new things to try during the year—a list of goals for the coming year. You don't need to wait for the year to begin to create a new list of healthy risks, though. You can do this anytime and add to it as you cross things off.

Healthy risks are anything just outside the comfort zone. Ice skating, skateboarding, skiing, learning to sew, spending longer periods of time away from home, jumping from swings, conquering monkey bars . . . the options are endless. Sit with your daughter and brainstorm the things that you've both wanted to do but always avoid for some reason. Once you have a good list of fun risks to take, write them on Popsicle sticks (one challenge per stick) and place them in a jar. Each time you find a free afternoon, grab a stick and go do it—together. When your daughter knows she has your unconditional support, she'll be more likely to put one foot in front of the other and go for it. And it's a lot of fun!

Rose-Colored Glasses

When I was in high school, I begged my parents for sunglasses with rose-tinted lenses. I was obsessed with them, and for good reason. The minute I put those glasses on, the world seemed a happier place. Life felt manageable. Even on the foggiest days, optimism existed in the rose-colored sky that magically appeared when I wore those shades. I miss those glasses, but these days I have young girls create their own rose-colored glasses to view the world through a different lens.

With a little light cardboard (or even construction paper) and some pink cellophane wrap, your daughter can craft her own rose-colored glasses to inspire optimism when self-doubt comes crashing in. While she works on them, talk about the fact that self-doubt affects absolutely everyone at times. It's perfectly normal to wonder where you fit or how you compare. The important thing is to circle back around to positive thinking. That's where the rose-colored glasses come in handy.

Before you head outside to try them out, ask your daughter to describe three positives from the day. They can be anything from "A friend laughed at my joke" to "I remembered my spelling words!" Sometimes we need time to work through the negative thoughts before we find the positive. That's okay. It also helps to remind her that small positives are still positives. Once you've discussed a few positive thoughts from the day, head outside and look through those rose-colored glasses. Talk about how things tend to look different through a different lens. Take some time to view the world in rose, and discuss how you feel afterward. Then harness that optimism and set some new goals.

Mountain Climber

While some girls are risk takers from the start, all girls can learn to step outside their comfort zones and gradually push their own limits. I like to talk about mountain climbing when encouraging girls to take little risks here and there. When you stand at the bottom of a big mountain, it's natural to wonder how you'll get to the top. It feels overwhelming at first, but you put one foot in front of the other and take breaks at the rest stops along the way. It's the same with taking new risks. You start small and take one little risk at a time, with time to stop and reflect after each new risk.

Have your daughter draw a large mountain on a piece of paper and color it in as she sees fit (for tweens, google some photos of mountains and start with a photo collage). Next, ask her to think about some small chances she's wanted to take but hesitated to follow through on for one reason or another. Have her write them along the mountain, one after another, until she reaches the top. Add a rest stop at the top to take a break and think about how each risk turned out. Add a few more healthy risks along the trail leading back to the bottom. Your daughter can post this mountain in her room and check risks off her list as she takes them. Be sure to check in with her and talk about how she felt after taking those chances.

Jealousy Smoothie

Have you ever read *Enemy Pie* by Derek Munson?[4] You should. It's a great story for girls and boys that addresses bullying, misunderstandings, and mending fences. In it, a boy's father promises to make enemy pie to put a stop to unkind behavior by a peer. The only catch is that his son has to spend an entire day with his enemy to make the pie work. In the end, the pie is actually a delicious cherry pie, and the boy makes a new friend. After reading that book to girls, I ask them to create a recipe (a real one) for a jealousy smoothie to use the next time they're feeling jealous of a friend.

I find that girls have an easier time working through negative emotions when they have something to do while they talk. Many girls also experience big feelings of guilt when they're feeling jealous because they are generally told to be kind and nice. We have to put an end to this practice. It's okay to feel jealous sometimes! It's what we do with the feeling of jealousy that matters.

Here's how the jealousy smoothie works: For each jealous feeling, you add an ingredient to the smoothie. "I can't believe she won the friendship award at school" = vanilla yogurt. "Her parents buy her everything she wants so she has the coolest stuff" = strawberries. You get the drill. You add the ingredients to the blender as your daughter vents her feelings, and when you hit the "mix" button, you talk about ways to change her jealous thoughts to positive thoughts. You might say something like "You always tell me how friendly she is to other kids, so it probably felt good to be recognized for kindness" or "Tell me about some of your favorite things in your room and why you love them." In the end, your daughter works through her negative emotions *and* ends up with a yummy treat to share with Mom. You dump the negative thoughts, mix up some positive thoughts, and share a special moment as a result.

Ice Cream Cone Compliments

Alert: This one is perfect for groups!

I find that girls get so caught up in comparisons that they don't make much time for compliments. Instead of sharing what they view as a strength of another girl out loud, they internalize negative feelings about themselves. When we teach girls to build each other up out loud, they learn about the power of looking for positive attributes.

You can do this one as a family, in a classroom, or in any other group. Ask your daughter to cut enough cones out of construction paper so that each person in the group has one. Write your name on your cone. Next, cut enough ice cream scoops (in a variety of colors) so that each person can give one scoop to every person in the group. Ask each group member to write one (thoughtful) compliment for each person in the group on a scoop and sign it. I might write, "You always empathize with your friends—Mommy" on my daughter's scoop, for example. Finally, deliver your compliments, tape them together to make an ice cream cone, and read them out loud. This activity always brings smiles to faces and teaches kids not only to look for the positive but also to share it out loud.

Choices!

An easy way to help girls increase their risk taking is to let them make some decisions on their own. I can't tell you how many girls complain that they never get to choose anything (sometimes even what to wear) and they just have to do what their parents tell them to do. Sure, kids have to follow directions, and parents do a lot of organizing because they're in charge, but girls can and should make their own decisions when it comes to important stuff like sports, activities, friendships, etc.

With girls living fairly scripted lives, they feel somewhat powerless. Handing over the power of choice to your girls (big and small) empowers them to step up to the challenge of making their own decisions and taking healthy risks. Try a few of these:

- Hairstyle (please, I'm begging you, let them choose their own hairstyle)

- Clothing
- Sports
- Activities and clubs
- How to spend free time
- Reading material

I never would have guessed that my daughter wanted to play lacrosse (or that she would want to dye her hair red), but she thought about it and gave lacrosse a try, and it quickly became her new favorite sport. That only happened because I stepped back from making suggestions and let her find her way. Choice is a powerful tool for young girls.

Discover Passion

One thing I see over and over again is that parents push for girls to find an interest. Sometimes it's a sport, but it can also be art, an instrument, or even fashion design. It's great for girls to find their interests, but specializing at a young age tends to backfire. We make the mistake of assuming that passion involves just one thing, but girls can be passionate about any number of things.

Let your girls follow their sparks and try new things. Taking one season off or sitting out one painting class isn't a game changer, but finding a new passion just might be. My daughter is passionate about cooking right now. She loves everything from finding new recipes to shopping for ingredients to chopping and cooking. Will she grow up to be a famous chef? Probably not, but she is learning to care for herself, and she's having a lot of fun (and enjoying a spike in self-confidence) while doing it.

Allow your daughter the freedom to step back from the organized activities and explore other interests. You never know where passion lurks until you have the time and space to discover it.

Thought Stopping

The negative inner critic is one of the greatest obstacles to taking healthy risks and trying new things. That little voice that whispers, "No way, you can't do this," has the power to stop girls from taking that first crucial step outside the comfort zone.

Thought stopping is an easy tool that girls can use to stop the negative inner critic and focus on positive thoughts. I always joke with girls that while it might feel strange to talk to yourself, it's actually the best way to get out of a negative headspace! The best part is that they can do it without uttering a sound. It's as easy as 1-2-3:

1. Stop! That's not true.
2. I am brave [or substitute other positive attribute here], and I can do this.
3. It feels good to try new things!

By using thought stopping, girls can disrupt the negative thought pattern and refocus on a positive thought. They replace the negative inner critic with their inner truth (I am brave) and move forward with determination instead of feeling paralyzed by "what-ifs."

Building courage takes time and practice, and even the girls who love to climb the tallest trees and jump from high places can have fears lurking beneath the surface that hold them back in other ways. Empowering girls to take small steps toward healthy risks helps curb the self-doubt and quiet the inner critic that often holds them back.

CHAPTER 4

Perfect Girl Syndrome

I am careful not to confuse excellence with per-
fection. Excellence, I can reach for; perfection is
God's business.
—*Michael J. Fox*

"I'm trying to get perfect grades, so I can't miss any homework."
Gracie was only in third grade when she became fixated on perfection.

"You're nine, Gracie; you don't have grades."

"But I have report cards. And I want them to be perfect."

For Gracie, perfection meant order. It also meant working toward
her goals and keeping her parents happy. She had her whole life planned
out, and she wasn't willing to deal with any missteps along the way. The
only problem with her perfect plan is that failures, no matter how small,
really upset her. She struggled to cope with both her own mistakes and
the mistakes of others. A missed word on a spelling test caused her to
take practice tests every day of the week so that she wouldn't miss
another word for the rest of the year (she didn't). That was her own self-
inflicted punishment, but when a group project proved challenging because some group members didn't share her work ethic, she nearly lost
a close friend over it.

Gracie didn't have a ton of fun during that time. She threw herself into studying, practicing her tennis skills (she also aspired to be the perfect player), and putting together perfect outfits. She had it all figured out, with one exception: Her anxiety spiked during this time. Her need to control everything triggered more than just a fear of failure; it also propelled her into a constant state of worry. She had to be hyper-vigilant in accomplishing her daily to-do list in order to maintain her carefully created version of perfection. It was overwhelming, at best.

Striving for perfect grades is one thing (however misguided at age nine), but striving for perfection in other areas of life can be down-right dangerous. Body image concerns start a lot earlier than most parents think. In fact, even preschoolers understand that people tend to judge others by their appearance. Sadly, unless they learn otherwise, these early ideas can last a lifetime. That bears repeating: The messages girls internalize when they're young can stick with them as they grow.

A recent report by Common Sense Media shows that more than half of girls ages six through eight report that their ideal weight is less than their current size.[1] According to the report, five- to eight-year-olds who thought their moms were dissatisfied with their bodies also expressed dissatisfaction with their own. You might be thinking, "Not my kid," but don't gloss over this one without giving it a second thought. The mom of a second-grade girl was shocked when her daughter looked up at her and asked, "Do my legs look too big?" Girls hear and internalize messages from a wide variety of sources. While some girls talk openly with their parents, others engage in a silent struggle as they try to make sense of what they're learning.

Not all girls who worry about their bodies and experiment with new eating patterns develop eating disorders, but according to a report published in *Pediatrics*, eating disorders and hospitalizations for eating disorders are on the rise in children under the age of 12.[2] The mother

Parent-Teacher Conference

Be aware of these sneaky signs of eating issues among young girls:

✿ Negative body talk.

✿ Self-conscious about eating in public or in big groups.

✿ School lunch is uneaten more often than not.

✿ Counts calories or repeatedly asks about calories.

✿ Mealtimes are a constant battle (won't eat certain foods, skips meals, asks to eat alone).

✿ Talks about weight or body shapes of peers and other adults a lot.

✿ Changes in eating patterns: cuts food super small, chews one bite for a very long time, attempts to hide food.

✿ Changes in behavior and/or temperament: irritable, depressed, pulling away from peers, trouble sleeping.

✿ Weighs self constantly.

✿ Hides food in room to sneak-eat later.

✿ Becomes fixated on exercise.

✿ Big changes in weight.

of the second-grade girl was right to seek help when her daughter expressed concern about the appearance of her body. The sooner we intervene and help young girls develop body kindness and work through their emotions about their changing bodies, the more likely they are to make healthy choices and seek help when they're struggling in the future.

The difficulty with tackling perfectionism in young girls is that it isn't limited to one aspect of their lives. Some struggle with their appearance and engage in disordered thinking about their weight and ideal bodies, some are fixated on grades and transcripts (or how they look on paper), some take perfectionism to the field, and some (like Gracie) deal with a little bit of everything. One study of adolescent girls in grades six to 12 (from two independent girls' schools) found four overarching sources of significant stress: pervasive experiences of pressure to perform, narrow constructions of success, peer competition, and misalignments in expectations between girls and their parents.[3]

Children today are surrounded by a superkid culture, and it's even more prominent among girls. There is pressure to reach perfection in all areas: perfect grades, perfect appearance, perfect performance as an athlete, and perfect community service projects. The secret to success, it seems, is being perfect.

They even encounter it on social media. I can't tell you how many parents tell me their girls have no interest in social media, only to discover secret accounts on multiple platforms. Apps like Snapchat and Instagram (and a long list of other social apps—by the time parents get hip to them, many kids have moved on to the latest and greatest) fuel the need to showcase your sizzle reel.

What's worse, girls are conditioned to judge each other in these forums, and often those snap judgments result in unkind behavior between girls. As in, they "rate" each other based on looks and vote one another out of "beauty" contests (and yes, this is happening *before* the recommended age of 13). They call out their "besties" in their profiles, but edit those lists almost daily, and based on every little interaction. They friend and un-friend based on what they see, how girls rate them, and what happens in real life. The interplay between social media and the school day results in a tangled web of social wins and losses that complicate the day-to-day lives of even the most socially savvy girls.

Yes, perfect girl syndrome permeates the social lives of girls. All of that perfection, as it turns out, actually increases mean girl culture.

It's enough to make your head spin. We can't sit back and watch it unfold, though. We have to get in there and find the root cause of the perfectionism so that we can help girls learn to work through (or take a stand against) perfect girl syndrome.

Parent-Teacher Conference

Not sure if your girl is a perfectionist? Look for these behaviors:

* ❀ Highly anxious or upset about making mistakes.
* ❀ Avoids, procrastinates on, or has difficulty completing assignments.
* ❀ Fear of embarrassment or humiliation (or negative evaluation).
* ❀ Gives up easily.
* ❀ Rewrites assignments often.
* ❀ Distorted or rigid thinking (e.g., doesn't see what peers or adults see re: success because of impossibly high standards).
* ❀ Overgeneralizes failures.
* ❀ Avoids answering questions in school in an effort to avoid being wrong.
* ❀ Overly cautious on assignments (spends extra time on homework).
* ❀ Meltdowns or angry outbursts when things don't go as planned.
* ❀ Dissatisfied with level of work that others view as acceptable.
* ❀ Risk aversion—avoids trying new things for fear of making mistakes.

Where Does Perfectionism Originate?

All girls are different, and it's nearly impossible to find one single cause of perfectionism among young girls. Did you know there are also different kinds of perfectionism? It's true.

Self-Oriented Perfectionism

Self-oriented perfectionism occurs when girls set unreasonable expectations for themselves. In this case, young girls tend to engage in punitive self-evaluation, self-blame, and overgeneralization of their perceived failures. They expect perfection and fall apart when they come up short.

Socially Prescribed Perfectionism

Socially prescribed perfectionism occurs when girls perceive that others require them to be perfect. In this case, young girls tend to have a strong need for approval from others, experience anticipatory anxiety related to potential negative evaluations from others, and fear they won't be able to meet the high expectations of others. Whether they misperceive the expectations of others or hear the message that perfection is expected, these girls have a need to please and earn stellar evaluations from the adults in their lives.

Perfectionism comes at a hefty cost. One study found that self-oriented perfectionism is significantly associated with depression and anxiety, while socially prescribed perfection is associated with depression, anxiety, social stress, anger suppression, and outwardly directed anger.[4] I see these very issues over and over again with elementary school girls. Whether they feel the need to meet their own self-prescribed and unrealistic expectations or the expectations they feel others place upon them, the end result is symptoms of both anxiety and depression. More often than not, they describe feeling hopeless.

Parent-Teacher Conference

Perfectionism stems from a number of sources and appears to result from a combination of inborn tendencies and environmental factors:

✿ Temperament—some girls have perfectionism built into their personalities.

✿ Messages they hear about success, achievement, and failure.

✿ Highly critical parents, coaches, and/or teachers.

✿ Academic pressure.

✿ Excessive praise and/or demands.

✿ Parental love is conditional upon achievement and success.

✿ Adults modeling perfectionism.

For years, I worked with a girl we'll call Bella who struggled with socially prescribed perfectionism. Her perfectionism was triggered by a difficult relationship with her dad. He was hard to please on a good day, and the more she met his expectations, the higher his expectations climbed. As it turned out, he was a perfectionist himself, and he felt that his high standards were the key to his success. All he wanted was the same, if not a higher, level of success for his daughter. He had good intentions, but because he modeled distorted thinking (nothing was ever good enough unless it was "perfect") and constantly increased his expectations, she was made to feel like she was never quite good enough. Her perfectionism became so all-consuming that it negatively affected her education, her peer relationships, and her family relationships. It took a lot of hard work to help this little girl to accept and learn from her

Parent-Teacher Conference

Extreme perfectionism can trigger a number of mental health disorders, including the following:

- ✿ Performance anxiety
- ✿ Social anxiety
- ✿ Eating disorders
- ✿ Depression
- ✿ Anxiety
- ✿ Obsessive-compulsive disorder
- ✿ Suicidal thoughts and suicide

mistakes *and* to stop spending all of her emotional energy on pleasing others.

It's a bit overwhelming, I know, but in understanding how girls perceive themselves and what causes them to engage in perfectionism, we can help them figure out their unique triggers and how to step away from the pursuit of perfection.

One area to consider is the messages girls hear in the home. Are you overly critical of yourself when you don't meet your own expectations? How do you handle failure? Are you overly focused on grades and results when it comes to your kids? Research shows that early experiences—such as the messages they receive and hear about success, achievement, and failure—do play a role in how girls perceive expectations.[5] For example, children with highly critical parents show a greater likelihood of showing perfectionistic traits. When girls feel like their parents are watching and evaluating everything they do, they learn to strive for perfection in an effort to avoid negative input.

In Bella's case, her perfectionism stemmed from an effort to please and impress her dad. When efforts to impress seemed to fall short, she increased her perfectionism. There was another factor, though, that likely played a role in her perfectionism: Her dad was a self-described "perfectionist." While some of Bella's behavior might have been learned or developed as a response to her father's evaluations of her, perfectionism can actually run in the family. Research shows that maladaptive perfectionism is inheritable and that genetic factors play a role in associations between anxiety and maladaptive perfectionism.[6] In short, parents can pass down both their perfectionist tendencies and the anxiety that accompanies that perfectionism to their kids.

As I mentioned earlier, all girls are different, and perfectionism isn't restricted to a single source. Temperament also plays a role in perfectionism among young girls. As often as I see the pressure placed upon young girls by overly critical parents, I see just as many baffled parents who can't figure out why their girls engage in self-oriented perfectionism. As one mom said, "I always tell her that I'm proud of her and that I just want her to be happy; I don't know why she puts so much pressure on herself!"

I can identify with the daughter of that mom because, once upon a time, I was that girl. I vividly remember nearly falling apart at school while working on a second-grade project. It was a book (my first book!) about a witch who makes a poisonous brew but accidentally uses soap flakes instead of poison. When I attempted to draw the picture of the witch looking shocked by her mistake, I couldn't get it right. I erased and drew and erased and drew until my eraser made a small hole in the middle of the witch's face. I was devastated. When my teacher saw my distress, she looked at the paper and said, "What a great idea! Do you want to use the hole punch to make her surprised mouth look *really* surprised?" Her intervention helped in the moment, but ahead of me was a long road of internal pressure and redoing assignments obsessively, well into high school. It wasn't parent pressure or a high-stress academic environment that triggered my perfectionism at a young age, though. That was simply who I was until I learned to cope with my fear of falling short. It was built into my temperament.

Taking your daughter's personality into consideration can provide important clues to her perfectionistic behaviors. Girls considered "highly sensitive" or anxious and girls with low self-esteem are all at risk of falling into the perfect girl syndrome trap.

An important thing to remember about perfectionism is that it is fueled by anxiety. Perfectionistic kids are worried kids. Your daughter might not appear worried. In fact, she might go to great lengths to hide her worry. Worrying, after all, doesn't fit the model of the "perfect" girl. She might seem stubborn or unwilling to accept help. She might seem lazy or unable to move beyond procrastination. She might even seem highly irritable. More often than not, young girls struggling with perfectionism are overcome with anxious thoughts, trying desperately to avoid failure.

Combine an anxious temperament with external pressure and you have a recipe for extreme perfectionism. A heavy emphasis on performance, both at home and at school, can contribute to perfectionistic behavior. Girls are increasingly judged by their test scores and other measurable achievements. In the words of an eight-year-old girl who struggled with the concept of teamwork in noncompetitive soccer, "I *have* to score at least two goals before I pass because that's how I show my parents that I'm good." Another complicating factor there? Her parents paid her per goal. I later learned that she was also paid for "perfect" tests. When young girls feel as though they are put on display for the results they produce, *and* they get paid for it, they conclude that their value is tied to their achievements. That's a lot of stress for a young girl.

Even when parents don't buy into perfect scores and high achievement, some girls feel the pressure in the classroom. A third-grade girl told me that her homework takes longer than it should because her handwriting is "messy" when she's tired, and messy handwriting results in a lower grade. She constantly rewrites her assignments until she considers them "perfect." While it's important to help young girls reach for their potential in the classroom, grades and achievements shouldn't be the primary source of evaluation. When young girls learn that the process of discovery is more important than the perfect score, they are more inclined to take risks in the classroom setting. When their self-worth gets tangled up with grades, on the other hand, they back down from new challenges and hyper-focus on perfection, instead.

How Does Perfectionism Affect Our Girls?

In addition to the fact that perfectionism puts girls at risk for anxiety, depression, and other mental health disorders, it holds our girls back. When girls get wrapped up in perfectionism, they are afraid to try new things; they take fewer risks both in the classroom and on the field (or in other activities); they work slowly (in an effort to get everything "right"), which triggers feelings of frustration; they miss opportunities due to fear of failure; they have difficulty working in groups because they don't trust their peers to hold themselves to the same high standards; and they are less likely to seek the help they need to thrive (in the academic setting and beyond) because they don't want to appear incapable or incompetent.

Perfectionists spend so much time worrying about how others will judge them and how they will measure up to their own expectations that they miss out on the important business of childhood. The third-grade girl who spends excessive amounts of time on her homework loses time to play, connect with family and friends, and enjoy the gift of boredom. The soccer player who can't even consider passing the ball to her teammates until she proves her worth to her parents and coaches misses out on opportunities to grow as an athlete and to make friends (what she considers "mean" behavior by teammates is actually their frustration with her tendency to hog the ball). And the girl who only wants to please her father is robbed of the opportunity to follow her own dreams and find her own passions.

Perfectionism negatively affects learning, friendships, family relationships, and emotional health. When girls strive to fit into the perfect girl mold, they live in a bubble of heightened stress and decreased overall happiness.

Breaking Down the Myth of the "Perfect Girl"

When I run empowerment groups for girls, I always carve out time to talk about the myth of the perfect girl. I begin by asking one question: Who knows a "perfect" girl? Without fail, hands shoot high in the air. When I ask them to start yelling out traits that perfect girls share, they are practically jumping out of their seats. *The best at soccer! Really smart! Tons of friends! Answers a lot of questions! Pretty! Cool clothes!* The list goes on and on.

When we break their ideas down point by point, I always find that young girls tend to hold themselves to impossible standards, and that they receive input from home, the media, books, peers, and even magazines they find strewn around the house or waiting rooms. Young girls, you see, are collectors of information. They might not always ask for clarification on the bits of information they find, so it's up to us as parents to check in with our girls frequently to help them process the information flooding their brains and potentially distorting their beliefs.

It takes time and repetition to break down perfectionism, but each conversation is one step closer to helping your daughter learn to embrace, and even celebrate, mistakes.

Parent-Teacher Conference

Kicking perfectionism to the curb doesn't have to be an overwhelming process. Remember this three-step plan:

❀ **Educate:** Teach (and reteach) your girls about the myth of perfection.
❀ **Model:** Show your girls that everyone makes mistakes by highlighting your own failures.
❀ **Empower:** Encourage your girls to learn from their mistakes and talk back to that pesky worry center in their brains that has a tendency to catastrophize (see page 112) and seek perfect results.

Name It

I always tell young girls that if they can name it, they can deal with it. We don't need to sugarcoat what's happening. In fact, I find that teaching girls the meaning of perfectionism and the feelings beneath the behavior actually helps them to understand it. It's kind of like finding out that you have a virus when you thought you had strep throat. Knowing that it's a virus doesn't make you feel any better in the moment, but at least you know what you're dealing with and what steps you can take to begin to heal.

"Perfectionism" isn't a bad word; neither is "anxiety." When we take the time to help girls understand how their brains are wired and why they strive to meet unreasonable expectations, they can begin to explore adaptive coping skills that work for them by helping them reduce their anxious thought patterns and perfectionistic behaviors.

Don't be afraid to use big words with young girls. Anxiety isn't

Parent-Teacher Conference

Try this description of anxiety to help girls understand how their brains work:

"When you are focused on getting something done perfectly, it's because the worry center in your brain is very active. We all have a worry center. Sometimes that worry center can be very useful. It reminds us to look both ways before crossing the street or to hold a hand in a crowd. Other times, the worry center becomes very loud and upsets us. When this happens, we experience anxiety. When the worry center gives us information that isn't true, we feel scared and overwhelmed. We have to help calm the worry center in our brains so that we don't feel anxious."

This description of perfectionism is also useful:

"Some kids, and even some grown-ups, have a voice inside of them that tells them to do everything perfectly. It makes them really critical of themselves and of other people. When this happens, kids feel unhappy and very worried. It also makes kids feel like mistakes are really awful and scary. It takes the fun out of everything we do!"

nearly as scary as it sounds when parents provide an accurate description that girls can process.

Celebrate Your Mistakes!

Perfectionists tend to view the world through a very narrow lens. They are likely to describe their moms, and even older sisters or older female cousins, as "perfect." This tendency is magnified when young girls don't see their role models making mistakes on a regular basis.

Girls live in a world of constant corrections. From the classroom to the playing field to almost any other extracurricular activity, girls receive a steady stream of input that provides corrections for their mistakes. What the adults in their lives intend to convey is that mistakes can be fixed. What girls hear is "You're doing it wrong. Again."

To help girls flip their understanding of mistakes from "I'm wrong" to "I'm learning," start by pointing out and celebrating your own mistakes and failures. I can't tell you how many fits of laughter have resulted from my daughter helping me correct my typos or how many little girls have sat on my couch and soaked up every word when I share a story of a simple, everyday mistake (like forgetting to take the trash out and having overflowing trash cans for a week that invited a family of raccoons to practically move in).

You might think those little mistakes you make aren't worth sharing, but those are the stories that normalize the concept of microfailures and small mistakes. Girls need to see their role models at their best, at their worst, and in between. Showcasing your sizzle reel teaches your daughter that perfect is best; highlighting the outtakes empowers your daughter to accept the fact that mistakes and failures are part of growing up and moving forward.

Talk Back

Remember those cognitive distortions from chapter 1? We need to review a few of them here. Perfectionists live in a secret world of cognitive distortions. They might look like they have it all together on the outside, but that pesky worry center is on high alert most of the time, screaming out negative thoughts.

Does your girl engage in black-and-white thinking? Many young perfectionists do. Things are either right or wrong, perfect or a failure, good or terrible, and the list goes on. They fail to see the shades of gray between the extremes because they are focused on results.

Catastrophizing is another popular cognitive distortion among perfectionistic girls. These girls have a tendency to exaggerate the consequences of minor mistakes. They expect the absolute worst-case scenarios to occur most of the time, and they ask a lot of what-if questions ("What if I forget everything on the test? What if my teacher hates my report?").

Then there are the girls who rely on overgeneralization. They form general conclusions based on one small event or mistake. "I got a seventy-two percent on my spelling test. I'm terrible at spelling! I will *never* learn to spell!" I see this one a lot in my office. When perfectionists get wrapped up in results, they make the jump from mistake to total and complete failure without taking any other factors into consideration.

The best way to tackle these cognitive distortions is to teach girls how to reframe their thoughts. Cognitive distortions trigger a cycle of negative thinking, which causes girls to engage in self-criticism. Helping girls dissect their negative thoughts and reframe them from a positive perspective breaks the cycle of negative thinking.

In the case of a girl who overgeneralizes, for example, it helps to teach her to zoom out and discuss what factors contributed to the negative event. "I failed my math test. I'm terrible at math" can be reevaluated as "I was tired and unprepared for the test. I can ask for help and study more for the next one." In empowering girls to take control of negative thinking, we teach them to move away from perfection and refocus on the power of learning instead.

It's important to break down this myth of the perfect girl when they're young. Can they grow up to reach their dreams and be who they want to be? Yes. Is perfection a realistic goal for young girls? Absolutely not. Girls who strive for perfection fail to ground themselves in reality and, in doing so, set themselves up for a lifetime of disappointment.

While it might be tempting to try to "toughen up" young girls because life is hard and full of obstacles (I can't tell you how many parents suggest this as the antidote to perfectionism), remember this: Our job as parents is not to make our girls tough so that they can fight back against the harsh realities of growing up girl; our job is to support them and help them thrive so that they can rise above the negativity and create a better narrative for girlhood for years to come. You can't change the temperament of your daughter, but in taking the time to understand it, you can learn how to help your daughter work through the feelings beneath the perfectionism.

I like to remind my daughter that some of my best ideas were born from the failures that came just prior. We learn from our mistakes and missteps, no matter how painful that might be. When we stop focusing on perfect, we make room for new, and sometimes better, ideas.

Girls Can!

Paint the Big Picture

Perfectionism causes kids to zoom in on small things. For Gracie, a perfect report card was a step toward meeting her lifelong goals. What were her lifelong goals? At nine, she wanted to become a lawyer to fight for animal rights. When I asked her to paint her big picture (literally— okay, with markers, not paint), she found that hyper-focusing on that one report card was actually distracting her from her long-term goals. She was so concerned about grades in school that she never thought about doing something to work on her assertiveness skills (something any good lawyer needs), like acting in the community play.

Got a perfectionist on your hands? Not to worry, this is common among young girls. Ask her to paint her big picture. Perhaps her goal is to make a club soccer team someday. Zooming in on one game won't get her there, but thinking about the big-picture steps to get there (practicing, playing on her town team, taking breaks to rest, learning the rules of the game) just might. When we teach girls to keep the big picture in mind instead of narrowing in on individual moments, they are better able to cope with the ups and downs that occur along the way. You can't always play the perfect game, but that doesn't mean you can't reach your overall goals.

Play Bounce Back

Whether or not you think your daughter is a perfectionist, it's perfectly normal for young girls to experience negative thoughts at times. Girls are under a ton of pressure right now, and sometimes that pressure triggers self-criticism. Teach your daughter to break her negative thought cycle with this simple game.

Grab a basketball or playground ball and head outside with your daughter. Talk about the fact that everyone has that inner voice that sometimes gets a little too critical. Share some of the things your inner voice says about you to illustrate the point. Ask your daughter to describe a negative thought she had during the day. She should bounce the ball to you when she shares her thought. Next, help your daughter reframe it. Catch her negative thought and bounce back a positive thought when you return the ball to her. Ask your daughter to help you reframe your thoughts by bouncing back positive thoughts to you.

In engaging in positive reframing *with* your daughter, you normalize the negative thought cycle that can occur at times while teaching her how to refocus on the positive. This little gem, known as *cognitive reframing*, is a strategy that will last a lifetime.

Nurture Your Body

Given the fact that perfectionism can lead to disordered eating, it's essential to empower girls to make healthy choices and find balance early on. Things to avoid: talking about weight, diets, and restricted eating. If you're shaking your head, I understand. Who talks to little girls about diets? As it turns out, a lot of parents do.

You might think your self-criticism goes unnoticed, but trust me on this one: Your daughter is watching you very carefully. When you describe your legs as "fat," she hears it. When you mention needing to "lose a few" to fit into your bathing suit, she's listening. When you make negative comments about your shape, size, or appearance, she's taking it in.

It's important to teach young girls to nurture and be kind to their bodies. Girls grow and change at a rapid pace, and no two girls are the same. Teach your girl to understand what her body can do for her. I often ask girls to draw the outline of a body and label the parts that help her thrive. Strong leg muscles help her run fast. Her healthy heart helps her remain active. Her growing brain helps her learn. Once she labels the body, we talk about what she needs to do to care for and nurture those important body parts: eat healthy foods, and play outside for muscle strength!

Teaching young girls to "eat a rainbow" helps them think outside the box when it comes to making healthy choices and developing a healthy relationship with food, but the best way to empower young girls to nurture their bodies is to get them in the kitchen. Involve them in the whole cooking process, from finding recipes to buying the groceries, to cooking the meal.

True Beauty Collage

It's one thing to tell young girls that beauty comes from within, but seeing it on paper is a much more powerful experience. Some girls struggle to internalize this message because it is too easy to get caught up in wondering how we measure up. Whether they're looking at their peers or seeing some version of perfect on a favorite show, it can be hard to step back and think about what it means to find the beauty in life.

I use collage with young girls to work through a lot of different issues, but using collage to illustrate true beauty is one of my favorite strategies. For the best results, keep some large paper available—as in big enough to trace your daughter's body. You can do this exercise on a smaller scale, but I find that the life-size collage is very powerful.

Once you've outlined your daughter on the paper, get out the old magazines or look for appropriate images online. Ask your daughter to step back and think about the real beauty of the human body. What can her body do for her that sets her apart? What value does each part of her body hold?

One client thought long and hard before filling the head with books and art supplies; drawing her family and friends in the heart; putting images of soccer, running, and bike riding on the legs; and covering the arms in words and art to represent her creativity. In showcasing inner beauty through the collage, girls see the many ways their bodies bring beauty into this world. It's not about fashionable clothes and a thin waistline—it's about strength, intelligence, creativity, and play. It's about the many parts that make up the whole. It's about finding the beauty in individuality.

Wheel of Strengths

Fun fact: I have never once made a chore wheel for my house, but I have made a wheel of strengths. It's natural for girls to get caught up in comparisons. They see what their peers are doing and wearing and playing with, and they begin to evaluate themselves against their peers. It happens. The problem with comparisons, however, is that when we get caught up in how we think others are outperforming us, we forget that we have our own individual strengths.

Creating a wheel of strengths with your daughter helps her refocus her thoughts on her own unique traits and positive qualities. Instead of wondering how she compares to others, she can spin the wheel and think about one of the many strengths she brings to the table.

Using a white paper plate, have your daughter choose her favorite colors, then divide the plate into sections, with one color for each (try six to eight sections to start). On each section, your daughter writes one positive quality. Keep in mind that labeling strengths can feel overwhelming at first, particularly if your daughter isn't used to doing it. She might need a little help to get started. Examples might include: helpful, knows a lot about science, has a great memory, empathic to others, fast runner, loves to cook, etc. Once the plate is full of strengths, cut out an arrow using cardboard and attach it to the plate using a thumbtack or paper clip. Spin the arrow to see where it lands, and talk about that strength. Point out times you've watched your daughter tap into that particular positive quality and how it helps her thrive in the world.

Two Journals

I always recommend two kinds of journals to young girls: a mother-daughter (or father-daughter) journal to communicate those hard-to-describe thoughts, and an affirmation journal to help combat negative thinking and excessive worries. The first is a wonderful communication tool that helps girls open up to their parents without feeling judged or watched. Many girls choose to use this as a daily conversation starter with their parents. They might, for example, write a note to Mom or Dad before bed, leave it for the parent to read, and look forward to a response in the morning. This gives girls the opportunity to share thoughts they might otherwise feel reluctant to share because opening up can be anxiety-producing, particularly if it includes tricky topics like bullying, mistakes, or negative emotions. The second helps girls refocus on their positive traits and their dreams and goals when they're feeling down.

Take your daughter journal shopping and encourage her to spend the last ten minutes before bed each night writing a few sentences about the best part of her day, her strengths, and her goals for the future. By ending the day on a positive note, girls are able to let go of some of the negativity they might have experienced during the day and fall asleep with hope-filled hearts.

Paper Crumple

You can talk to your girl about perfectionism for hours and feel like you're not getting anywhere, but adding a visual changes the whole dynamic. Kids respond to visuals and hands-on activities, particularly when dealing with emotions.

Ask your daughter to choose a piece of construction paper and cut it into her favorite shape. Next, ask your daughter to name a self-criticism that popped into her head that day. When she says it, ask her to make one crumple in her shape. Ask for another negative thought or perceived failure and put another crumple in the shape. Keep doing this until the shape is all crumpled up and looking a lot less perfect than it did when she began the experiment. Talk about how this is what it feels like inside when we let perfectionism take over. Each time we put ourselves down for a mistake or make an unfair comparison, we crumple our own hearts and feel sad and anxious as a result.

Bonus tip: For best results, do this project with your daughter by crumpling your own shape. This normalizes the process and helps girls feel less scrutinized.

Create a Mantra

I recently told a group of girls that when I'm feeling overwhelmed and thinking that I can't do something, I make up a song in my head to remind myself that I can do it. They laughed. Then they wanted me to sing. After we enjoyed a little humor about singing out loud versus singing in your head, we talked about the power of mantras.

Sometimes a simple phrase can change the way we approach difficult tasks. When girls are overwhelmed with pressure, both internal and external, they get stuck in the moment. They hyper-focus on getting the desired result and feel deflated when they don't reach their goals. Establishing a mantra, or a few mantras, helps girls tap into positive thinking when perfectionism looms. Ask your daughter to come up with her own personal mantra to talk back to perfectionism (an example might be "When I work hard, I achieve my goals"). Have your daughter paint that mantra on a canvas or create a colorful poster out of it to hang on her wall, and put a smaller version in her pencil box to take to school each day.

CHAPTER 5

Sporty Girls, Artsy Girls, Bossy Girls, and Girly Girls

Definitions belong to the definers, not the defined.
—*Toni Morrison*

Labeling kids is certainly nothing new in the world of parenting. Introverts are labeled "shy" or "quiet," extroverts are labeled "spirited" or "outgoing," kids who love sports are the "athletic" ones, and those buried in books are "clever." I find that, in general, parents do this for positive reasons. Parents see the whole picture—they know what their girls are made of—and they want others to see it too. The problem with labels, though, is that they can be limiting.

Olivia's mom struggles to avoid labeling her. Olivia is, in fact, a quiet kid. She's anxious in large settings and prefers to observe. That's okay. A lot of young girls are very similar to Olivia. The problem is that the minute Olivia enters a new situation, her mom labels her. She does this to explain why Olivia is the way she is. She also does it to get ahead of the judgments—if she calls Olivia out first, other people can't judge. It's flawed logic, but it comes from a good place. Olivia *hates* the labels. She feels like the labels—even the good ones ("She's super creative!")—are the only thing people see about her.

Labels can be positive, and those might seem benign (is it really such a bad thing to label my kid "creative"?), but they can also be negatively charged. Here's the thing: Young girls can and do internalize these labels, positive or negative. Sometimes that works out in the end. If a "loudmouth" does become a CEO one day, that "bossy" label won't seem like such a big deal. But what about the young girls who get labeled in a more negative light early on?

What about the "mean girls" *and* their "victims"? Some girls are naturally more assertive than others. These girls tend to emerge as the leaders of the pack. While there can be positive leaders in the early years, mean girls can and do rule the recess yard. At 10 years old, Amanda fears recess every single day. A girl who was once her "best" friend assumed the power position over time. When Amanda walks out to recess these days, she has two choices: do what her "best" friend says to do or lose best friend status and sit alone. There are six or seven girls in the group on any given day, and they are the only friends Amanda has ever known. When Amanda dared to come forward about the mean girl behavior, she was quickly labeled a victim. And that mean girl? The teachers keep a close eye on her, but she continues to live up to her label.

We have to be careful about the labels we create for children. We even have to be careful about the labels our girls create for themselves. I've had many young girls carve out very specific labels—some of them not favorable ("I'm dumb"). And let's not forget about the labels girls create for one another ("loser"). Labels can quickly become a self-fulfilling prophecy. I've had so-called "mean girls" sit on my couch and tell me that people already think they're mean, so there's no point in being anything else (plus, it's fun to feel powerful), and "victims" hide out in my office so that people won't point and stare and call them wimps.

When Julie first walked in, she appeared closed off, angry, and unwilling to engage. She spent the first few sessions staring at her feet and responding to me with one-word answers whenever possible. She was hurting, but she didn't know where to begin. When her mother initiated treatment, she described Julie as "angry and negative all the time. She hates everything." Julie was only eight years old when she began therapy. It's hard to hate *everything* when you're eight. As it turned out, Julie actually liked a lot of things. The problem was that nobody ever asked.

They signed her up for softball and expressed disappointment when she quit. They signed her up for volleyball and got mad when she didn't like it. They tried almost every sport in their community and became highly frustrated when Julie expressed dislike on any level. Early on, Julie's parents thought she seemed athletic. A fast runner as a toddler, she was always playing tag and engaging in rough-and-tumble play with the boys in the neighborhood. For this reason, Julie earned the "sporty" label. Sadly, what she really wanted to do at eight was learn to knit.

When we put girls in a box early on and hyper-focus on that one part of them, we limit their potential and carve out a future that they might not even want.

Why Do We Label Kids?

There are a number of reasons behind labeling, and to really understand the "why," we have to dig beneath the surface and figure out how our children's behavior affects us. One mom recalled her embarrassment and frustration when her daughter didn't interact with other moms at a party. "They're trying to say 'hi' and be friendly to her, and she's rude. She just ignores them." That mom felt that her daughter's behavior reflected poorly on her parenting. Instead of taking her daughter aside to remind her how to interact with adults at a party, she made a sarcastic comment that her daughter carried with her for years to come.

Parents fear judgment just as much as kids do, and offering an explanation for the way a child behaves helps ease the worry on the part of the parent. In the case of the so-called "shy" girl, the behavior in question isn't necessarily negative, but it might make other people feel uncomfortable. I once heard a mom label her young daughter a "motormouth" in an effort to explain why her daughter talked over other kids almost constantly. "Needy" or "clingy" are labels earned when kids stick close to parents in social settings or interrupt adult conversations to get attention. All of these labels (and many more) are used to explain behavior so that others won't judge or criticize.

Distancing is another reason parents throw labels around. As was the case for the little girl who was "rude" to her mom's friends, the mother used a sarcasm-laced label to describe her daughter in an effort to distance herself from her daughter's lack of social graces. She was embarrassed and frustrated, so she made a joke and slapped a label on her daughter as if to say, "What can I do? That's who she is!"

Parents also use labels in an effort to communicate their expectations to their kids. This generally involves positive labeling. "You're so smart! I know you'll ace that test!" sounds like the comment of a supportive parent, but where does that leave the girl? What happens when she doesn't ace the test? Is she no longer considered smart? Is she a disappointment? Expectation labeling is also used in social settings. "Making friends is your specialty!" and "You're the most polite girl around!" are examples of positive labels meant to inspire kids to put their best foot forward, but they also put kids in a narrow box wrapped up with a bow of high expectations. In other words, these "positive" labels sure do make it difficult to fail.

When parents label their girls, they give them a title they have not chosen for themselves. In essence, parents say to their daughters, "This is who you are. Be this." Labels carry with them preconceived ideas about the traits and characteristics belonging to the individual. When a girl is labeled as shy, for example, other people assume that she keeps to herself, doesn't talk much, and prefers to avoid large social gatherings. In labeling young girls, we set specific expectations for them, and it can be hard to break from those labels over time.

What's So Bad About Labels?

When girls create their own labels, nothing. Some girls try on several different labels as they explore their interests and try to find their passion(s) in life. They might self-identify as athletes, musicians, artists, writers, or even nerds (yes, this is still my own personal label of choice). You might find that these self-created labels change monthly, weekly, or even daily. Much like the constantly changing career paths of early childhood (doctor! teacher! fashion designer!), middle childhood can be a time of rapidly shifting identities. This is, in fact, a very healthy part of child development.

Labels become harmful when other people create those labels for girls and call them out as such. This isn't restricted to parents. Teachers, coaches, grandparents, and even peers can create labels that leave a lasting impact on young girls.

Both positive and negative labels can become self-fulfilling prophecies for girls, so we have to be particularly careful about the words we use to describe them.

Parent-Teacher Conference

Fifteen negative labels to remove from your vocabulary right now!

1. Lazy
2. Scattered
3. Procrastinator
4. Distracted
5. Clingy
6. Needy
7. High maintenance
8. Dramatic
9. Shy
10. Bossy
11. Irresponsible
12. Slow-poke
13. Difficult
14. Stubborn
15. Reckless

The Problem with Negative Labels

Ella's mother consistently referred to her as "difficult." "She's just not as easygoing as the others," she told me over and over again. "They go with the flow; she always has some issue to deal with." Some of these statements were made by phone when Ella was in school, but she repeated these statements in my office. While it sounds like her feelings about her daughter are baked-in resentment, it was actually quite the opposite. This mom felt that no matter how hard she tried, she just couldn't provide the emotional support that her daughter seemed to need. This mom felt like a failure, and she deflected those feelings by creating a label for her daughter that explained some of her behavior.

When parents (or other adults in their lives) view girls through a negative lens, their evaluations of them are more critical. They expect them to act in a certain way, and they look for evidence that they are correct. Instead of looking for positive change or providing the support young girls might need to make a change, adults put them in a box and assume the undesirable behavior will continue.

Girls pick up on these negative belief systems and internalize negative core beliefs as a result. They take on those labels and live up to them. The girl who is consistently described as "lazy," for example, will continue to act in the manner that her parent or teacher expects. The "disruptive" girl in the classroom has no motivation to raise her hand or change her behavior because she knows her name is already written in the disruptive column. When Ella's mother wasn't in the room, Ella told me that she gave up trying to improve her communication with her mom because she didn't want to bother her anymore.

By now you've probably heard of Carol Dweck's work on growth mind-sets versus fixed mind-sets. In a 2012 interview on the matter, Dweck broke it down as follows: "In a fixed mind-set students believe their basic abilities, their intelligence, their talents, are just fixed traits. They have a certain amount and that's that, and then their goal becomes to look smart all the time and never look dumb. In a growth mind-set students understand that their talents and abilities can be developed through effort, good teaching, and persistence. They don't necessarily think everyone's the same or anyone can be Einstein, but they believe everyone can get smarter if they work at it."[1]

When we apply Dweck's theory on fixed mind-sets to labels, we see the danger of labeling girls early on. When girls internalize the labels given to them by parents, teachers, coaches, and other adults in their lives, they believe that they can't change. Instead of operating on the assumption that they can learn, grow, and change, they believe that fixed traits keep them from progressing beyond a certain level. In a nutshell, they get stuck, and they stay stuck because they believe their abilities are limited.

The Problem with Positive Labels

"You're so smart! You're such a great student!" Ever find yourself making these exclamations in response to something great that came home from school? Been there (oops). It can be hard to avoid getting caught up in the moment, even though sometimes the immediate responses that come naturally can actually do more harm than good.

In fact, Dweck's research applies to the positive labels we bestow upon our children as well. When girls consistently hear things like "You're smart" and "You're a great student," they tend to develop fixed mind-sets. They believe they're smart, and that's great, until they encounter a challenge. That's when they struggle with the fixed mind-set. Instead of thinking, "I need to work a little harder at this one," they think, "I guess I'm not that smart after all." In failing to live up to the positive label, they lose their carefully constructed identities.

Positive labels can be a significant source of stress for young girls. While phrases like "talented soccer player" and "gifted student" are meant to build girls up, they can actually place undue pressure on girls. What happens when the talented soccer player has a mediocre season? What happens when the gifted student fails to perform? The pressure to live up to positive labels can trigger feelings of anxiety when girls encounter challenges, as well as feelings of hopelessness when they fail to meet the expectations.

One more problem with positive labels is that they can be limiting. Girls will strive to meet the expectations of the labels given to them, but they will also internalize the message that those labels define them. If you consistently refer to one daughter as "the artsy one" and another as "the sporty one," those girls will likely work hard to live up to those labels without stepping outside their comfort zones to try new things.

In her work on empathy development, Michele Borba, EdD, addresses the problem with labels. "What we say about our children helps define who they are and the type of people they believe themselves to be," explains Borba. "Too much praise can make kids more self-centered, more competitive, and more prone to cut others down. Too little encouragement can erode self-esteem."[2]

The bottom line is that the goal is to raise multidimensional kids who make up their own minds about their strengths and interests. To do that, we have to give them the opportunity to explore their own identities on their own terms. If we slap labels on them, we stop forward motion. If we take a wait-and-watch approach, we give them the gift of time and space to learn about themselves.

Labels Play into Mean Girl Culture

Labels pop up all over mean girl culture. When I ask girls to name some of the labels that girls use to hurt other girls, they offer many. One girl rattled off, "losers, nerds, tattlers, teacher's helpers, gross girls, boy-girls, pretty girls," and many more without taking a breath. In mean girl culture, girls are categorized into groups based on a number of factors, including appearance, interests, good girl or bad girl behaviors, and many more.

When we label girls, we teach them to label others. Even when we focus on what we think are positive labels, we still send a dangerous message: Group girls by labels. We need to teach girls to get to know the whole girl instead of focusing on certain behaviors or characteristics so that girls aren't so quick to judge and dismiss others who don't fit into their preferred categories.

Why Identity Development Matters

"My dad was an awesome basketball player, and he still plays basketball all the time after work, so my parents really want me to be an awesome basketball player too. They think it will help me make friends and get into college." Lia is eight years old and not particularly interested in sports. What she really wants to do is act in a play, but her parents say she has to wait until the summer, when she'll have more time. The thing is, the reason Lia has no time is that she has to play basketball year-round, even though she doesn't like it. She doesn't have many friends on the team, and she tells me that she isn't that talented. "My parents think I haven't been trying and I could score more points if I tried."

Identity development can be a tricky business during early and middle childhood. On the one hand, girls enter this world with their own temperaments. How we interact with the world around us has a lot to do with personality and development. On the other hand, all kids are susceptible to environmental factors, such as messages they receive from parents, teachers, religious institutions, coaches, and others. In short, identity development is a long and arduous process with both internal ("I'm a great problem solver!") and external ("My coach doesn't think I'm good enough") factors at play.

And we can't forget about the issue of peer influence. In many cultures, from about the age of seven and on, children enjoy greater responsibility, independence, and time spent with peer groups. While this broadens their worldviews and offers them new and exciting information, it also puts them in a position to constantly compare themselves to others. We see this in very young girls, even preschoolers. When the comparison is favorable in that they find common ground ("We both love to draw animals!") or have shared similar experiences, girls feel competent and are inspired to learn and grow together. When the comparison is unfavorable, however, girls are left feeling inferior to their peers. This can negatively affect identity development.

I can't drive this point home enough: Young girls make their own comparisons about how they measure up to other girls, and they look to other girls for peer input. Parents can and do affect the self-worth of their girls, but peer influence is a powerful force in girl world. As Rosalind Wiseman, parenting educator and bestselling author of *Queen Bees and Wannabes*, explains, "What is often overlooked is that it is the girls themselves who are the enforcers of these cultural rules in their day-to-day lives. They police one another, conducting surveillance on who's breaking the laws of appearance and clothing, boys, and personality."[3] While you might be shaking your head because surely your girl isn't caught up in appearances or boys just yet, I would caution you to think twice. Girls tell me stories of tricks played on other girls in front of the class to get a laugh from the boys . . . in third grade!

As girls grow and learn, they are constantly pushing the boundaries of what they feel they can do and accomplish. They encounter new people, new role models, new obstacles, and new environments on a regular basis. Take a moment to think about how it must feel to start over every single school year in a new room with a new teacher and a different group of peers. Now add a new team with a new coach and new teammates, or a new musical with a new director and new castmates. Girlhood is full of inconsistency. Trying to find your place and figure out who you are is a monumental task, one that comes with significant setbacks at times. The fact that girls feel the need to measure up to other girls or worry about the judgments of the adults in their lives only complicates matters further. Talk about an emotional roller coaster!

Sometimes a simple shift in language makes a big difference. Describing your daughter's lacrosse game as fun to watch because it was

Parent-Teacher Conference

Ask your girl these questions to help her work through her feelings about her identity:

✿ What makes you unique?

✿ What are three of your strengths?

✿ What are you interested in right now?

✿ Do you have a goal you want to work on?

✿ What are your dreams for this year?

fast-paced and exciting and the team worked well together changes the message you send. Instead of your daughter hearing "You're the best player and your team can't survive without you," she hears "You're part of a great team that plays well together!" It's a subtle difference on paper, but a big difference when it comes to reducing the pressure we unknowingly put on girls at times. This kind of language also takes the focus off labels and results (negative or positive), and promotes positive identity development.

Praise is not the enemy, and pointing out your daughter's strengths won't necessarily cause her to be self-centered and lack empathy, but when we use labels and misplaced praise to put girls in a narrow box and place that box on a very high pedestal, we do them a disservice. First, we send the message that they're best, which does lead to self-centered behavior. Second, we set them up for disappointment and failure without teaching them how to cope. Impossibly high standards for young girls tend to result in impossibly low feelings of self-worth. We owe it to our girls to find the happy medium and let them form their own identities as they grow.

Girls Can!

Inside-Outside

Identity development is a gradual process and is closely tied to the development of self-esteem. In fact, sometimes girls get so wrapped up in how they feel about themselves in relation to others (as in how others might judge them and how that affects their self-esteem) that they don't always show their true colors. They have the outer layer that they share with the world (the star athlete!) and the inner layer that they keep private.

While we all have things we want to keep private, it's important to encourage girls to share some of that inner layer. A young girl might be the quintessential "sporty" girl on the outside, but she might have other interests and talents hidden in the inner layer that don't fit the label but just might be her true source of passion.

Give your daughter a piece of paper and ask her to draw a medium-size circle in the middle and a much larger circle around that. Ask her to fill that outside layer with all the great things that she shows the people she encounters each day. Perhaps she loves math, has a good sense of humor, and plays the violin. This is the "outside" stuff that feels safe to share. Ask her to fill the inner circle with the things she doesn't usually share. Maybe she writes poetry, knits, or collects interesting rocks. This is the "inside" stuff that she keeps to herself. Talk about why she hesitates to share some of the inside stuff and what might happen if she did open up. Would she feel more in tune with her passions and interests if she didn't keep so many things hidden? Would sharing her inside stuff paint a more complete picture and make her feel more confident as a result?

I find that this activity empowers young girls to work through their feelings about their emerging identities while fostering a strong sense of self. When girls no longer fear judgment about their choices and interests, they work toward their goals with confidence.

Use Descriptive Praise

Have you ever heard the phrase "Praise the actions, not the actors"? This is a great mantra to stick in your pocket so that you can avoid the pitfalls of misplaced praise. I'll be honest; it can feel weird at first. When your instinct is to exclaim, "You were great out there!" it's really hard to say, "I liked the way you passed to your teammate!" instead. As I mentioned earlier, that subtle shift says a lot to your daughter. It's specific, so she knows you paid attention. It's focused on the action, so it doesn't set her up to try to be the best player every time.

I often encourage parents to practice using this phrase with young girls: "I love watching you _____ because _____." For example, when my daughter has an Irish dance competition, there are no guarantees. You win some and you lose some, and all you can do is your best. I can often be heard saying, "I love watching you dance because your smile lights up the room and shows me how happy you are." In using this phrase, I communicate to my daughter that I love watching her dance because I know that she feels happy and confident when she dances. If she wins, great. If she loses, she got to have fun doing her thing that day.

Talking Points

Sometimes young girls have a hard time opening up about their hopes and dreams. To put yourself out there and share your deepest darkest secrets, even with your mom, is a risk. To that end, sometimes girls retreat inward during the school-age years and quiet down a bit.

Internalizing emotions can negatively affect self-esteem as girls struggle to balance the need to please others and fulfill the roles they feel they've been assigned with their secret wishes and the parts of their identities they keep hidden. Parents can help draw girls out of their secret worlds by engaging with them in fun and stress-free ways and, in doing so, strengthen their voices and identities.

**SOME POPULAR TALKING POINTS
AROUND HERE INCLUDE:**

❀ What is something you want to learn how to cook?

❀ What's the best movie you've ever seen?

❀ You have to travel across the country—airplane or car?

❀ Name someone you admire and tell why.

❀ If you wrote a book, what would you title it?

Using talking points is a great way to get to know your child better without any pressure. I know, I know, you already know your child. But do you? Kids can be secret keepers (I had a whole invisible school that my mom didn't know about until last year). Helping girls truly open up and share their secret hopes and dreams helps put an end to living up to labels. It gives girls the opportunity to shine from all angles. Make some fun talking point cards and put them in the center of the table at meals. You know, those silly questions that actually lead to eye-opening answers, like "If you were stuck on a deserted island and you could only have three things, what would they be?" or "If you could have dinner with one person, living or dead, who would you choose?" Bring those down to kid level to get to know the inner workings of your child a bit better.

Confident Hearts

It's really hard for young girls to filter out the input they hear from so many different sources. Girls often tell me that they know in their hearts that they are being (or trying to be) true to themselves, but sometimes the white noise around them causes them to make different choices and back away from their strengths and dreams. Ugh. Fitting in is no easy task. Neither is suppressing the urge to fit in.

Have your girl create her very own confident heart as a reminder that she is exactly who she is meant to be. Cut a large heart out of cardboard or paper. If you use cardboard, which is great because it's sturdy, be sure to have your daughter cover it with colored paper of her choice. Next, ask your daughter to think about her strengths, her dreams, her hopes, and what makes her unique. Ask her questions to understand her thinking as she fills her heart with her strengths and goals. When it's finished, talk about how it feels to get those inside feelings down on paper, and discuss ways to bring those things to the surface each day.

Mother-Daughter Groups

A great way to empower girls to work together is to form mother-daughter groups. When girls form peer groups, the natural instinct of the parent is to step back and let girls work through any obstacles independently. This is a mistake. When girls begin to pull away and spend more time with peers, it's time for parents to find ways to connect and keep the relationship thriving. You hear a lot about unconditional love and open and honest communication when it comes to raising young girls. The first step to applying those things to your mother-daughter relationship is to strengthen your bond.

Community service: Some areas have wonderful mother-daughter community service groups available, but if you don't live in one of those places, be the change you hope to see. Start a group for moms and daughters to come together once a month to complete a community service project. Get a few other moms involved to spread out the organizational tasks and get your group off the ground.

Book club: Mother-daughter book clubs can be a ton of fun. Have each mother-daughter duo make one recommendation to get your book list started. Move the group from house to house (or park to park) each month for a change of scenery, and put the girls in charge of finding a craft or project to go with the book when it's their turn to host.

Label Confetti

Talking about this stuff can be intense for young girls, so it helps to make it a little silly sometimes. Get some small sticker labels and a marker and ask your daughter to think of all the labels she can come up with for you, write them on stickers, and stick them on your shirt. Some might be positive, but some might be negative. After you look over the labels and talk about how you feel to have those labels stuck to you, peel them off one by one and tear them up. When you're done tearing them to pieces, take your "label confetti" and throw it in the air in a ceremonial dumping of the labels!

If your daughter is up for it, have her stick her own labels on her shirt and follow the same steps so she can also rid herself of the labels that don't actually define her.

Weekly Challenge

When kids struggle with "picky eating" (talk about a hard label to get rid of), experts recommend working on one new food at a time and trying that food several times before giving up hope. It makes sense. Sometimes your first experience isn't the best because you go in with low expectations.

When it comes to moving girls out of those narrow boxes, I recommend doing one new thing a week. It doesn't have to be a big thing. Sometimes spending a little time finding Waldo provides a new challenge that teaches girls that they are capable of problem solving.

Create a challenge board at home so that you and your daughter can motivate each other to try one new thing per week. Report in on the results and whether or not you are willing to try that thing again. What did you learn? How did you feel? Do you recommend that someone else try that thing? Why or why not?

In helping girls find ways to step away from labels and focus on their many positive qualities instead, we empower them to work toward their own goals and step outside those boxes to embark on new adventures.

❀

CHAPTER 6

Finding Me: How to Build an Authentic Self

Why fit in when you were born to stand out?
  —*Dr. Seuss*

When parents think of peer pressure, they tend to think about things like drugs and alcohol, smoking, sex, cyberbullying, and dressing or acting a certain way. You know, things to file away for middle school (maybe). I find that parents don't think about peer pressure in the elementary-school-age years, but it does happen. A lot. No, they're not swiping alcohol from unsuspecting parents, but they are using peer pressure to get what they want from their friends, and peer influence can affect how girls view themselves in relation to others.

Eileen's mom called me because her once happy seven-year-old daughter no longer wanted anything to do with first grade. Her mom feared that the academics were just too much and wondered if she needed to get a tutor. In first grade. On the third round of a therapeutic board game, Eileen started talking. "The girls are mean. They tell me if I don't play what they want to play at recess, they won't be my friend." A hierarchy was in place, it seemed, and Eileen didn't fit in. As it turned out, she didn't want to play the role of the little brother

Parent-Teacher Conference

How does peer pressure manifest in young girls? Watch for these signs:

- ✿ Changes in attitude
- ✿ Rejection of previously close friendships with no explanation (or as one 12-year-old said to her mom, "We just don't hang out anymore, okay?")
- ✿ Withdrawal from parents and family activities
- ✿ Sudden fixation on material goods
- ✿ Rejecting family customs and traditions
- ✿ Secretive behavior

in a daily game of "family." In her eyes, the choices were clear: Do what they want or fake sick. She went with sick.

A 2013 study published in *Child Development* shed some new light on the fact that peer groups and peer pressure do emerge in the elementary school years.[1] Researchers at the University of Maryland found both positives and negatives when conducting this study. On the bright side, forming small peer groups early on provides social support and gives kids the opportunity to stand up to pressure and negativity. On the not–so–bright side, however, groups sometimes impose unfair standards on members, and where there's an "in group," an "out group" isn't far behind.

What Changes in the School-Age Years?

It should come as no surprise that girls seem to change almost daily as they work their way through the school-age years. As one mom said to me, "Just when I think I know exactly what she's into and who she wants to hang out with, she comes home with a new friend and a new after-school activity to try. Who can keep up?" For many girls, dipping their toes into independence for the first time is exciting. Gone are the days of wearing the frilly dresses Mom picked out when they weren't watching or playing with other girls simply because they live next door. Suddenly girls see possibility and opportunity around every corner. They develop strong feelings for what they like and don't like, and they aren't afraid to share those thoughts.

As exciting as it is to grow up, it's also a lot of work. It isn't always easy, and middle childhood is packed with social, emotional, and cognitive changes. Think back to your daughter at age three and then consider your daughter at age eight, ten, or even thirteen. An enormous amount of growth and development occurs during those years.

SOCIAL/EMOTIONAL CHANGES

- Self-concept grows, and they begin to explore their identities.
- Observe and compare themselves to their peers.
- Form stronger, more complex relationships.
- Build relationships with adults outside of the family unit (coaches, teachers).
- Experience peer pressure.
- Become more aware of their changing bodies.
- Might begin to prefer friendships with their own gender.
- Think independently and have their own opinions.

CHANGES IN THINKING AND LEARNING

- Increased attention span.
- Increased focus on interesting tasks.

Parent-Teacher Conference

Find small, low-pressure ways to connect with your girl.

❀ Go out to lunch.

❀ Watch a movie together (*Put your phone away!*).

❀ Go hiking.

❀ Cook something together.

❀ Create a photo book together.

❀ Kick around a soccer ball.

❀ Ask your daughter to teach you something (like making a friendship bracelet or creating a photo collage).

❀ Run errands together.

- Face more academic challenges.
- Begin to understand differing points of view.
- Responsible.
- Right and wrong can be very narrowly defined—have a strong sense of morals, largely based on personal experience.

Though many girls begin to move toward peers during middle childhood, they continue to need support and guidance from their parents. A strong parental presence during these years has a protective effect against peer pressure and the stress that often accompanies the changes, listed above and on the previous page, that girls undergo during this time period. While some of you are no doubt shaking your heads because your daughters seem to be all friends all the time, girls tell me that they don't know how to tell their parents how much they need them. Communicating emotions and interpersonal needs can be difficult during this time.

Parent-Teacher Conference

Many kids love technology, and even 10-year-olds enjoy connecting via text these days. We don't have to completely restrict the use of technology, but we do have to teach balance and safety when interacting in the digital world. Try these tips:

❀ **Ask questions:** Instead of hyper-focusing on rules, ask your daughter which apps she's interested in and why. Find out how she interacts with technology and what she gets out of it.

❀ **Create healthy boundaries:** Declare tech-free zones (dinner table, anyone?) and set time limits (young girls do not need iThings in their bedrooms). Power down one hour before bedtime. Also? Walk the walk! Follow your own rules to set a healthy example.

❀ **Talk about the downsides:** Technology can be a lot of fun, but it also has negatives. Eyestrain, headaches, neck and back pain, and sore hands can all be traced back to excessive tech time. Although kids do use technology to connect, there is a disconnect that occurs when they don't engage in face-to-face communication. Talking about the pros and cons enables girls to make healthy choices on their own.

❀ **Bring back single tasking:** I know, I know, you're a great multitasker! I used to say that too. Here's the deal: The human brain doesn't really multitask; it task switches. It can task switch quickly, but it isn't very efficient. Teach your girls to focus on one thing at a time. If they are *engaged in technology, it should be one gadget at a time. My husband and I are sometimes cited for the "no phones while watching TV" rule (and have our phones placed on a high shelf as a result), but establishing these boundaries does teach healthy habits (that our girls can then reteach to us).*

Technology Matters

It doesn't matter what the rules are regarding age and Instagram, it seems, because I know 11-year-old girls (and some even a little younger) who spend *a lot* of time creating swoon-worthy photos to share with their peers. They also make music videos, other short videos, and photo collages of their current friends. You know what else they do? Use their profiles to call out the "in" crowd. Alex became fixated on this part of social media early on. Girls used their profiles on several social media accounts to list their "besties." When she made the coveted list, she felt good. But when she got into a fight with two of her friends over the attention of a boy, she was promptly removed from those profiles. That hurt. She was pushed out and she knew it. And the worst part was that all the other kids saw it play out online.

As girls grow and begin to experiment with independence from the family, healthy friendships play an important role in their development. Girls who feel good about themselves and feel connected to their peers (even if it's only one close friend) are better able to reject negative peer influence and make positive choices for themselves. In other words, they don't feel the need to follow the crowd because they know in their hearts that they have the ability to make good choices.

The Role of Empathy in Peer Relationships

Empathy plays a starring role in positive peer relationships and standing up to peer pressure (or helping a friend stand up to peer pressure). When I ask groups of girls if they know what empathy means, I usually get some version of the following response: "Understanding how other people feel!" That's a great start when it comes to understanding empathy, but we can't stop there. Empathy is actually fairly complex, which is why it takes time and repeated exposure to teach empathy to kids.

As girls tell me over and over again, empathy does involve understanding how another girl feels by putting oneself in that girl's shoes (or "perspective taking," as we call it in the field). It's not just "You're sad. I've been sad, so I get it." To truly tap into empathy, girls need to learn to take the perspective of their friend in need. "You're feeling sad because your dad is traveling for the whole week and you miss him. I would feel really sad if I couldn't see my dad every day, so I can imagine how sad you must feel right now."

Another key element of empathy development is self-awareness. Sometimes a friend struggles with something that triggers emotions, but one girl's emotions might be very different from the other's. When girls are taught to distinguish their own feelings from the feelings of others, they are better able to listen to their friends and understand the issues at play.

As a school-based counselor, I did a lot of peer therapy. In peer sessions, kids had the opportunity to work through bumps in their friendships in a safe environment with some much-needed guidance. I had one pair of middle school girls who frequently asked for peer sessions, not because they wanted to get out of class together, but because, though they were "best friends," they were also complete opposites. One had a "Get over it" attitude when arguments ensued, while the other was highly sensitive and often felt overwhelmed with emotion.

I helped these girls learn to step back from their own emotional responses in an effort to listen to the needs of the other.

In a nutshell, they took turns identifying their feelings, stating their needs, and coming up with strategies to repair the friendship. It wasn't easy, and some days I wondered whether or not we'd made any progress at all, but in the end, it worked. I will never forget the day they popped by unannounced to let me know that they wouldn't need any more peer sessions because they were, in fact, playing the role of "Kate" at recess to help other girls learn to get along. They had learned enough and were ready to share their knowledge with their peers.

A great way to teach perspective taking at home is to use books and TV. When girls are immersed in a book or show that appeals to them, parents can use those characters to point out facial cues, nonverbal cues (like body language), and verbal cues to help girls stop and think about how the characters are feeling and why they might be feeling that way.

In fact, one study showed that books can be a great vehicle for empathy development.[2] For this study, 110 school-age children (average age of seven) were split into two groups to read illustrated scenarios based on emotional scripts. One group engaged in meaningful conversation about emotional understanding, while the other group was asked to draw a picture about the story. After two months, researchers found that the group that engaged in conversation outperformed the other group in emotion comprehension, empathy, and theory of mind. These positive outcomes remained stable over a six-month period. Teaching empathy works, and it's as easy as reading a few books and talking.

One more important component of empathy involves helping girls learn to cope with, or regulate, their own emotions. In the case of the peer counseling example, the "Get over it" girl had a tendency to become frustrated when her highly sensitive friend cried over things she considered "no big deal." Her frustrated response involved repeating the same statement over and over in an increasingly loud voice until she finally stormed out of my office to take a break. It's nearly impossible to empathize with a peer when you can't regulate your own emotional responses. I spent a fair amount of time teaching that girl to use visualization techniques to calm her frustration, but I taught her friend how to verbalize her feelings without blame. Using "I" statements helped her convey her feelings and needs without blaming her friend for all her negative emotions. (See chapter 9 for tips on teaching girls to express and cope with their emotions.)

Building the Authentic Self

Watching girls find their peer groups, declare independence, and become individuals is a beautiful thing. Sometimes I feel like I'm constantly in awe of my daughter. I love hearing her stories and seeing her move from the quiet observer to the assertive go-getter (and sometimes back again). Sometimes I still see the little preschooler in her, but other times I see her moving forward and finding her way.

Girlhood isn't a direct path from A to B. Middle childhood brings with it ups and downs, challenges and successes, friendships and loneliness, and even separation and returning to the nest. The best thing we can do for young girls during this time is support them. They need our guidance. They need our unconditional love. And they need every ounce of patience we can muster. They also need the freedom to make mistakes, to take their own paths, and to say no to our advice and intervention when we know that saying yes would be significantly easier. In other words, they need to learn on their own, at their own pace.

Parents hold the gift of hindsight in their back pockets. We've been there. We've solved that problem. We've stared down peer pressure and made the right (or wrong) choice. Because of this, we sometimes feel the need to lecture, inform, or run in for the fix (or maybe all three). In our hearts, we want to protect our girls from failure, heartache, or loneliness. We do these things to change the trajectory for our girls. But in doing these things, we deprive our girls of the opportunity to build their own authentic selves. They need to do this. They need to find their voices, follow their dreams, and learn how to solve problems in their own ways. They have to figure out who they are and what they're made of, and to do that they need us to step away from the director's chair and play a supporting role in their day-to-day lives instead.

The best way to do that is to get in touch with our own emotions that crop up during this parenting journey. I can't tell you how many moms sit in my office and recall their childhood memories of social exclusion or public humiliation. They want their girls to avoid these obstacles, so they engage in social engineering. They cultivate friendships for their girls, work out conflict on their behalf, and push them to join more teams and more activities because the more they do, the more opportunities for friendship they have. I get it. And in some ways, it makes sense. Some girls have difficulty making new friends. What's the harm in helping?

What I hear from the girls is that sometimes those friendships that are made on their behalf aren't the ones they would choose, that it's embarrassing when a mom steps in to solve the conflict, and that they're exhausted from too many activities. One girl looked up at me with tears in her eyes and said, "I just want to hang out in my room and draw."

Parental pressure is no joke. I see it a lot, and I've even experienced it at times. If we want to teach our girls to go their own way and be individuals, we have to model that in our own lives. If our girls see us caving to the pressure to fit in and keep up, they will learn to do the

Parent-Teacher Conference

This is what your daughter needs when the going gets tough:

❀ For you to listen without judgment

❀ Unconditional love

❀ Hugs

❀ Uninterrupted time together

❀ Brainstorming together. Young girls look to their parents for help solving difficult problems, but they want help, not directions.

same. To help our girls live authentic lives, we need to live our own authentic lives. (Incidentally, this lesson on authenticity also makes a great comeback when your daughter complains that she has the earliest bedtime in the universe—"I don't mind being different. Early bedtime works for us.")

Beyond dealing with our own issues and sources of pressure and stress in this world of parenting, we also have to listen to our girls to help them discover and follow through with their passions. The wonderful thing about being a young girl today is that there are endless possibilities. Sure, some girls love team sports and want to sign up for three sports every season (but please limit them to one), while others love science, technology, art, cooking, theater, or any number of other things. And there are clubs or classes for just about everything.

Resist the urge to plug your daughter into what every other girl in town is doing, and give her the gift of discovery. Take a break from the culture of busy and let her try things at home or test out different activities before making a commitment. A 10-year-old girl begged (*begged*) her mom to let her take a sewing class for months, but the class conflicted with ballet. She was over ballet; she liked the kids, so she didn't mind going, but she was also willing to give it up. When she finally took a month off from ballet to take the sewing classes, her spirits were instantly lifted. She felt at home in the sewing class. That basic class led to a fashion design for dolls class, which led to a design class in which she made herself a skirt. She did return to ballet at some point, while also continuing her design classes, and in doing so, she found her path.

How the Push to Conform Plays into Mean Girl Culture

Conformity, and engaging in sports and activities simply because other girls do the same, sends the message that sameness is preferable to being different. When girls don't have the opportunity to explore their own interests and desires, they get caught in a cycle of going with the flow and doing what everyone else is doing. What does this mean for the outliers? For starters, it means they struggle to fit in. It also gives girls in the "normal" crowd perceived power over the girls on the outside. In short, conformity drives mean girl culture.

It's important to teach girls to embrace and celebrate differences, as well as to learn from one another. Groups shouldn't form solely based on outside activities, and self-worth shouldn't be wrapped up in fitting in with one specific group. When girls have the freedom to try out a wide variety of friendships and showcase their interests and talents, they learn to blaze their own trails and take pride in their individual differences.

Girls need opportunities to try all kinds of things, but not all at once. Take a season off from a sport and try something new, or simply increase free time and see what discoveries your daughter makes on her own. Specializing in anything at an early age, be it a sport or other activity, is more likely to result in burnout than future success. We have to step away from the pressure to fill the downtime so that girls can figure out who they are, who they want to become, and what kind of a future they want to enjoy. If we want to raise girls who are resilient and compassionate, we have to start by giving them the opportunity to follow their own paths and make their own decisions.

Group dynamics are tricky business during the school-age years, and girls need help learning to cope with and stand up to peer pressure. They also need to be encouraged to build an authentic self. Girls can lose their dreams and goals when they feel "stuck" in a certain group. A wide variety of friends is a good strategy, but don't stop there. The earlier we talk to our girls about pressure, empathy, and kindness, the more empowered they are to act as change makers as they grow.

Girls Can!

Introduce the Concept of Peer Pressure

A lot of parents tell me they don't want to start talking about peer pressure before their kids encounter it because they don't want their kids to worry about things that aren't yet a problem. In some ways, this makes perfect sense. "Live in the moment" is a phrase thrown around a lot these days, and for good reason. When we live in the moment, we enjoy our girls just the way they are today.

The flip side of this is that information is helpful for young girls. Instead of waiting for negative peer pressure to arise, parents can get ahead of it by introducing the concept when they're young. When parents use age-appropriate language and take developmental level into consideration, they can help girls understand the meaning behind peer pressure and how to stand up to it. Try this:

"Sometimes a friend might ask you to do something that you don't want to do or to leave out a friend at recess. She might ask you the same thing over and over again. It's okay to say no to a friend or even a group of friends, and it's also a good idea to ask an adult for help if you're not sure what to do."

Sometimes young girls engage in peer pressure not because they're trying to act "mean" but because they want to get their needs met. This is typical in the early elementary years and can last through middle childhood. It's a mistake to jump from one bad choice to "mean girl," but I see it happen. If your daughter experiences peer pressure or some kind of early relational aggression, resist the urge to label the other child, and try to talk about the "whys" instead. Why do you think your friend asked you to do that? What was happening at the time? I wonder how she could have been feeling. When we help girls talk through the situations instead of labeling and moving on, we empower them to act as change makers the next time they encounter these behaviors.

Note: You know what your child can handle. Some girls are highly sensitive and have difficulty regulating their emotional responses to difficult topics. In that case, proceed with caution. Introducing these concepts takes time—avoid piling a bunch of information on your daughter all at once.

Teach Refusal Skills

Parents spend a lot of time teaching young children to follow rules and listen to others, but they don't always teach them how to refuse something. Refusal skills play an important role in standing up to peer pressure. It's hard to do when you're young, though. The path of least resistance is tempting when standing up to negativity might mean losing your status within the class.

Try practicing these refusal tactics with your daughter:

- Broken record: Teach your daughter to choose a stance and repeat it over and over again until the person applying the pressure walks away or shifts gears. When my daughter's friends wanted to leave another girl out, I taught her to say, "She's really fun. Let's play with her too," until the other girls ran out of excuses.

- Ask questions: Kids who pile on the pressure don't expect their victims to ask questions. Practice responding to pressure with "Why do you want me to do that?" or "Why are you asking me that?" or "What good would that do?"

- Keep the door open: If your child doesn't want to engage in the negative behavior but wants to preserve the friendship, teach her to say, "I don't want to do that, but if you change your mind and want to do something else, let me know."

- Call it like it is: Sometimes the best way for young girls to confront pressure is to call it like it is. Teach your child to keep it short but honest when dealing with pressure: "That's mean," "That's cheating," and "That's against the rules" are all simple statements that get to the point.

Create a Personal Billboard

One of my favorite ways to help girls begin to discover what makes them unique is to create a personal billboard. This is a great activity to do one-on-one, but it also works well in groups. When I use this activity in groups with girls, I pair them off and have them interview one another to get to know their individual strengths and create billboards for each other.

Why a billboard? Billboards are used to draw attention to things and showcase reasons to buy certain products or attend certain events.

Creating a personal billboard helps girls internalize a positive message: You are unique, and you are someone worth getting to know! It's a fairly simple project. Ask your daughter to think about what makes her different from her peers, what strengths she has, and what her personal goals are. Once she has a good list, ask her to design an eye-popping billboard to showcase all that great stuff. Talk about the things she writes down, and ask her questions to engage her in conversation. In doing this, you send two powerful messages: I enjoy listening to you talk about your hopes and dreams, and you are special to me just the way you are.

Set Limits

Middle childhood is no time for passive parenting. I know that it's hard to set limits, and it can be exhausting when your daughter constantly pushes your limits. Bottom line: Her job is to push limits and test boundaries; your job is to stick to your limits. This comes up often with technology (if you feel overwhelmed by finding that magical balance between too much and not enough, you are not alone), but it also applies to family responsibilities, bedtimes, and healthy habits.

If you don't set and adhere to limits for your daughter, how can you expect her to set limits with her friends when she needs to? Setting limits isn't just a matter of getting the chores done and eating vegetables. When you set healthy limits, you teach your daughter how to set and stick to personal boundaries out in the world. One day, she might need to say, "No, I won't leave out my friend," and she will only be able to do that if she understands the concept of limits.

Identity Circles

Sometimes girls struggle to identify who they are because they wear different faces in different circumstances. I once worked with a girl who was a force on the soccer field. She was tough as nails, confident, and a great team player. Her teachers saw a completely different girl at school, though. At school she kept to herself, appeared reluctant to engage in classroom discussions, and seemed anxious about getting her work corrected. Her mom described her as silly, talkative, and energetic at home. This girl showcased three different personalities in three different places. When I asked her which description was the best fit, she said, "I think a little bit of all of them."

Identity circles help girls think about how they see themselves and how others perceive them. Grab a sheet of paper and draw a small circle in the middle. Ask your daughter to write her name there. Next, ask her to draw a circle large enough to fill with descriptions about who she is at school, and connect that circle to the center with a line. You'll want to complete one circle for school, one for home, and one for any other place your daughter spends a lot of time (the playing field, band, etc.). Finally, ask her to complete a "true you" circle. Who is she on the inside? What does she wish others knew about her?

This project helps girls discover the ways they shift and change while considering who they truly believe themselves to be.

Self-Addressed Letter

Sometimes it's hard for young girls to talk about things like identity formation, hopes and dreams, and peer pressure. Young girls tend to be parent pleasers by nature, and girls tell me that fear of disappointing parents and other adults holds them back from sharing their innermost thoughts. Fear not; the more time you spend connecting with your daughter and listening without judgment, the more likely she is to begin opening up.

In the meantime, self-addressed letters can help. Explain to your daughter that letter writing can be a calming activity, and sometimes it helps to put your feelings down on paper, even if the letter is just for you. Encourage her to write a monthly letter to herself to spend time connecting with her inner self. She might need some sentence starters to get the words flowing. Try some of these:

- Something great that happened this month was . . .
- I felt really happy when . . .
- I felt sad when . . .
- Something I really want to try is . . .
- I wish my parents knew . . .
- I don't like it when . . .
- I love to daydream about . . .

Good Friend, Great Friend, Not a Friend

One thing I hear from girls a lot is that friendships can be confusing. Sometimes friends do unkind things, and girls aren't sure if the friendship is over or if it's just a bad day. Sometimes girls don't know how to communicate their feelings or concerns, and their attempts to resolve a conflict backfire. Some girls are all too willing to give endless chances to a friend who isn't being kind because it's exceptionally difficult to walk away from a friend.

Role-playing is a great way to help girls work through their feelings of confusion and uncertainty about uncomfortable peer interactions. Ask your daughter to help you come up with a list of scenarios that happen at school, in activities and sports, and even on the playground. Write them on individual slips of paper and put them in a hat. Ask your daughter to pick one and to assign characters for each of you. Play out the scenario, including the unkind behavior and attempts to resolve the conflict. Dressing up to get into character sometimes helps reduce the intensity of emotions that can occur when working through difficult topics.

After you've played out the scenario and attempted to resolve the problem, take turns evaluating each character. Is character #1 a good friend, a great friend, or not a friend? What about character #2? Why did you evaluate them the way you did? What could each character do to get a different evaluation?

Read Together Every Night

It seems like the moment kids learn to read independently, parents step away from reading together. This is a mistake. Reading together is a great way to connect with your daughter, and many books provide conversation starters to help kids think about peer pressure, being authentic, and finding their passion. Watching a character develop on the page increases empathy and helps girls consider their own inner selves.

For younger readers, the Clementine series is both entertaining and full of obstacles and issues that girls face during middle childhood. The Ramona series is a classic option and full of opportunities to discuss empathy and identity development. For older girls, the Harry Potter series is packed with identity development, friendship issues, and individuation. When I ask girls for recommendations, they almost always include Roald Dahl books as well, but when it comes to books, the possibilities are endless. For tweens, I always recommend scouring the Good Reads recommended lists together. What one girl loves, another might not enjoy at all. Put in the time to make new reading discoveries together, and read together or side by side to stay connected.

I always encourage parents to choose the slow and winding road when it comes to young girls. Just because your daughter shows a talent for the piano doesn't mean she wants to play it constantly. It's okay to step off the treadmill (also known as the path to success), try new things, and put self-exploration first. At some point, your daughter will find her passion (or passions) and become focused on that. For now, give her the opportunity to find her own way at her own pace.

❁

CHAPTER 7

Reaching for the High Bar

Forget about the fast lane. If you really want to fly,
just harness your power to your passion.
—*Oprah Winfrey*

The good news in the world of girls is they are hearing some very positive messages these days. Girls are encouraged to follow their dreams and reach for the high bar. *You can be anything you want to be,* whisper (sometimes overzealous) parents over and over again. Indeed, society is stepping up to the plate. STEM camps and coding classes for girls are popping up everywhere. Web sites and resources intended to inspire young girls are readily accessible. Girls are playing tons of sports, and opportunities to learn skills for the future are everywhere. Girls *can* get on the fast track to success—all they have to do is set goals and work hard.

What's the downside of this girl power generation? Pressure. Supergirls feel an intense amount of pressure to be everything and get into Harvard (or Stanford or Yale . . .). According to a teen ethics poll of 787 teens 13 to 18 years old, 44 percent say they feel a strong pressure to succeed, and the pressure is felt more often by girls than boys.[1] A Temple University study found that girls are more at risk of interpersonal stressors, which thereby increases their risk for depression. Specifically, girls tend to ruminate more about their stressors, and that can trigger feelings of depression.[2]

In our quest to lift girls up and encourage them to shatter glass ceilings, we've added just a tad too much pressure to the mix. Girls face achievement pressure across multiple domains of their lives. In school, they feel pressured to make the grade. Girls are consistently evaluated by their outcomes, and sometimes parent expectations are unreasonably high. I can't tell you how many parents express concern when one grade is "lower" than the rest. Outside school, girls are expected to be "well rounded." They need to play a sport, find a creative outlet, volunteer, have a group of friends, and take on household chores to work on being "responsible." Here's the bottom line: High expectations are healthy. Unreasonable expectations can be damaging. Find your daughter's baseline, and set expectations accordingly.

Success doesn't occur when girls work themselves into the ground. Success occurs when girls reach for their goals along with a healthy side of balance.

Kate wanted to be the first in her family to attend an Ivy League school. She made this declaration at the impossible age of nine. I don't know about you, but I don't know a ton of nine-year-olds with super specific life goals. Her parents cheered her on. Her grandparents, aunts and uncles, and family friends cheered her on. She played every sport she could play, joined every club available, and studied long past a reasonable bedtime every night. She spent little time with friends outside of her carefully selected activities, and she never slowed down. This began at age nine. By 17, Kate had a 4.0 GPA and two varsity letters, but she was fried. And she didn't get into the Ivy League. While Kate definitely looked good on paper, and certainly seemed like a great candidate for the Ivy League, she never took the time to find her true passion. Her only goal was to get into an Ivy League school. Beyond that, she didn't have a clear path. She worked herself into the ground to make the grade, but she failed to stop and think about her hopes and dreams for the future.

What Triggers Stress for Girls?

It might seem like childhood is generally fairly stress-free, but I find that a lot of kids are under stress these days. A national survey on childhood stress in America found that 72 percent of children frequently showed negative behaviors linked to stress during a 12-month period in 2015.[3] From social issues to parent–child relationships to academic and extra-curricular demands, many young girls are running on stress, and not many of them are given lessons in coping.

Parent-Teacher Conference

Watch for these common causes of stress for young girls:

* ✿ Family discord/home environment
* ✿ Illness in the family
* ✿ Death in the family
* ✿ Divorce/separation
* ✿ Academic struggles or pressure
* ✿ Homework
* ✿ Peer problems and/or peer pressure
* ✿ Bullying
* ✿ Sibling rivalry or sibling bullying
* ✿ Hectic schedules
* ✿ Poor sleep habits
* ✿ Insufficient downtime/lack of free-play time

Friend or Foe?

One mom in New York reached out to me when her child refused to go to school several days in a row. When she met with the teacher and talked to a few other parents to try to piece it all together, she was shocked. Her child was being bullied. In preschool. The tears, screaming, and flailing limbs weren't an attempt to manipulate. This child was under stress and scared to return to a school she once loved.

It might be hard to believe that peer problems can escalate in a preschool environment, but social exclusion (and other forms of relational aggression) can occur in young children. Results of one study showed that girls exhibit more relational aggression than boys (who are more likely to engage in physical aggression) in preschool, that children primarily direct their aggression at same-sex peers, and that relational aggression in early childhood is positively associated with peer rejection later on.[4] Statements such as "You can't play with us today" or "I don't want to be your friend anymore" seem like normal friendship errors that can be corrected with a quick apology, but repeated exposure to this kind of relational aggression (even at the preschool level) can cause increased stress levels for young girls.

As girls move into the elementary school years, relational aggression can increase. While parents and teachers are often on the lookout for lunch table rejection (parents are hardwired to ask about lunch to make sure girls aren't excluded from the lunch table), I find that recess rejection is fairly pervasive in the early elementary years. On the playground, girls can wander off from the watchful eye of the recess teacher and engage in exclusion and other acts of unkindness that cause significant stress for young girls. In middle childhood, being left off the guest list for a birthday party can be downright devastating, and being "frozen out" by a group of girls can trigger feelings of low self-worth, anxiety, and/or depression.

Parental Problems

Parental relationships play an important role in the lives of girls, and poor parent-child relationships can be stress-inducing for young girls. In fact, a recent study showed that "pushy parenting" when it comes to academic and extracurricular performance negatively affected the academic success and social/emotional well-being of middle school students. The same study showed that children who believe their parents value kindness and compassion as much as or more than academic success actually have higher grade point averages and suffer from less anxiety and depression.[5] In their overzealous efforts to help secure successful futures for their children, it seems, pushy parents unknowingly trigger stress that leads to poor outcomes.

Pushy parenting isn't the only parenting style that results in high stress levels, though. Authoritarian (or strict and highly controlling) parenting is linked to anxiety, depression, poor social skills, and other behavioral problems.[6] This harsh style of parenting is low on parental responsiveness (a.k.a. not very nurturing) and focused on high (sometimes beyond developmental capability) expectations and performance. In this rigid emotional climate, open parent-child communication is generally not available, making it difficult for young girls to feel connected to their parents or to seek help when they encounter obstacles. The result? Girls feel pressured, resentful, and frustrated. It's a recipe for low self-esteem, stress, and anxiety.

Home Life

Addison was convinced that her parents were headed for divorce. (They weren't.) Week after week, she shared her concerns about "fighting" and "anger" and "yelling" at home. It was true that her parents were under stress and arguing more than normal. It was also true that her parents were low on patience and yelled at times (they felt terrible about it and made great efforts to manage their own stress, but it was hard). What Addison left out of her stories was the fact that she knew all of this because she spied on her parents a lot. She sensed tension between them, as school-age girls do, and made it her goal to "investigate" the problem. While they tried to save their heated debates for late at night and behind closed doors, Addison kept herself awake at night to listen in and find out what was going on and if it might be her fault.

Addison isn't alone. Stress trickles down in families, and when kids don't have all of the information, they tend to do two things: They focus on the worst-case scenario (divorce), and they assume they are at fault in some way. Some kids become pleasers who follow their parents around trying to make everything right again. Others become detectives who try to piece together the clues and, in the process, internalize the stress they encounter. Addison was the latter.

When it comes to family discord or separation or divorce, girls do take on the stress that exists within the home. It's not limited to parental fighting, though. Sibling relationships can include excessive teasing and taunting, and even bullying. Yes, you read that right. Siblings can and do bully their siblings. Left unchecked, this behavior can trigger stress, anxiety, and depression.

Loss of a family member or a close loved one is an obvious source of stress, but having a friend or family member with an illness (even if you feel like your daughter is protected from it) can increase daily stress levels for girls.

And we can't forget about financial stress on the family, job loss, and moving. All of these family issues can trigger feelings of stress and anxiety that are difficult to manage independently.

School Stress

It used to be that school included a healthy balance of academics and enrichment. Sure, there were always tests, quizzes, and evaluations.

But recess was plentiful; PE, art, and music (the so-called "specials" of today) were guaranteed; and the day wasn't quite as intense. The average school day today is packed with academic instruction, and many schools have short recess periods and lack PE. Kids are sitting for longer periods and learning at a rapid pace. While many kids are capable of surviving this kind of school day, it does take its toll. When parents call me with concerns about evening meltdowns that seem to come from nowhere, my first thought is always "stress."

Some girls internalize their stress throughout the day but don't necessarily "struggle" in school. These girls fly under the radar because they generally follow the rules, complete their work, and appear stable. They fall apart night after night, but they put themselves back together and do what they have to do during the school day. Other girls experience stress at school, not because the day is long and lacks sufficient downtime, but because they deal with academic obstacles and other school-related stress. These are the girls who "act out" or "lose focus" in the classroom. They're not really acting out, of course; they're overwhelmed and frustrated, but the adults don't necessarily see the stressors hidden beneath the behaviors.

However, it's not all bad. Not at all. In fact, young girls are learning some amazing things these days. Fourth-graders are doing dissections. Third-graders are learning the art of poetry. History lessons are hands-on and exciting in many schools. There are new and exciting ways to learn math. There are many positives to the shift in education, but even positive shifts can lead to stress, and that's why we have to tune in to how our girls are faring from an emotional perspective each day.

School stress is complicated, and no two girls experience stress in the same way. That makes it hard to spot. I encourage parents and teachers to try to find patterns of behavioral changes, but the best thing we can do is talk to our girls about stress. When we help them understand their physical symptoms of stress and connect triggers to emotional and somatic responses, they can learn to seek help both at school and at home. To do that, we need to understand how stress and pressure manifest in young girls.

How Does Stress Manifest in Girls?

Girls don't come home from school saying, "I feel stressed out. I need help." They might come home and say they're not feeling well. They might claim exhaustion or headaches. They might appear irritable or low on patience. More often than not, though, they don't say much of anything at all. They experience stomachaches, headaches, and other physical symptoms, but so does the average school-age kid on any given day. Parents don't necessarily think "stress" or "pressure" when kids complain of stomachaches because, well, we're all familiar with the stomach flu, right?

Physical symptoms aren't the only signs of stress in young girls. Many parents share concerns about behavioral changes that seem completely out

Parent-Teacher Conference

If you notice a pattern to these physical symptoms, consider your daughter's stress level:

✿ Frequent stomachaches

✿ Frequent headaches (including migraines)

✿ Muscle pains (kids tense their muscles when stressed)

✿ Frequent trips to the school nurse

✿ Other physical complaints with no known medical cause

Parent-Teacher Conference

Girls also show these behavioral changes when under stress:

- ✿ Sleep disturbance
- ✿ Irritability
- ✿ Mood swings
- ✿ Isolating
- ✿ Refusal to participate in normal daily activities
- ✿ Refusal to go to school
- ✿ Frequent complaints
- ✿ Clingy behavior
- ✿ Changes in eating habits
- ✿ Skin picking or hair pulling
- ✿ Bedwetting
- ✿ Stuttering

of character. To hear Harper's mom tell it, Harper shifted from a confident and "easygoing" second-grader to an "argumentative" third-grader almost overnight. After ruling out a number of possible reasons for this change in demeanor, she later discovered that test anxiety was the culprit and the third-grade year was full of tests and assessments.

Stress can be an emotional roller coaster for young girls. Because children naturally experience emotional shifts throughout the day as they encounter highs and lows (I'm excited! I'm frustrated!), changes in the emotional baseline can seem "normal." Patterns of new and different emotional reactions (or intensified reactions), however, should not be ignored. The most recent statistics on suicide rates in the United States show that the highest percent increase for the female population was in the 10- to 14-year-old age group.[7] Any symptoms of stress, anxiety, or depression or major changes in behavior need to be evaluated.

> Sometimes I cry at night and I don't even know why. I'm not sad. I just cry.
> —*A third-grade girl*

Not every negative behavior is a sign of stress. Everyone is entitled to a bad day or sometimes a few bad days in a row—even kids. But a negative *pattern* of behavior can point to stress and/or too much pressure.

Stress Exacerbates Mean Girl Culture

When girls are under stress, they sometimes project it onto others. While many parents say that their daughters store up their stress and let it all out at home, many girls tell me that girls take their stress out on each other. Sometimes this comes in the form of the heated "My life is harder than your life" discussion. Other times, girls lash out at

Parent-Teacher Conference

Watch for these emotional symptoms of stress:

- ✿ Frequent crying with no known trigger
- ✿ Angry outbursts
- ✿ Fearfulness
- ✿ Anxious behaviors
- ✿ Separation anxiety
- ✿ Aggressive behavior

other girls because they've hit their maximum stress level. Stress also fuels the fire of unhealthy competition.

We all hear the stories of kids surviving the stress of the school day only to explode or fall apart when they get home, but girls tell me that sometimes waiting until the end of the school day is hard. A fourth-grade girl ended up in my office because she felt ostracized at school. She was funny, generous, and bright but couldn't hold on to a friendship for more than a couple of weeks. As it turned out, she was known for projecting her stress onto her friends. That's what was behind her behavior, anyway. What her friends saw was a girl who blamed her friends for everything, acted jealous, and "threw fits" on the playground. Other girls stayed away from her because of her hurtful behavior.

When I help girls stop focusing on their own sources of stress and empathize with other girls under stress, they are able to slow down and consider how the cycle of stress affects their friendships. When girls vent their stress and talk about ways to work through it with other girls, they can actually help each other cope. This works well when I'm mediating a group of girls. When girls are left to handle these emotional shifts without the benefit of stress management strategies, however, mean girl culture thrives.

The Balancing Act

> I want to give her opportunities. I don't want her to hold
> herself back from things.
> —*Mother of a fifth-grade girl*

It's no big secret that we live in a pressure-filled world and kids face a ton of stress these days, but girls seem to pay a higher price. In lifting them up and directing them toward that coveted high bar, we sometimes forget to teach them the art of balance. That's not to say that they shouldn't reach, because they should. But they should reach when they're ready and willing and driven by their own passion. The truth is that parents can't force their kids to find passion. Passion, like it or not, comes from within.

That mom who wants her daughter to have opportunities isn't alone. I hear that from a lot of moms, and I get it. I want my daughter to know that she has opportunities and that she can try any number of activities until she finds her true passion. She can have one passion or ten. She *can* reach for and grab that high bar. I don't want her to back down because something is new or hard or different or (gag) "comes naturally" to boys. But I want her to find those things on her own terms. I want her to find her way when she's ready.

The big secret here is that there is no "fast track" to success for our girls. In fact, fast-tracking them plays a huge role in pressure, stress, and, ultimately, burnout. Fast-tracking girls tends to be counterproductive. When girls are constantly pushed beyond their developmental levels or overwhelmed with the stress of overscheduling and overdoing, they don't enjoy the "success" that parents so desperately want them to experience.

The truth about reaching for the high bar is that it's a balancing act. When girls are given the opportunity to pursue a multitude of interests over the course of time, they can take the time to immerse themselves in different activities and find their strengths and weaknesses, likes and dislikes. When the pressure to succeed is replaced with a license to explore, girls have the emotional space to figure out who they are and what makes them tick. When parents remove the race to the finish line from the equation, girls are given the gift of time.

I recently exclaimed to a group of nine- and ten-year-old girls, "This is a great time to be a girl!" They immediately erupted in cheers while jumping up and down. Then we got down to the business of balancing the world of opportunity with the pull to slow down and enjoy girlhood. Girls often describe feeling stuck. They want to do all the cool things, but they also want to play with their friends, take walks outside, and ride their bikes as fast as possible on a hot summer day. They want to go to that interesting science camp, but they also want to build with LEGOs, draw, or just hang out at home.

Supergirl culture doesn't have to result in a generation of girls too stressed to access the wonderful opportunities and possibilities that await them. In teaching girls the art of balance, we can empower our girls to take on the world one small step at a time.

Remember Kate, who so desperately wanted to get into an Ivy League school? When the rejections came in, she felt her dreams crashing in around her. She couldn't understand how it had all gone so wrong. When she came up for air, however, she decided to focus on the opportunities she actually had before her (not the ones in her carefully constructed fantasy of perfection). She visited a few of the colleges that had accepted her and fell in love with one of them. In that moment, she finally ripped off her cape and decided to live the life that actually existed instead of always striving for some version of "better." It was, without a doubt, the best thing that could have happened to her.

Girls Can!

Set Manageable Goals

Goal setting is an important skill. It comes in handy when planning for the future, for sure, but it also helps girls manage their day-to-day lives. The problem is that in our success-driven culture, we sometimes set unrealistic examples of goal setting for our girls, when we should be teaching them to set age-appropriate and manageable goals.

The good old-fashioned flow chart is a great way to illustrate goal setting. You place your overall goal in the top box and then break it down into manageable pieces. If the goal, for example, is to make the club swim team, you start by coming up with three smaller benchmarks to help make that goal a reality. Those can even be broken down into several smaller tasks within the benchmark (e.g., "Do more conditioning" becomes "Do planks and push-ups three times a week").

When girls learn to break down larger goals into manageable parts and follow through on each step, they are empowered to set and meet their own goals.

Teach Relaxation Skills

There's an app for everything these days. Gratitude journal? There's an app for that. Worry journal? There's an app for that. Mindfulness training? There are tons of apps for that. You know what there isn't an app for? Carving out time to practice the art of balance and relaxation.

Mindfulness and deep breathing are great strategies for calming the senses and remaining present, but girls also need to learn to balance downtime and fun time with their quest for success. Journaling provides stress relief and the space to dream. Daydreaming actually helps people recall information. In fact, one study found that when people are engaged in simple tasks that don't require full attention and their minds wander (daydream), they use their idle resources to tap into their working memory and think about other things.[8] And reading is always a great escape. No two girls are the same, and finding a relaxing ritual that works and appeals to your daughter can take some trial and error. Try a few of these strategies at home (no classes necessary!):

- Painting/drawing/sketching/coloring
- Writing poetry

- Baking
- Knitting (one of my personal favorites)
- Photography
- Yoga (yes, there's an app for that)
- Playful exercise (swings, homemade obstacle courses, etc.)

Visualization

I love to teach girls visualization. I start by telling them that guided visualization can help with everything from meeting their own personal goals to coping with worry to getting to sleep at night. When we engage our minds in visualization exercises, we give our bodies permission to let go of internalized stress while helping our minds focus on positive imagery.

Girls hear a lot about visualizing "success" these days, but I prefer to teach them to visualize the process. You don't always win the gold medal or ace the test, but you can put forth your best effort and learn new things along the way. To that end, visualizing the process (whether it's taking a test or competing in a swim meet) helps girls focus their positive energy on effort, not results.

Ask your daughter to sit comfortably and take three deep breaths. A great way to teach deep breathing is to breathe in for a count of four, hold for four, and release for four. After a few deep breaths, ask your daughter to focus on her muscles. Is she carrying any stress in her legs and feet? If so, flex and relax, beginning with the feet, to release the tension. Continue with hands and arms as your daughter shifts into relaxation.

Next, describe in detail the scenario your daughter is worried or stressed about. Paint the backdrop. Talk about her strengths. Remind her of her hard work leading up to this point. Lead her through the process, one detail at a time, focusing on things that she is prepared for and that are within her control (e.g., she can warm up her muscles before the race by swimming four practice laps). In working through the process step-by-step in their minds, girls feel calm and confident.

Hopes and Dreams Board

Truth be told, I've always disliked the idea of a bucket list because it feels so final. It also feels like a to-do list that won't likely get done in a timely manner because it's full of nonessentials that are sometimes fairly far-reaching. I definitely want to visit Ireland, for example, but it's not in the cards this year. A hopes and dreams board, on the other hand, provides a visual representation of things that can be accomplished on any given day (no expensive plane tickets required).

I encourage girls to create their own hopes and dreams boards. When I recently asked a group of girls to name one thing they want to learn but never have time to practice, more than half of them yelled, "Ice skating!" without even thinking about it. Girls have wants and ideas that get pushed aside because their lives are busy enough already, or they're so tired when they finally do have downtime that they would rather do nothing at all.

Creating a hopes and dreams board for their rooms gives girls the chance to get those wants out in the open. When they do this, they are more likely to prioritize those secret dreams when opportunity strikes. They can also share those wants with you so that you can help them try new activities and get unstuck.

Play Past Life Successes

When girls feel pressured and experience stress, they tend to focus on the worst-case scenario. *I'll fail my test. I won't score a goal. The kids will laugh at my project.* Negative thinking can be powerful. So can tapping into positive events from the past.

I like to play "past life successes" with girls when the "what-ifs" trigger negative thoughts. It's a simple process.

- State the current trigger.
- Name the worst-case scenario taking up space in your brain.
- Share a past life success: What success from the past shows you that you're capable of jumping this current hurdle?
- Past lessons applied today: Name one thing you did to make that past experience a success that might help you with your current problem.

Often, a shift in thought process helps girls break the pattern of negativity clouded by "what-ifs" and replace it with memories of success and confidence.

Balance Beam

I'm always in awe of the Olympic gymnasts during the balance beam event. They appear calm and in control, even when they slip or miss a step. Of course, years of practice and carefully choreographed routines play into that appearance, but to the viewer at home, it looks like a dance.

To teach girls about creating balance in their lives, we have to help them understand the give-and-take of matching busy activities with downtime, family with friendship. Have your daughter draw a balance beam on a piece of paper. Divide the beam into an equal number of one-inch sections. Ask your daughter to name some of the activities that keep her feeling busy. Examples might include birthday parties, sports, after-school classes, etc. Write one busy activity per square in half of the squares on the beam, all in a row. Take a breather to talk about how busy that beam looks. Ask your daughter how it feels when she has an action-packed week with little time to herself.

Next, ask your daughter to name her favorite downtime activities. This can include anything from snuggling with a parent to reading to drawing to playing outside. Fill in the remaining boxes with relaxing downtime activities. Talk about how those activities feel soothing and rejuvenating.

Finally, comment on the beam. Though it might technically be "even" because there are equal numbers of each activity, it isn't "balanced." The way it's drawn, your daughter moves from a series of very busy and potentially high-pressure activities to a series of downtime activities. To truly create balance, the two kinds of activities should alternate along the beam. Redraw the beam together so that it reflects a healthier balance.

Promote Calming Hobbies

One of the challenges of helping girls find balance is that everything feels super important right this very minute, and many things feel like stepping-stones to the future. I can't tell you how many parents talk to me about finding opportunities that will look good on college applications . . . when their daughters are in elementary school.

Hobbies are the antidote to winning at all costs. When girls find hobbies, activities they do for fun and relaxation, they are better able to fight stress and cope with the pressure they face on any given day. Whether it's gardening, needlepoint, making friendship bracelets, or turning your kitchen into a chemistry lab, encourage and promote hobbies. Talk about the power of letting go of expectations and evaluations and engaging in activities simply because they're fun.

Release Negative Energy

When stress builds up, girls internalize negative energy. Eventually, that energy comes out. I've found that parents expect this to happen with boys, but assume that girls don't have the same experience with storing negative emotions in their bodies. Not true. Girls tense their muscles, hold in their feelings, and experience physical symptoms of stress. They need to let their stress out.

There are tons of ways to redirect pent-up stress, but I find that the following are crowd-pleasers:

- Pound Play-Doh
- Jump in mud puddles
- Throw wet paper towels (outside)
- Dance to loud pop music
- Yell for 30 seconds behind a closed door
- Play bounce off: Bounce a Nerf ball against the wall. Vent one frustration as you release, and replace it with one positive thought when you catch it.

When girls have strategies to release their negative energy, they are better able to work through their stressors. When girls can conquer their triggers of stress and maintain a healthy balance, they can finally reach for that high bar—the one that appeals to them and reflects their dreams and goals. Parents can't push girls across the finish line to a lifetime of success and happiness, but they can guide their girls and support them as they challenge themselves to reach for the sky.

❖

CHAPTER 8

Find Your Voice!

It took me quite a long time to develop a voice, and
now that I have it, I am not going to be silent.
—*Madeleine Albright*

In 18 years of working with young girls, I've found that many
young girls struggle with assertiveness skills. We teach girls to be kind
and compassionate. We teach them how to be respectful. We teach
them to listen, and we teach them to take turns. What we also need
to teach them . . . is how to speak up. It's not enough to encourage
them to raise their hands and answer questions in the classroom. It's
not enough to encourage loud and boisterous play on the field. Girls
need to learn (at an early age) that their voices matter. They need to
learn how to assert their feelings, thoughts, needs, and ideas. More
importantly, they need to learn to state those things with conviction.

A 2010 study published in *Developmental Psychology* looked at
gender variations in children's language use. Researchers analyzed
speech that is considered to be gender stereotyped, including talk-
ativeness, affiliative speech (speech that promotes social cohesion), and
assertiveness. On average, girls were more talkative and used more affiliative speech than boys did, and boys used more assertive speech

than girls did.[1] Where girls talk often and use inclusive speech patterns to draw others in, boys pounce with assertive communication and get their needs met.

I recently asked a group of girls if they have ever been in a classroom or other setting where the teacher or activity leader asked a question and the boys were jumping out of their seats and calling out answers while the girls remained in their seats raising their hands politely. In this all-girl group setting, nearly every girl jumped up and down and shouted, "*Yes!*" One by one, they shared their experiences and talked about how frustrating it is when boys "take over" because they aren't afraid to be loud, even if they're being inconsiderate of the rest of the class. Years of research normalizes what girls experience every single day: Elementary and middle school boys receive eight times more attention than girls.[2] When boys call out, they are rewarded with listening. When girls call out, they are reminded to raise their hands. When boys don't engage in classroom discussions, teachers encourage them. Girls, on the other hand, tend to feel invisible.

Mia struggled to communicate her needs in the classroom. She loved her teacher and had tons of friends, but she would much rather suffer in silence than bother her teacher with the fact that she couldn't make any sense of her math. So she suffered. When a particularly low math test score came home with an offer for extra help from the teacher, Mia's mother took action. As it turned out, Mia was afraid that her lack of understanding might create extra work for her teacher, so she just kept trying on her own, hoping it would make sense at some point. By the time she admitted this to me, she was weeks behind and needed several days of one-on-one help from her teacher to catch up. Mia was too polite to assert her own needs.

Indeed, girls continue to be socialized to be kind and polite, while boys are often given the benefit of the doubt because, you know, boys will be boys (and other clichés that make no sense). A British parenting

Web site, Netmums, conducted a survey of 2,500 mothers to determine whether mothers treat their daughters differently than their sons. The results were startling: 88 percent of mothers surveyed admitted that they treated their sons differently than their daughters; 55 percent of mothers said they have stronger bonds with their sons; and 21 percent admitted that they are more critical of their daughters.[3] Lacking an emotional bond with Mom *and* coping with high levels of criticism is a recipe for low self-esteem in young girls. And girls with low self-esteem struggle to assert their needs.

Ellie is the perfect example of a young girl who couldn't find her voice to deal with friendship issues. A simple misunderstanding during fourth-grade recess period left Ellie iced out of her peer group for weeks. She decided to play outside her group, so the three other girls turned their backs, telling her in no uncertain terms, "We're not talking to you anymore." When I asked her what had happened, she told me that she hadn't seen the other girls—it was raining, and she assumed their class was inside. The other girls saw her, and they took swift (and nasty) action. In our session together, Ellie identified several phrases that *would* have been perfect. She hadn't used them in the moment, though. When the other girls attacked, she was stunned. She stood, silent, and watched them leave her behind. When she finally tried to talk to one of them later in the day, that girl simply rolled her eyes and walked away.

What Is Assertive Communication?

The problem with being too assertive is other girls might think you're a know-it-all.
—*A fourth-grade girl*

Parent-Teacher Conference

Many girls lack a basic understanding of the mechanics of assertive communication. Teach your girl these steps:

❀ Stand tall.

❀ Make eye contact (and hold it!).

❀ Use a calm, clear, and firm voice.

❀ Say no without guilt or anxiety.

❀ Listen (use nonverbal cues like nodding to show you're listening).

❀ Share your concerns with confidence.

I find that young girls often confuse "assertive communication" with "aggressive communication." In an effort to appear "kind," to please others, and to avoid being misunderstood as "angry" or "aggressive," girls hold back when they should assert themselves. For Ellie, the thought of asserting herself caused her to panic. She was sure the girls would misunderstand her intentions and view her as "a mean girl," so she stood, silent, while her friendships fell apart right before her eyes. Once Ellie began to understand and practice assertive communication, however, she was able to repair those friendships.

Teaching assertiveness, or the skill of confidently expressing your wants and needs without imposing those wants and needs on others, takes time and practice. Assertiveness is closely linked to self-esteem, fear of rejection and/or criticism, being seen as capable or incapable, and fitting in with others. Girls who use assertive communication with ease tend to be high in self-esteem and more confident about their place in

Parent-Teacher Conference

Define it!

Assertiveness means recognizing and standing up for our own rights and expressing our own needs while at the same time recognizing the rights and needs of others.

the social hierarchy, whereas girls who struggle with self-esteem and worry about how they might be perceived by others are less likely to assert their thoughts and needs. For some girls, the potential pitfalls ("I spoke up and my friends laughed at me") are too risky. They stand in silence because they don't feel like they can cope with rejection or embarrassment.

We all want our girls to speak up, to ask for help when they need it, and to free themselves from the emotional baggage that sometimes causes them to silence their voices when they should be speaking up. We all want our girls to proceed through life with confidence and certainty. For most girls, however, building assertiveness skills is a long-term goal.

What Other Styles of Communication Do Girls Use?

Being assertive doesn't come naturally to everyone. Some girls are more passive in their communication style, while others are more aggressive.

The trouble with passive communication is that girls hold back their true feelings and opinions. In doing this, they often feel like others take advantage of them, and other people can't really get to know them and connect with them. Anger and resentment can build

Parent-Teacher Conference

Not sure whether or not your daughter needs help with assertiveness skills? Go through this checklist with your daughter. If you find that more than half of these boxes are left empty, it's a good indicator that your daughter struggles to assert herself. Talk about each statement (even the ones she checks) with your daughter to help her consider areas where she might need guidance and practice.

- ❐ I am comfortable meeting new people on my own.
- ❐ I can say no without feeling guilty or anxious.
- ❐ I can express my feelings clearly.
- ❐ I can ask for help when I need it.
- ❐ I can share my beliefs without worrying about what other people will think of me.
- ❐ I can acknowledge and take responsibility for my mistakes.
- ❐ I can express my opinions and stick to them, even when my friends disagree.
- ❐ I can speak confidently in a group.
- ❐ I believe that my needs are as important as the needs of others.
- ❐ I believe that my ideas are important.
- ❐ I can delegate tasks to others within a group.
- ❐ I value my own ideas and know that I have information to share.

up for passive communicators, which later results in fractured relationships. One more side effect of passive communication? It can lower self-confidence. When girls think their opinions and feelings don't

Parent-Teacher Conference

Watch for these signs of passive communication in your daughter:

❀ Hedging (lessening the impact of thoughts)

❀ Frequently stating "I don't know" or "I'm not sure"

❀ Difficulty projecting her voice

❀ Resists speaking in groups

❀ Apologizes frequently, sometimes for no reason

❀ Lets others make decisions but later feels regret

❀ Answers questions with "I'm not sure if this is right, but . . ." or "I might be wrong, but . . ."

❀ Difficulty making eye contact (often looks down)

matter, they feel invisible. They can even experience symptoms of depression and/or anxiety.

Communication style is part personality and part learned behavior. While some girls tell me they fall back on passive communication because that's what "feels right" to them, they can learn to communicate in a more assertive manner. Things that hold girls back from developing assertive communication skills include lack of self-confidence, people pleasing, worrying about peer or adult rejection, sensitivity to criticism, and preference for avoiding conflict.

I once overheard my daughter mumbling (somewhat under her breath) that it's easier to just go along with her brother's ideas than to try to convince him otherwise. I sat the two of them down to role-play assertive communication and active listening. In working through the scenario (and a few others, for good measure) with a mediator, they were able to practice skills they both needed to work on and come to a resolution that pleased them both. (Have I mentioned that Rome wasn't built in a day?)

Aggressive communicators have their own issues to confront. Girls who use this style of conversation tend to dominate conversations and lack listening skills. These are the girls who take over the lunch table and miss social cues from their peers. They also give their opinions forcefully, which can leave others feeling hurt or disrespected. This can make it hard to make and keep friends. While aggressive communicators can sometimes get others to follow them and do things for them, they are also at risk of being disliked by their peers.

There are a number of factors that contribute to girls developing an aggressive communication style early on. For many girls, the desire to have their needs met or their feelings heard drives their behavior. I find this is often the case when girls feel invisible or ignored at home. That was the case for Sawyer. She referred to her brother as "the annoying one" who "needs constant attention." She felt that his cries

Parent-Teacher Conference

If this describes your daughter, she is most likely using aggressive communication:

❁ Interrupts frequently

❁ Dominates conversations

❁ Uses a loud voice to communicate

❁ Uses body positioning to appear strong

❁ Uses sarcasm when she disagrees

❁ Uses put-downs

❁ Appears insensitive

❁ Gets into arguments frequently

for attention (he was prone to lengthy tantrums and hitting) drowned out her existence. This was an exaggeration, but it was how she felt. She coped with her lack of attention at home by demanding attention at school. She knew that her behavior at school was off-putting for some of her peers, but she didn't stop. It was nice to feel like she was attended to, for once.

An aggressive communication style can also result from overconfidence (praise junkies beware!), lack of empathy for others, and poor listening skills. I always caution parents that empathy and listening skills are life skills that require frequent practice. These aren't skills that can be developed in a single conversation. Girls need frequent input, and they need parents to model these skills for them every single day.

A Note About Boundaries

Personal boundaries are closely tied to assertiveness skills. Boundaries help create healthy relationships by establishing personal (and physical) space between people. The boundaries we establish become guidelines to help us treat one another with mutual respect. For children, boundaries also play a role in setting limits.

Establishing and adhering to boundaries isn't always easy. Parents tend to think of boundaries as an imaginary line around them that defines the space between parent and child, but I find those lines are often blurred. Parents cross boundaries at times (like when we try to solve problems for our kids), and many kids are hardwired to push boundaries (as in, "No, I'm not tired at all, so I'm staying up"). That's part of the learning process (for parents and kids!). Even though boundaries are sometimes blurred, it's important to continue to talk about them with our girls.

Moms ask me a lot of questions about teaching girls to say no and to protect their bodies. I can't tell you how many questions I get about keeping girls safe from predators. The truth is there's no easy solution

Parent-Teacher Conference

Consider these healthy boundaries that you can teach your daughter:

✿ Safe body boundaries (all girls need to learn about safe touch and how to say no). This includes open and honest conversation about keeping the parts of the body covered by a swimsuit private. Always use correct terminology when discussing safe body boundaries.

✿ Physical boundaries around physical aggression and unwanted affection. This includes roughhousing, tickling (some kids do not enjoy this at all), and even holding hands.

✿ Listening boundaries (girls need to feel heard).

✿ Privacy boundaries (when your daughter no longer needs help getting dressed or going to the bathroom, step back).

to that one, but when young girls understand the concept of boundaries (beginning with those difficult safe-touch chats) and know that they have the power to create their own boundaries and assert them (even to adults), they learn to stand up for themselves and walk away from situations that feel uncomfortable in nature or appear to have blurry boundaries. Clear boundaries help girls get in tune with their instincts and trust their guts—skills that will last a lifetime.

Assertiveness Is Important!

I can't stress this point enough: Assertiveness skills are crucial to girls' development. I would know. I struggled with assertiveness for many years. I was one of those "avoid conflict at all costs" passive communicators well into my twenties, until I realized that to get where I wanted to go in life, I had to learn to speak up. News flash: It's really hard to unlearn passive communication and replace it with assertive communication when you've spent a lifetime hiding in the shadows.

Here's the deal: Girls confront social situations that require assertiveness skills several times a day. The mistake we make is that we think assertiveness is saved for things like bullying or defending a master's thesis. Not so much. Think about what it might feel like to try to order lunch in a crowded school lunchroom when you're being pushed down a long aisle without time to think and you just can't find the voice to communicate what you actually want or need. Think that's no big deal? Think again! If assertiveness doesn't come naturally, it can be hard to get your needs met in a loud, fast-paced environment (this, by the way, describes many elementary and middle school environments today).

Girls need to be able to speak up in the classroom, both when they require help and when they want to engage in class discussions. They need to be able to stand up to peers, spark conversations with friends, ask to join groups at play, and leave a group if something isn't right or if they want to join another group. Girls need to be able to communicate their needs to their parents, coaches, and other mentors. Girls need to learn how to ask for directions and for help in a store or other place in the community, and how to flag down assistance in an emergency. That's a lot of speaking up!

Speaking Up Breaks Down Mean Girl Behavior

One thing girls tell me is that it's really hard to stand up to mean girl behavior, even if it's coming from your best friend and it's not directed at you. I can understand that. Being a bystander is complicated at best, especially when you want to maintain your existing friendships. Speaking up does help unravel some of that unkind behavior, and the best way to fight lack of kindness is with what my girls sometimes refer to as "extreme kindness." It's true. It's nerve-racking to take that first step, but when girls speak up for other girls by way of stepping in and saying something kind (e.g., "Hey, I was hoping to hang out with you today"), they send a powerful message to the aggressor: Kindness wins.

The sooner we empower girls to find their inner voices and let them out, the sooner they will be able to separate, individuate, and make the world a better place. If the goal is to raise kind, confident, and resilient girls who take the world by storm, we have to begin by teaching them how to speak their minds.

When young girls learn *how* to use their assertive voices, they are more likely to stand up to negative peer pressure, perform better in the classroom, verbalize their thoughts and feelings to friends and family, and experience greater self-confidence. Girls who aren't afraid to speak up are better able to solve the daily problems they encounter along the way without looking for a rescue.

Girls Can!

Model It/Label It

I know what you're thinking: "Model it" is tired advice that you hear over and over again in every parenting thing ever written. I get it. It does feel tired. Is it really the best we've got? Well, yes, to some degree it really is.

Girls look to their parents to learn how to do stuff and work through complicated situations, particularly the ones that don't come naturally to them. If girls see their parents using calm, clear, and confident communication when seeking help with a flat tire, for instance, they learn that the best way to get help in an emergency is to remain calm and state their needs clearly. Check! If they witness their parent screaming and losing patience with the person attempting to help, on the other hand, they get the message that aggressive speech is useful in an emergency.

I encourage parents to do two things when modeling assertive communication: Show it in action and label it after the fact. Honestly, choose your moments carefully. Maybe the flat tire isn't the best time to work on assertiveness skills, but asking for help in the supermarket is. Once you've labeled an experience as assertive communication, talk about your voice tone, the listening skills you used, and your body language.

While you're at it, model and talk about ways to say no and when it's appropriate (and even essential) to say no, even to an adult.

Teach Personal Boundaries with Boundary Hoops

One thing I see a lot of these days is that young girls don't always understand personal boundaries. They don't know that they can create their own boundaries, and they don't understand the importance of respecting other people's boundaries.

I use hula hoops to help girls internalize the concept of personal boundaries. It's a simple process, really. Get two hoops, one for each of you. Step into the hoops and hold them at waist height. Tell your daughter that the circle the hoop makes around her is a boundary. What she decides to keep inside that boundary is up to her. The same goes for you. To help her understand, name some personal boundaries that you prefer to keep. One example might be knocking on a closed door before entering a room, and another might be saying "Excuse me" before interrupting a conversation (and only if it can't wait). For kids, a good boundary might be no hugging without asking or no pushing and shoving.

When we teach kids to establish healthy boundaries, and to respect the boundaries set within our own homes, we set them up to establish clear limits and assert their needs. Before you drop those hoops, walk an obstacle course side by side that might cause you to bump hoops. What happens when you cross a personal boundary? How can you fix the situation once you've crossed the line?

Feedback Filter

Passive communicators often live in fear of judgment, criticism, and/or rejection. They tend to be sensitive souls, and in an effort to avoid negative (and sometimes hurtful) feedback, they avoid stating their needs.

I like to teach girls to visualize a feedback filter (although I've had more than one girl actually draw a feedback filter as they imagine it might look). In filtering the feedback we get, we can sort the statements into constructive criticism (these statements can actually be quite useful when we analyze them), personal attacks (these are hurtful statements that don't help), and comments that we don't quite understand. When we visualize the filter, the first step is to throw away the personal attacks. Those don't help us grow and learn, and often leave us feeling sad. Next, we take a look at the constructive criticism. We repeat it back and consider what we might learn from it. Finally, we work together to try to understand the comments that don't seem positive or negative. Is there something to learn? Filter it into the constructive pile. Does it lack helpful advice? Filter it out to the recycling bin. We can always revisit that one later.

The feedback filter helps girls step away from the fear of rejection and judgment and learn to accept the feedback that occurs when they speak up, with comments that may be either positive or negative in nature.

Make a Persuasive Argument

There's nothing like trying to prove a point to bring out the assertiveness in a person. Children everywhere love to persuade their parents to push back bedtime, let them increase ice cream intake, and play just one more game. Because we often have to say no, many kids give up on persuasive arguments along the way. We should, however, embrace this strategy. No, I'm not saying you need to scoop out extra ice cream, but it doesn't hurt to discuss the effort that went into trying to get that scoop.

To practice the power of persuasion, including asserting ideas, give your daughter some funny scenarios and ask her to create a persuasive argument. An example might be "Take some time to think about it, and then give me your three best reasons why I should buy you a pet horse." This is a fun game that helps young girls practice asserting their thoughts in a fun and safe environment.

Community Practice

The best way to practice assertiveness skills is to get out into the world and put them into action. The key is to give girls the opportunity to use their voices without putting them on the spot.

The public library is always a great (and emotionally safe) place to practice asking for help. I have yet to meet a children's librarian who didn't jump right into action to help a child in need of a book. Parents get in the habit of doing things for kids because it comes naturally to us. We have to be assertive. We're always on! And if we're being honest, it's easier to step in and solve the problem than to teach a lesson in assertiveness each time.

Step back and give your daughter a chance to speak up the next time you make a visit to the library. Give her a specific request: "Would you please ask the librarian where you might find some books on sharks?" Practice with her before you send her off. Remind her to pay attention to those boundaries (she might need to wait in line) and use a calm, clear voice.

Other great places to encourage your daughter to seek help are the grocery store or a toy store. I recently caught myself ordering dinner for my daughter at a restaurant. I got halfway through the order when I thought, "What on earth am I doing? She's perfectly capable of ordering her own meal!" I stopped the order and cued my daughter to take it from there. With a smile, she finished the job for me. Old habits die hard, but it's time to put our daughters in the driver's seat of life.

Confident Voices

Ever watch tween programming that showcases tween girls acting like they don't know much of anything at all? Every once in a while, my daughter asks me to preview a show that she hears about from her friends. More often than not, I can hardly make it through five minutes without practically erupting in exasperation. *Why* must the media continue to promote the "dumb girl" persona? Luckily, we've found some great series on Netflix and Amazon, but the tween girl voices lacking assertiveness and catering to the needs of the boys in other shows are hard to shake (thankfully my daughter understands that "previewing" doesn't mean she will ever get to watch—you see what I did there? Boundaries!). I do, however, show her short clips at times to let her decide what different voice tones actually communicate.

It's hard to describe how to use a confident voice, but you can make a game of it. Write mini-scripts that mimic situations your daughter might encounter at school. For example, perhaps a girl wants to join a lunch table, but the group is ignoring her while she stands there holding her tray. First, act out trying to get attention by using a passive (quiet, unsure, nervous) voice. Have your daughter play the role of the girl sitting at the lunch table first. Let's say she can't even hear the passive voice. Next, shock her with an aggressive voice (loud! imposing! possibly angry!). Check in with your daughter to see how that voice affected her. Finally, use an assertive voice (calm, clear, confident).

Talk about which voice worked the best and why; then trade roles and have your daughter attempt the three voices using a different social script. Spend time afterward talking about how it felt to use each voice, and how the other person reacted in the moment.

A great follow-up to this is to use clips from all kinds of TV shows (cartoons, cooking shows, etc.) to analyze voice tone, body posturing, and assertiveness skills. Try to find one passive communicator, one aggressive communicator, and one assertive communicator in each show.

Newscast

A great way to practice using your voice and sharing it with the world is to have your own news hour. Gather some girls or just do this one as a family. Brainstorm the top stories of the weekend, craft news blurbs, set up a news desk complete with coffee mugs for water, and get that iPhone ready to record.

I've done this one with girls' groups and just with one girl in my office. When you're on camera, you have to practice projecting your voice, sitting tall, and making eye contact. The more girls practice these assertiveness skills in a fun setting, the more likely they are to use them out in the world.

Some girls are naturally more assertive than others, and assertiveness skills require time, practice, and patience. It's worth putting in the time with your daughter, though, because girls who can assert themselves are confident, socially successful, and equipped to handle and confront peer pressure; they stand up for their friends and are willing to take healthy risks as they reach for their goals.

❖

CHAPTER 9

Express Yourself!

But feelings can't be ignored, no matter how unjust
or ungrateful they seem.
—*Anne Frank*

We all experience moments when our emotions seem to
control our actions. Perhaps we yell when we could have taken a few
deep breaths and remained calm. Sometimes we say things we wish
we could take back or put something in writing that is better left un-
written. When people are under stress, emotions can feel "out of
control," and sometimes we react before we think.

Despite the fact that people of all ages and both genders do this
from time to time, for some reason, when young girls react out of
sheer emotion, they are labeled "dramatic." I've seen it in schools. I've
seen it on playgrounds. I've even seen it in my office during family
sessions. When two boys have a screaming match on the basketball
court, they are tired, overscheduled, or stressed out. But when two
girls put on a similar show? Well, they're just being dramatic.

Take Rosie, for example. Rosie is highly sensitive to what she perceives as "rejection" or criticism. When another child doesn't laugh at
her joke, for example, she experiences a strong negative emotional

reaction. She lashes out (with words, not hands). I watched her in the classroom one day as she tried to manage her strong emotions. It was a holiday party day, and the kids were all running on excitement. Rosie made a craft for a friend. The friend, busy with another friend, shrugged her off when she delivered the craft. Rosie crossed her arms, stomped her feet, and used a loud (read: aggressive) tone of voice with her friend. The classroom teacher swooped in to talk to Rosie privately, just as the girls rolled their eyes and referred to Rosie as "dramatic." The damage was done.

Recent research on how adult men and women process emotion sheds some light on the differences in emotional reactions between the sexes. One study found that subtle differences in brain function explain why women react differently than men to negative images.[1] Researchers measured the brain activity of women and men using brain imaging while the participants viewed images that evoked positive, negative, or neutral emotions. Blood samples were also taken to determine hormone levels in study participants. What they found is that the subjective ratings of negative imaging were higher for women than for men. High testosterone levels were linked to lower sensitivity, while higher feminine traits (including psychosocial gender role variables) were linked to higher sensitivity.

There was one other significant (and new) finding in this study: The dorsomedial prefrontal cortex (the area of the brain involved in cognitive processes like perception and reasoning) and the amygdala (the area of the brain known for detecting threat and processing fear and sadness) were strongly connected in men. The more the two areas interacted, the less participants reported sensitivity to the negative images. Researchers determined that this connection between the two areas appeared to be modulated by testosterone (the male hormone). In short, men and women do react to negative emotions differently.

As it turns out, those so-called "overreactions" we see in young girls might be attributed to a combination of brain functioning and lack of emotion-regulation skills. The truth is that self-regulation skills develop gradually, so it's important for parents and educators to have realistic expectations for young girls. It's also essential to remember that no two girls develop at the same pace, so comparisons are futile.

We socialize little girls to be respectful and quiet. We shush them when they raise their voices and tell them not to worry when they express fear. We are so prepared for them to play the part of the drama queen that we attempt to head them off at the pass by dismissing their concerns and complaints. In essence, we teach them to suppress their emotions.

Ivy learned at an early age that expressing her anger (at seven she was known for long, loud tantrums) would only lead to more anger. Her tantrums were often met with stiff consequences. Her parents felt that the consequences (no TV for a week, plenty of time alone in her room, canceled play dates) worked, in that her tantrums became infrequent. The problem was that Ivy spent all of that "in-between" time trying desperately to suppress her emotions. The tantrums erupted when she couldn't stuff her feelings for one more minute.

Ivy didn't need consequences for tantrums. She needed to learn how to verbalize and cope with her big emotions. For Ivy, tantrums were actually an expression of emotion. It was the only way she knew to get her feelings out.

What Is Emotion Regulation?

Emotions play an important role in our lives. Emotions often affect our actions, reactions, and choices. For young girls, emotions can play a role in choosing friends (I feel happy with that girl so I want to play with her again), problem-solving strategies, focus (it can be very difficult to focus on a task when your emotions are not in sync), and

Parent-Teacher Conference

Remove these dismissive statements from your repertoire right now:

✿ Stop crying.

✿ Don't whine.

✿ Be a big girl.

✿ Move on/get over it.

✿ Don't worry/you worry too much.

✿ You're so dramatic/don't be a drama queen.

✿ Stop overreacting.

thinking. While children are often conditioned to suppress emotions (don't cry, don't be mad, don't worry), learning to balance, or "regulate," emotions will actually help kids with social skills, academic success, and emotional health.

Jennifer Lehr, author of *Parent Speak*, refers to dismissive statements as clamping down on kids' feelings. "We grown-ups seem to be really comfortable telling children who aren't okay that they're actually just fine," says Lehr. "That might be because we're ill-equipped to handle unhappy feelings and tears. We also may not realize that telling a child (or anyone) to stop feeling their feelings is unhealthy."[2] Both solid points by Lehr.

We can't possibly teach our girls how to cope with and regulate those big, messy, sometimes complicated emotions if we're too busy telling them to stop having feelings at all. The key to regulating emotions is learning how to feel them and what to do with them, even when it's really, really hard.

"Emotion regulation" is a fancy term to describe the way we consciously (or sometimes unconsciously) influence which emotions girls have, when they have them (girls might suppress certain emotions during the school day to avoid embarrassment, for example), and what they do with those emotions. When girls lack emotion–regulation skills, they might scream when they're angry. When they begin to develop those skills, they are more likely to take a deep breath or walk away from a trigger.

Parents often ask me why girls continue to repeat the same patterns of behavior (e.g., yelling, talking back, verbal aggression) when those behaviors don't have positive outcomes. This behavior is typically viewed as "stubborn" or "willful." It's not. Repeated behaviors are not an attempt to upset or annoy parents or other people.

Maura struggled with this every single day. At nine years old, Maura was full of frustration. The majority of that frustration stemmed from the fact that Maura had a difficult time making friends. Maura was always described as "funny" and "talkative" by her teachers, but other kids seemed to experience her as "domineering" and "aggressive." She liked to control conversations because she felt that telling stories and sharing ideas was the best way to connect with other girls. The problem, of course, was that her inability to let others take the lead was off-putting to her peers. Combine that with her lack of regulation skills (she had a tendency to "flip a switch" from calm and friendly to angry and verbally aggressive), and it was a recipe for social isolation.

Parent-Teacher Conference

Here's the short version of emotion regulation:

Regulating emotions is the ability to express and cope with emotions in a way that is constructive, rather than impulsive or hurtful.

Her parents worked hard to practice social skills with her. They role-played things like joining groups and practicing listening skills, thinking that would help Maura learn to be a better friend. But day after day she complained about mean girls and being left out (and her teacher backed it up with her behavioral reports). While social skills practice was a good idea in theory, Maura wasn't ready for that yet. What she needed first was to learn how to verbalize and process her negative emotions. It was anxiety that drove her poor social skills (she worried obsessively about being liked and fitting in), compounded by poor frustration management that compelled her to act out the moment she felt rejected by peers. She engaged in these behaviors over and over again because she didn't know what else to do.

Girls engage in repeated behaviors when they're caught up in the whirlwind of emotion and don't know how to cope. Similar to the toddler who kicks and screams when exhausted, hungry, or overstimulated, older girls fall back on unsophisticated regulation strategies when they are overwhelmed with negative feelings because they haven't yet learned how to regulate their emotions in a more adaptive manner.

Build a "Feelings Vocabulary"

I usually just say "fine" when people ask me how I feel because it's too hard to make other people understand.
—*A sixth-grade girl*

It's no big secret that putting feelings into words is a great way to manage negative emotions. This is why "Use your words" is one of the most common phrases heard on the tot lot. The first step to learning to regulate emotions is to name them. While that might sound like a fairly simple concept, I find that many school-age and middle school girls struggle to name more than two or three feelings. When girls are taught to slow down in order to recognize, consider, and label their emotions, they are better able to cope with the triggers at hand. In fact, research shows that the act of naming feelings actually begins to soothe the amygdala, reducing emotional reactivity.[3]

When girls have sophisticated feelings vocabularies, they are better able to understand both their own emotional responses to events and the emotional responses of others. They are better able to discriminate between emotional states and communicate their feelings to others. Knowing how to verbalize their feelings helps girls hit "pause" on emotional responses and access appropriate strategies to cope with their feelings or seek assistance. This increases their capacities for empathy, compassion, and forgiveness.

Teaching emotional or "feelings" vocabulary is often overlooked as girls shift from early childhood to middle childhood. When school and extracurricular activities become the primary focus, feelings are often unintentionally shoved aside. While most girls learn to label emotions like happy, mad, and sad early on, many girls miss out on the subtle gradations in between because they don't know how to label them.

There are many ways to work on increasing your daughter's feelings vocabulary. A great place to start is by describing her emotions as you see them. When parents tap into empathy and connect with their daughters during emotional moments, girls learn to make sense of the feelings swirling around inside them. Talk about facial expressions, body language, and other nonverbal cues. Girls look to their parents to help them when they're feeling "stuck." Sometimes they need help unlocking the clues to their own emotions so that they can begin to calm themselves.

I always recommend learning one new feeling a week as a family. Young girls love to learn new words because words are exciting and powerful. The more words you know, the better equipped you are to

Parent-Teacher Conference

Young girls experience tons of emotions. Add more sophisticated words to your own feelings vocabulary to help your girl learn new terms.

Anxious	Lonely	Grateful	Embarrassed	Loving
Frustrated	Annoyed	Agreeable	Guilty	Relaxed
Joyful	Fearful	Impatient	Overwhelmed	Jealous
Thoughtful	Stubborn	Brave	Ignored	Disgusted
Affectionate	Friendly	Confused	Hurt	Surprised

express yourself. Start by choosing a feeling out of a hat. First, ask one family member to act out the feeling using only facial expressions and nonverbal cues. Next, have a different family member describe the meaning of the feeling and provide an example. Finally, work together to draw a picture of that feeling, then tape it to the fridge so you can all practice using it throughout the week.

The goal of building a feelings vocabulary is to normalize the range of emotions that girls experience. If you only use the chart when your daughter experiences negative emotions, those are the feelings that will stick with her. If you use it to identify all kinds of emotions (yes, even "bored"), your daughter will learn that all feelings are important.

Something I hear from parents fairly regularly is that they often try to hide or mask their feelings from their daughters because they don't want their daughters to see them upset or hurting. Honestly? This is a mistake. When our girls only ever see us experiencing positive emotions, they build us up to be perfect people who never experience pain or heartache. They think that we can handle anything. While the supermom persona might feel good for the mom in the scenario, it leaves the young girl feeling like there's something wrong with her for experiencing negative emotions.

While I certainly don't suggest treating your daughter like your best friend and confiding every adult-size problem or issue you encounter, it is a good idea to label your emotions. Instead of hiding in the bathroom when you're frustrated, say, "I feel frustrated because [briefly state the reason]. I need to take five minutes to calm down and try again." When moms and dads do this with their daughters regularly, girls learn that we all experience highs and lows, and it's perfectly normal to feel like you're coming unglued sometimes. When parents show their feelings using "I" statements with strategies attached, girls internalize positive ways to cope with negative emotions.

Parent-Teacher Conference

The "I" statement is a powerful parenting (and teaching) tool. It might feel odd at first, but practice using "I" statements daily to get used to it. It's easy:

I feel [insert feeling here] because [trigger]. I need [coping strategy] to feel better.

One note: Avoid blame. Even if you're losing your patience because your daughter won't stop talking back, blaming her for your negative emotions won't help. You feel frustrated because you want to be heard. Say that.

Scaffolding

Helping girls develop emotion-regulation skills involves bridging the developmental gap between what they already know and can do (perhaps your daughter can label five emotions, but not 10) and more complex skills. That's where scaffolding comes in. You want to support your daughter in internalizing more complex and adaptive coping skills as she grows. To do that, you have to figure out what she already knows and where she can reasonably go from there. Again, age-appropriate expectations are important here. If your daughter can accurately label and describe two or three emotions, you begin by adding two more feelings words (not 20) to begin to expand her vocabulary. It takes time and practice to learn and process this information. If you rush it, she'll miss it.

Scaffolding emotion-regulation skills helps girls learn by watching, practicing, and receiving cues and feedback when using skills in real time. It might sound like a lot of work, but it helps girls with complex skill acquisition. One study found that use of scaffolding to teach emotional regulation in a classroom setting had positive results. Students showed improved behavior control and demonstrated on-task learning (or improved focus), better peer interactions, and more assertive behavior.[4]

Sometimes strategies read in a book feel completely unattainable at home. I understand that. Scaffolding sounds like a technique that requires some kind of advanced degree, but really it can be broken down into four easy steps.

☐ **Model it:** You want your daughter to learn to verbalize her emotions and choose a coping strategy that fits the feeling. That's emotion regulation in a nutshell. Dust off your acting skills because the first step is to model it. You can do this by using the "I" statements we just talked about or you can play-demonstrate.

Check for understanding after you've modeled the skill. Example: I feel so frustrated because this homework is hard! I think I might scream! Instead I'll go outside and jump rope or walk until I feel better.

☐ **Role-play it:** (FYI, role-play can feel totally awkward for parents but is a real crowd-pleaser with girls. Let go of your insecurities and try it.) Now you want to get your daughter in on it. Come up with a scenario that elicits a certain reaction from your daughter (maybe "no screen time" results in tears?) and role-play it with your daughter. Be sure to include at least one specific coping strategy to practice. Take turns being mom and daughter. Again, check for understanding.

☐ **Cue it:** By now your daughter knows at least one strategy to cope with negative emotions. Resist the urge to "fix" or "check out" when you see frustration (or another negative emotion) emerging and provide support instead. Sit near your daughter and keep your voice calm and even. Cue her to verbalize her feelings and use a strategy. Stay with her. This could take time.

☐ **Gradually move away:** You know your daughter best. She might need you to cue her once or twice, or she might need your side-by-side support and cues for two months. Assess her baseline (what generally happens when she experiences negative emotions?) and proceed from there. If one strategy isn't working, go back to the role-play stage and try another. The goal is to gradually step back from the cueing stage and give your daughter the opportunity to manage her emotions independently.

Emotion regulation develops over the course of childhood and continues to mature throughout adolescence. These skills play a critical role in mental health and contribute to academic success and the development of social skills. Girls with advanced emotion-regulation skills boast better school performance, positive peer relationships, and fewer symptoms of anxiety and/or depression. In learning to process and cope with a wide range of emotions, girls figure out how to manage the ups and downs of girlhood. The lack of emotion-regulation skills, commonly referred to as "emotional dysregulation," can result in depression, substance abuse, aggressive behavior, and poor school performance. It makes good sense to teach our girls *how* to regulate their emotions and what to do when the chips are down instead of encouraging the suppression of emotions.

Girls Can!

Volcano of Emotion

A volcano is a great metaphor for the suppression of emotions. Most kids know that it takes time for a volcano to erupt. The lava burns and bubbles until it reaches the surface and dribbles down the side, sometimes erupting quickly but sometimes moving slowly. This is what happens when we stuff our emotions over and over again. At first, we don't really notice. After a while, the emotions build up until we are ready to erupt. At that point, misplaced anger is common.

Have your daughter draw a volcano on a piece of paper. (Tweens might prefer to build a volcano and use a chemical reaction—get out the vinegar!) Color it for fun while you talk about the metaphor. Next, ask her to write down the things she hasn't expressed that made her feel mad, sad, or upset in some way. It can be anything, big or small—being left out at recess or not getting an invitation to a party, test anxiety, or relational aggression, for example. As she starts to fill the volcano with those suppressed feelings and triggers of frustration, point out how full it is. Talk about what might happen when those feelings finally make it to the surface. This is a great exercise for working through the day-to-day feelings that girls are socialized to push down and get through.

Play "Connect the Dots"

When emotions run high, kids tend to forget how they got from point A to point B. Rational thought disappears when anger kicks in, and this makes it difficult to calm down independently.

I like to teach girls to learn to "connect the dots" when they're calm so that they can think clearly about the situation when they're angry, frustrated, or overwhelmed. Here's how it works:

- Thoughts create feelings.
- Feelings create behavior.
- Behavior reinforces thoughts.

Once the cycle begins, it can be hard to stop. I cue girls to practice breaking the cycle by whispering (calming tones work best when kids are under stress), "Connect the dots." This reminds them to stop and think about what thought triggered the original feeling that set the negative cycle in motion. If they can identify the trigger point, they can step back, count to 10, and consider alternatives.

Popsicle Sticks Feelings People

One thing I know for sure is that kids love to make stuff out of Popsicle sticks. One session with a second-grade girl resulted in this strategy. She was mindlessly gluing sticks together to keep her hands busy while telling me about an incident with her peers that involved teasing and isolation. At one point, I commented that her sticks resembled a person. She added a sad face because she was feeling sad. We proceeded to make seven more while talking, and she ended up with a box of feelings people.

Let me give you a crafting tip so you can avoid learning the hard way (as I'm known to do): Glue dots are the best invention ever. Using Popsicle sticks, glue dots, felt, string, and markers, help your daughter create her own box of feelings people. Work together to build one feeling person at a time so that you can talk about the true meaning of the feeling and how that feeling might look. Listen more than you talk to understand how your daughter processes emotion.

The next time your daughter needs a little feelings TLC, ask her to get her box of feelings people and use them to attach feelings to events and talk about strategies to move from negative emotions to positive ones.

The other great thing about creating feelings people is that your daughter can also use them on her own. As she becomes more comfortable expressing and sitting with difficult emotions, she can use the people independently to think about and work through her feelings.

Play "Guess My Feeling"

Pro tip: Add a blindfold to any game and kids get really excited. One way to help kids move from needing a feelings chart or feelings dolls to analyzing emotions out loud is to play "Guess My Feeling." This is a great game to play as a family, in a group, or even in the classroom.

The guessers wear the blindfolds. The actor sits in the middle of the circle and chooses a feeling from a hat. The actor has to act out the feeling using words, physical actions, and voice tone. For example, if the actor pulls "frustrated" from the hat, she might stomp her feet, raise her voice, and say something like, "I can't believe I lost my homework! Now I won't get a stamp on my card, and I won't get a prize (change to 'I won't get a good grade' for older girls). Ugh! This is horrible!" The guessers have to listen carefully and draw connections between actions and feelings.

This game helps girls listen for cues and make connections between actions and reactions. Those are actually fairly complex emotion-regulation skills to master for young girls, but they can be fun to learn when you're immersed in a game.

How Big Is My Problem?

It's no big secret that young girls can be catastrophic thinkers at times. When they don't know how to regulate their emotions, they tend to jump to the worst-case scenario each time something negative occurs. My friend didn't include me on a group play date? She hates me! My teacher didn't call on me in class? She thinks I'm dumb! Girls do this when they don't have the necessary skills to evaluate the severity of a problem and find a solution that works.

Have your daughter make her own "How Big Is My Problem?" solution chart to determine what she needs to do in the heat of the moment. Here's a general idea of how it should look, but let your daughter get creative and add her ideas. (I've seen tween girls doodle amazing charts using these guidelines.) When girls feel they're in control, they're better able to access their strategies when they need them.

- **RED:** Big problem! This is an emergency. I can't handle this on my own.
- **ORANGE:** Medium problem. This is hard to manage, but I can wait for help. While I'm waiting, I will try to think of one possible solution.
- **YELLOW:** Small problem. I might need some support, but I will try three solutions before I ask for help.
- **BLUE:** No problem. I can handle this on my own.

Once your daughter finishes the chart, go through it color by color and add specific scenarios for each. A red problem might include being bullied (verbally or physically) at school. It needs to be addressed immediately, and your child needs help solving the problem. Orange might be a sibling argument or academic stress—something that causes discomfort for your child. Yellow is fairly mild. Perhaps your child had a disagreement with a friend at school or is frustrated with a challenging homework assignment. Blue is anything your child can already handle.

When girls practice assessing the severity of their problems *before* reacting, they take the time to pause and process the whole scenario. When they do this, they have the opportunity to label their emotions (thus calming their emotional responses) and choose a strategy. One young girl used this chart for about six months. In the beginning, she talked about being in the red zone a lot. Her problems felt big and overwhelming. After about three months, she came in and announced that she'd hadn't experienced a red problem in days. It only got better from there.

DIY Stress Ball

I know, I know, some of these ideas are real mess makers! Believe me, I've spent hours picking up the pieces of failed DIY stress-relief tools. The good news is that I've learned from my mistakes and can give you instructions that work!

Girls love to make their own stress balls. I have baskets of stress balls in my office that I'm willing to give away, but I always find that girls want to make their own. It all goes back to ownership: When they make them, they use them. It's also relaxing to engage in crafts and keep your hands busy while talking. Here's what you need:

- ❏ Two balloons
- ❏ Flour
- ❏ Small kitchen funnel
- ❏ Scissors
- ❏ Pencil

☐ Small spoon
☐ Optional: vanilla powder to add a calming scent

Start by cutting the end of the balloon so you can fit the funnel into the neck of the balloon. Be sure to leave enough of the neck intact so that you can tie it (double knots!) when you're finished. Insert the funnel and use a small spoon to get the flour through the funnel and into the balloon. Two tips here: (1) You'll need to use your hand to guide the flour down to the large part of the balloon. (2) If the flour builds up in the neck of the balloon, use the eraser end of the pencil to push it down. Continue adding flour until the balloon fits into the palm of your daughter's hand. Tie off the balloon. Place the second balloon around the first one to add a second layer (and avoid a flour explosion). You have to really stretch that balloon to get it around the first one, but it does work! Tie that one off with two knots. Voila! You have your own homemade stress ball.

You can add the vanilla powder in between scoops of flour to add that calming scent. You can also alternate the flour with dry rice to add a slightly different texture.

Encourage your daughter to keep her stress ball close by so she can grab it when feeling anxious, frustrated, or even bored.

Play "Say It or Think It"

I always tell young girls that we all say things we don't mean to say when we're running hot on emotion and not using our self-regulation skills. No one in this world is perfect, and we all slip up at times. Yes, even parents. It does help to practice identifying what thoughts you should verbalize versus the ones that will only hurt others.

For a long time, I worked with a girl who struggled to regulate her emotions. The moment she experienced any negative emotions at all, she yelled. Not only did she yell but she also used every bad word known to humankind. She blamed anyone and everyone for her problems, and she didn't stop to think about how her words might affect others. She just erupted in intense anger without warning. Needless to say, we played this game often in the early days of treatment.

Sometimes girls don't know where to draw the line between verbalizing their feelings and verbally attacking others. Many adults struggle to find this line, so can we really blame our girls for needing help with this skill?

You'll need to do some planning for this game because you need a list of statements that you've either heard your daughter make in the heat of emotion (though nothing that would embarrass or shame her) or more general statements that you think she might hear from peers or verbalize on her own. Half of them should be statements that you want her to say out loud (e.g., "I'm so angry right now!"), and the other half should be things that she shouldn't say out loud (e.g., "Sarah is the most annoying girl I've ever met!").

I like to make it into a game of *Jeopardy!* by creating categories (things said around friends, things said at home, things said when angry, etc.). Once you have the statements ready, the game is easy to play. Have your daughter choose a category, and read the statement out loud. Your daughter has to decide whether to "say it" or "think it." After the game, talk about safe times to say the "think it" thoughts. These might include in a journal, to Mom or Dad, or to herself in the privacy of her own room. They don't have to stamp out negative thoughts, but girls do have to learn when it's appropriate to verbalize a variety of negative thoughts. Sometimes that means waiting until they have a private moment with Mom or Dad.

Get Moving

Exercise changes brain chemistry. When negative emotions take over, encourage your daughter to get moving. She doesn't have to run three miles to shift her energy from negative to positive; she just needs to move. Try these:

- ❒ Jump rope for 30 seconds
- ❒ Do 25 jumping jacks
- ❒ Jog in place for 30 seconds
- ❒ Run a homemade obstacle course
- ❒ Get outside and dribble a basketball
- ❒ Do 15 wall push-ups (instead of push-ups on the floor, do them against the wall)

Emotional regulation can't be taught in a single sitting, and you'll have to work with your daughter to find the strategies that work best for her. Be patient. Share your own experiences. Most importantly, empathize often. This is hard work for your daughter! What will one day feel like a small blip on the radar feels huge and overwhelming to your daughter right now. The more you support her through the process, however, the better equipped she will be to handle the upsets as she grows.

❖

CHAPTER 10

Failing Out Loud and Other Acts of Resilience

I'm not afraid of storms, for I'm learning to sail my ship.
—*Louisa May Alcott*

"Are you okay with failing today? Will you survive if you make a mistake? Because you will make a mistake." A dance studio full of mixed-age Irish dancers stares up at their teacher as she repeats the questions. You can see from the averted gazes which ones are secretly petrified of failure. My daughter was once one of those nervous dancers—the natural-born pleasers who wanted to make the teacher proud. Three years into this sport, she's learned that the only way to get better is to take big risks in class, because failure on the dance floor only makes you stronger.

Standing helpless on the sidelines when your kid experiences failure is one of the more difficult parts of parenting, and yet giving kids permission to fail out loud and make big mistakes is one of the greatest gifts a parent can give. In a society where padded flooring sits under playground equipment, many parents go to great lengths to ensure that childhood is comfortable. They step in to problem-solve when the going gets tough, and they advocate tirelessly on behalf of their children for any number of reasons. It comes from a good place. Isn't it only natural to want to protect your kids from the hard parts of life?

This drive to build our children up by guarding them against discomfort (big and small) shouldn't come as news. Jessica Lahey, author of *The Gift of Failure*, wrote a whole book about this very topic. "Out of love and desire to protect our children's self-esteem, we have bulldozed every uncomfortable bump and obstacle out of their way, clearing the manicured path we hoped would lead to success and happiness," explains Lahey.[1] We take on the obstacles, and our girls have an easy ride to the finish line, right? Wrong. When parents insist on solving every problem and clearing every path for their daughters, they rob them of the opportunity to learn how to thrive in this world.

Susan is the mom who is always there with a solution. She has endless problem-solving ideas, it seems, and she never ever runs out of energy. She wants her kids to have the best possible childhood, and she will go to any lengths to make that happen. When she experienced pushback about some activity she wanted to bring to her daughter's school, she broke down. "I just want to create happy memories for them. I want them to look back and love their childhood." The problem is that you can't engineer happiness. And when your kids never really face adversity, they don't have the chance to work through hard stuff.

On the flip side, there are the kids who do their best to completely *avoid* failure on any level even when their parents don't interfere. They take the path of least resistance because they know they can handle it. As we saw in chapter 3, many girls avoid risk taking in any form. They also tend to obsess over grades and study more than necessary, often to the detriment of downtime, fun time, and simply being a kid time.

These failure avoiders bring it on themselves, and they limit their own possibilities in the process. The thing is, if you never leave your comfort zone, you don't really know what you're made of.

Bridget is a failure avoider. She flies under the radar because when she is engaged in something she knows she can do, she does it well and with enthusiasm. She practically jumps off the stage during school holiday concerts. It doesn't matter who you are there to support, you can't help but watch Bridget. Ask her to do something she doesn't normally do, however, and she responds, "I don't feel like it," or "I can't." When she confronts an obstacle, she shuts down and avoids it. When she confronts a failure, she falls apart. She enjoys playing team sports, for example, but she sobs each time her team loses a game. She enjoys playing sports for fun with her friends, but she cheats (even while playing tag!) if the game isn't going in her favor. She has no ability to cope with setbacks, no matter how seemingly meaningless the setback might appear.

Where Does Resilience Come From?

Parents often ask me if some kids are more naturally resilient than others. Is resilience something that we're born with? Can we nurture it in our girls, or is this one of those "you get what you get" scenarios? It's a little bit of both. In 18 years of direct practice with kids, I've seen varying degrees of resilience. I've seen very young girls thrive despite traumatic beginnings and teen girls fall apart over every tiny obstacle. I've seen one million (give or take) shades of gray in between those extremes. Yes, some girls come front-loaded with a greater capacity for resilience than others, but resilience can be nurtured in a positive home environment.

Research shows us that children can thrive despite adversity (even early trauma) if they have at least one supportive relationship with an adult. These reciprocal relationships help buffer kids against intolerable levels of stress and makes those stress levels tolerable. According to a report from the National Scientific Council on the Developing Child, resilience stems from the interplay between disposition (what you're born with) and external experience; positive relationships, adaptive capacities, and positive experiences all contribute to the strengthening of resilience in children.[2]

Building a Positive, Reciprocal Relationship

I recently found myself describing a mother–daughter relationship in the early tween years (nine to 10 years old) as a friendly tennis match (not a competitive one). A mother–daughter duo sat in my office filing complaints about one another. *She doesn't do what I ask. She doesn't spend time with me. She doesn't listen. She doesn't get off her phone.* Sound familiar? Please know that you're not alone. I have this conversation with parents (specifically moms and daughters) a lot.

In an effort to stop the negative back-and-forth complaint cycle, we talked tennis. I explained to this duo that when they ping complaints back and forth, they aren't working together. One hits over a complaint; the other feels bad, then matches the first complaint with one of her own, so they both feel bad. The relationship was grounded in unfulfilled expectations and resentment. They weren't hitting the ball back and forth to one another; they were hitting it *at* one another. And with great force.

We used the visual of that friendly tennis game to talk about what it means to have a positive and reciprocal parent-child relationship. You have to let the ball bounce, take a moment, and send back a stroke of equal measure to keep that ball in play. For this mother–daughter team, that meant reducing the focus on their individual wants and listening to each other's needs. Sure, a 10-year-old girl has to fulfill her responsibilities or deal with the natural consequences at times, but when this mom learned to prioritize the nature of their relationship over her need to raise a "responsible" kid who always does things right the first time, a reciprocal relationship emerged. They were able to enjoy that positive back-and-forth without throwing negatives at one another due to internalized resentment.

Research shows that positive parent-child relationships yield better outcomes for families. Results from a research brief by Child Trends shows that relationship quality is consistently and positively associated with a number of outcomes, including behavior, social competence, school engagement, mental health, and communication. Positive parent-child relationships yielded better outcomes across these domains.[3]

Parent-Teacher Conference

Parenting isn't easy, and sometimes we get so wrapped up in the mechanics of raising families that we push aside the relationship-building piece of the puzzle. I always ask girls what they need from their parents to feel supported, and these themes emerge:

❀ Listen more than you speak.

❀ Empathize (try to remember what it was like to be a young girl).

❀ Ask open-ended questions about fun stuff.

❀ Stop focusing on grades, sports scores, and other evaluations.

❀ Spend one-on-one time together.

❀ Tell them stories about when you were young.

Sometimes we have to hit the reset button on our parent-child relationships. Start by carving out time for those connected conversations.

The Importance of Problem-Solving Skills

Strong reasoning skills also contribute to increased resilience. When girls are able to assess and solve problems, they feel confident in their abilities to overcome adversity.

It's perfectly normal for girls to be unsure of themselves when they first attempt to work on a problem. That uncertainty can actually serve as a useful part of the process. Uncertainty causes us to step back and consider the problem through more than one lens before attempting to resolve it. When girls approach a problem with an instant solution, they are limited to that solution (which might or might not work). When girls learn that the process of problem solving is more important than getting the problem solved on the first try, they build resilience. They see, firsthand, the power of flexible thinking and multiple attempts.

Catherine struggled with problem solving. She was the "one and done" kind of problem solver. She generated one idea per problem, made one attempt, and accepted defeat if the attempt didn't produce the desired results. It didn't matter if it was a friendship problem, a homework problem, or some other kind of problem; she always limited herself to one attempt. When I asked for her reasoning behind it, she told me that her mom's rule was "try hard once." There's logic to that, and another side of the story. Catherine's mom wanted to gradually build up her problem-solving skills, so she made a rule that Catherine had to make one thoughtful attempt before asking for help. Catherine took that rule at face value and stuck to it. She encountered a problem, however, when her teacher enforced a "make three attempts before asking the teacher" rule for her third-grade classroom. Catherine had difficulty slowing down and thinking of alternatives because she was accustomed to instant strategies followed by immediate help. This was a big change.

One of the challenges of raising problem solvers is resisting the urge to intervene early in the problem-solving process. It's difficult to watch your daughter sit with discomfort and uncertainty. It's also hard to stand by when you see those miscalculations and mistakes (no matter how small) happening right before your eyes. But girls learn a lot from

Parent-Teacher Conference

With all the advice to "step back," you might be wondering what your role is in helping your daughter develop problem-solving skills.

❀ **Challenge:** Ask your daughter to break the problem down into smaller pieces and find a starting point. More often than not, girls become frustrated when a problem feels large and overwhelming.

❀ **Brainstorm:** Invite your daughter to blurt out every possible idea that crosses her mind (even the silly ones) that might address the problem at hand. Write them down as she says them.

❀ **Reflect:** Listen to your daughter talk about her ideas. Cue her to consider potential risks and benefits of each one.

❀ **Question:** Ask questions about parts of the plan that don't quite make sense to help your daughter rethink her strategy or clarify what she's doing.

❀ **Support:** Stand by and provide support by commenting on the process and pointing out efforts.

❀ **Review:** Help your daughter figure out what worked and what didn't. Talk about it and consider alternatives for next time.

Bottom line: You are the listener-in-chief of the problem-solving process.

those so-called "failures." When girls are given the space to consider what went wrong and rethink an idea, tweak it, or look for a new one, they build up both their problem-solving skills and their resilience. The more they do this, the less those missteps affect them down the line. They figure out what adults take for granted: We all make mistakes and miscalculations. It doesn't matter that we make them; what matters is what we choose to do with them.

Autonomy Is Essential

My mom thinks I need help with everything. It's annoying.
—*A fifth-grade girl*

If you want your daughter to be more resilient, you have to promote autonomy. Girls need to believe that they can accomplish a wide variety of tasks on their own. The only way to do that is to let them try.

I recently asked a group of about 20 girls who were seven to 10 years old to raise their hands if they enjoyed cooking with their parents. They all raised their hands. When I asked how many of them get to use sharp kitchen knives when assisting in the kitchen, only four kept their hands up. When I asked if any of them get the chance to cook completely independently, we were down to two. Sure, we need to teach girls to practice safety in the kitchen, and they need supervision when using the stove and knives, but most young girls are capable of learning how to use these things.

Cooking is one example, but I hear a lot of stories from girls about what they wish they could do versus what they're allowed to do. It's always important to consider both age and developmental level before handing over big jobs like lighting candles or hammering nails into the wall, but with proper instruction and assistance, girls can learn a lot of different skills. The best news is that the sooner you teach them, the sooner they take over.

Parent-Teacher Conference

Try these tips to promote autonomy:

- ☐ Give choices.
- ☐ Respect the struggle to learn.
- ☐ Hear her out when she's frustrated.
- ☐ Trust her to accomplish tasks without your input.
- ☐ Ask for her help when you have a problem.
- ☐ Relax! Learning is messy—don't sweat the mess.
- ☐ Encourage her ideas.

When girls experience autonomy, their self-confidence soars. Greater autonomy also results in greater self-determination. It's true: The more you let your daughter accomplish on her own (and without criticism), the more she will want to accomplish. Middle childhood is the perfect time to help girls work toward independence across all domains of their lives. Does this mean you push them out the door and wish them luck? Of course not. It means you help them find new challenges that you believe they can master (whether at home or out in the world) and give them a nudge to try while standing by with emotional support. In doing this you send your daughter a very important message (one that she will keep close to her heart for her lifetime): I believe in you.

Promote Sociability

You might be wondering what sociability has to do with building resilience and learning to fail. Well, a lot, actually. We can start with the fact that girls spend a good percentage of their time with their peers once they enter the school-age years. They're in school all day, five days a week. Many choose extracurricular activities that require some weekend participation. And let's not forget about parties, play dates, and "hanging out." While we think of resilience as a skill that we can work on in the safety of our own homes, the truth is that girls face tests of resilience out in the world each day. They need to learn to cope with setbacks and/or to ask for help more often than you might think.

When girls have the skills to elicit positive attention from others and to provide positive attention in return (sociability), they are better able to seek help when they need it and to work well with others. Girls spend a lot of time in groups, be it in class or during recess, and sociability helps them cope with problems within a group, work through pitfalls, and seek assistance if necessary. A few skills that help promote sociability include:

- Being empathic by listening carefully to others and reflecting back what you hear
- Helping others in need
- Being open to learning new ways to solve problems (this can be difficult for many)

Parent-Teacher Conference

Some potential setbacks girls experience away from home include:

- ❀ Academic struggles
- ❀ Friendship fails
- ❀ Embarrassment
- ❀ Negative interactions with adults
- ❀ Anxiety/worry
- ❀ Frustration

- Being a positive team member
- Giving and accepting honest feedback

The importance of sociability only increases as girls grow because girls are highly social beings. Or, in the words of Rachel Simmons, author of *The Curse of the Good Girl*, "Girls are deeply relational creatures, whose lives and stories are dominated by the people they sit next to, the parties they go to (or don't), the people they love the most, and the ones they can't stand. Girls are like seismographs, sensing the tiniest shifts in their relational landscape."[4]

It's imperative that girls learn to relate in a positive way in middle childhood so that they can cope with increased expectations and more complicated peer conflicts and issues as they get older. I always tell my daughter (and my clients) to think about being the good friend instead of worrying about finding a good friend. In being the friend she wishes to find and acting as an uplifter (instead of a squasher), she sets herself up for positive relationships with other girls.

If the goal is to raise autonomous, resilient girls who can cope with failure, setbacks, and emotional disappointments, we have to spend the early years helping them internalize the necessary skills to do just that.

Teach the "Growth Mind-set"

Over 30 years ago, Carol Dweck and her colleagues became interested in students' attitudes about failure. After studying thousands of students, Dweck came up with the idea of fixed and growth mind-sets.[5] Chances are you've heard these terms before, most likely in your child's classroom or during a back-to-school-night presentation. Many schools use the growth mind-set model to encourage students to grow into resilient learners, and for good reason. Take a look at the differences between a growth mind-set and a fixed mind-set.

GROWTH MIND-SET

- Believe that the mind is a muscle that can grow stronger with hard work.
- Desire to learn.
- Embrace challenges.
- Persist through setbacks and failures.
- Focus on effort to improve.
- Learn from criticism.
- Learn from the success of others.
- Achieve goals.

FIXED MIND-SET

- Believe that intelligence is a fixed trait.
- Desire to appear competent.
- Stop trying when confronted with a challenge.
- Ignore constructive criticism.
- Feel effort is a waste of time.
- Feel threatened by the success of others.
- Experience lower achievement rates.

Dweck might have started her research into this concept 30 years ago, but it still holds true. One recent study of seventh-grade students showed that the belief that intelligence is malleable predicted an upward trajectory in grades over a two-year period, while a belief that intelligence is fixed predicted a flat trajectory: "Children's beliefs become the mental 'baggage' that they bring to the achievement situation. Indeed, research suggests that negative experiences have lasting negative effects primarily when they affect an individual's beliefs."[6]

Encouraging girls to view the brain as malleable promotes free will, resilience, and autonomy. Teaching girls that they have control over their growing brains is empowering. They learn that setbacks are

Parent-Teacher Conference

Three tips to begin promoting a growth mind-set today:

☐ Give process praise—praise the efforts they make and the progress you see instead of the end result.

☐ Don't nag. Instead, provide constructive criticism that your daughter can apply to the task the next time.

☐ Focus on the journey. Your daughter can't just think her way into a growth mind-set. There will be setbacks and failures to accept and inspect together along the way. Be supportive of the journey and provide reminders about the power of the brain.

like bumps in the road—small discomforts that we can learn to work through (or around, as the case may be).

The only catch is that we have to be careful about how we teach this concept to our girls. As it turns out, parents can inadvertently send some very confusing messages. Sometimes the words that fly out of our mouths when we're excited are not the right words at all. "You're a natural soccer star!" is a setup for disappointment and unrealistic expectations, but "I really enjoyed watching you play" shows your daughter that her effort was the important part of the game. "It's okay, this just isn't your thing" tells your daughter to give up, but "What strategy can you try next time?" encourages her to keep working at it.

Fail Out Loud!

"Do you want to hear about one of my biggest failures *ever*?" "*Yes!*" scream 25 voices in unison. The girls stare at me in complete silence. No one dares to move. And I begin my story. I've had more than one failure in my 42 years, so I tell different failure stories to keep things interesting. It doesn't matter what story I tell; these girls want to hear how I coped, what I did to overcome the failure, and what drives me to keep on trying even when it feels like the cards are stacked against me.

I don't want my daughter to hear about failure because she doesn't know what that is.
—*Mother of a third-grade girl*

Girls experience failure. They might not call it failure, and parents might not view these setbacks as failures, but girls feel it. They feel it when they are rejected by peers. They feel it when they can't keep up with an assignment. They feel it when they get pulled from the soccer game to put the "best" player back in to score another goal. They feel it when they are considered the "best" player but they can't seem to get the ball in the net. Girls experience failure, but the message they hear over and over again is that failure isn't something we discuss. We move on and try again. We find excuses. We silence it. But we definitely don't discuss it.

Remember that Irish dance teacher who encourages her students to learn to accept failure? She also helps them learn to find the positive in failure. We can and do learn and grow from failure if we choose to look for positive changes we can make. My daughter worked tirelessly for a recent competition. She learned three new dances in 10 weeks, and she practiced on her own nearly every day of the week. She listened to her teacher's critiques and made changes. Her confidence grew in leaps and bounds every single week. When she took the stage, she stood tall and smiled from ear to ear because she knew she could do it. She didn't doubt herself for one moment. But when the results came in, they weren't what she'd hoped for.

I had two choices in that moment: Blame it on a bunch of external factors to try to reduce her discomfort, or be present in the moment and allow it to sink in. I chose the latter. I let her think for a few moments while she watched other dancers. I held her hand and waited for her to cue me to talk. All around her, girls her age were falling apart and expressing anger, but she was calm and thoughtful. "I know I did my best up there. I wish I'd gotten recalled." I hugged her and whispered the only thing I could: "I always love watching you dance. You've learned so much in two months, and you should feel proud of yourself for all you've learned. It's okay to be disappointed today. Tomorrow we'll figure out what to do differently next time." With that, she smiled and talked about her excitement about dancing with her teams the next day. The following week, her teacher reiterated my thoughts and encouraged her to get back out there and learn something new. So she did.

Failure should not be feared or avoided, and it certainly shouldn't be covered up. When we encourage girls to fail out loud, we teach them to learn from their mistakes, take pride in their effort, and get back in the game. Our girls look to us to make sense of these complicated issues. If their failures and setbacks send us into a panic, they will resist challenges and give up easily. If we remain calm, refocus on the positive efforts they've made, and provide feedback that they can use (or, better yet, help them figure out their own feedback), they become resilient, confident girls who take on challenges and resist the urge to give up.

Lack of Resilience Perpetuates the "Mean Girl" Dynamic

I've witnessed this in the classroom, in a group setting, on the playing field, and on the dance floor. When girls lack resilience and struggle to maintain a growth mind-set, they are quick to turn on other girls when the going gets tough.

Girls blame other girls for their own setbacks. They project their negative emotions onto their friends. They lash out in anger and frustration because they don't have the skills to cope with failure and upset. They don't know what to do with those ugly emotions that they've been conditioned to cover up and move away from. When girls don't know how to struggle, they take it out on other girls. And what happens next? Well, those girls who lash out get slapped with the ultimate self-fulfilling prophecy: the mean girl label. All because they never learned how to bounce back from failure.

The truth is that, despite parents' best efforts, young girls do face adversity, stress, and sometimes even (gasp!) failure on any given day. Parents can't protect their kids from every possible threat, but parents can build them up and teach them how to be more resilient.

Girls Can!

Replace "Why" with "How"

A simple shift in language can do a lot to help girls hone their problem-solving skills. When our kids come to us with issues that they believe they can't solve independently, the natural response of the adult is to ask a bunch of questions to get to the root of the issue. Often these questions begin with "why." *Why didn't they invite you? Why did the teacher give you that grade? Why didn't you ask for help?* "Why" questions are rarely useful when it comes to problem solving.

Resilient girls might not have all the answers, but they do have the ability to work through adversity. Sometimes they just need a little support. Change your "whys" to "hows" to empower your daughter to think like a problem solver. *How can you join that group of girls? How can you get help on that test? How can you fix that broken toy?* In shifting from "why" to "how," you put your daughter back in the driver's seat, and that will help her learn to try again.

Share Your Failures

Parents love to tell stories about their own childhood, and kids are a willing audience. It's great fun to hear what your parents liked to do and play and eat when they were young. But sharing the highlight reel isn't enough. We have to provide a balanced perspective if we want our daughters to feel okay with mistakes, mishaps, and complete, utter failures.

I love to tell my daughter about my biggest mistakes and embarrassing moments. She's heard the story about when I didn't make it to the bathroom in time at nursery school, but I've also told her about the art project that was a flop, being told I was "tone deaf" in front of my entire class, and the time my brother "saved me" from the boy who left candies in my cubby by barging into my class and telling my teachers. Our kids look to us to confirm what they experience often—that childhood isn't just a walk in the park. When we share our shortcomings, past and present, with our daughters, we relieve them of some of the pressure to be perfect.

Digging for Truth

When parents gloss over failures and setbacks, girls learn to hide the truth. You might not think of this common parenting practice as "lying," but it is. In refusing to acknowledge and accept failures and setbacks, we create a pattern of covering up the truth.

In my office and in my girls' groups, we dig for truth. I talk to girls about how there are often two versions to any given story: the success story we tell and the setback story we hide. We all do this. Think of one your success/setback stories. Share the success story first, highlighting your hard work and determination. Next, get down to the business of "digging for truth." Talk about the setbacks that got you there. Once you've shared your setback-to-success process, ask your daughter to share one of hers.

This simple talking game can be very powerful for young girls, particularly in groups (though I find it works well in a family environment too). Hearing the failures and setbacks of others normalizes the feelings girls experience when they confront failure. It also inspires them to be hopeful. Hearing both sides of the story from multiple sources shows girls that we all learn from our missteps, and talking about them is the best way to work through them.

Develop Challenge Phrases

Adults love to throw out clichés when things go awry, but I find that young girls respond better to creating their own challenge phrases. While clichés feel dismissive and almost sarcastic ("Don't cry over spilled milk"), challenge phrases inspire girls to keep working hard despite setbacks.

Talk to your daughter about the power of words. Positive words inspire us. Negative words bring us down and rob us of optimism and hope. It's up to us to reverse course on the negative narrative and choose words and phrases that remind us to focus, work hard, and learn from our mistakes.

It's important that your daughter create her own phrases so that they have a special meaning for her, but I've provided a few (shared by some of the girls I've worked with over the years) to get you started:

- Every challenge makes me stronger.
- Mistakes teach me new things.
- When I try, I learn.
- Achieving my goals is up to me.
- I know I can, I know I can . . .

Daily Three

One thing I find is that in an effort to increase responsibility, parents pile on chores and household expectations. Yes, girls should have specific responsibilities to contribute to the betterment of the family, but it's also important to keep those expectations healthy. Your daughter is in school all day and likely has at least one after-school commitment (though probably more) each week. Balance is important.

I recommend creating the "daily three." Choose three age-appropriate chores that your daughter can accomplish each day. For younger girls, the daily three might include: Make the bed, put the dishes in the sink, and clean up the toys. For older girls, the daily three might include: Empty the dishwasher, fold a load of laundry, and set the table. You know what your daughter is capable of, so start there. When we have realistic expectations about chores and responsibilities, we build autonomy. When we overwhelm our girls with a long to-do list each day, we build resentment.

Change the daily three monthly or even weekly to keep it interesting. Ask your daughter if there are any chores she likes. I had no idea that "folding parties" would be such a hit in my house, but my daughter insisted that laundry plus music can actually be a lot of fun!

Make a Shield

I've always loved the idea of shields when teaching girls to harness their inner strengths and tap into resilience. We think of shields as things that protect us from danger, but when those very protectors consist of our own strengths and positive qualities, we become our own protectors.

Have your daughter cut a shield in the shape of her choice out of sturdy cardboard; it doesn't have to look like a traditional hero's shield—it can be anything that makes her feel strong. Next, paint it. Encourage her to make it her own. Last, ask your daughter to cover her shield with the strengths, resources, and abilities that make her resilient and capable.

One third-grade girl divided her shield into sections. In one, she wrote her challenge phrases that inspire her to keep trying. In another, she drew pictures of the people who support her and build her up. In the last section, she wrote every single strength and talent she could think of. Her shield was packed with positivity. She marched out of my office confident, proud, and ready to tackle any challenge that came her way. Lesson learned: Be your own shield.

Coping Cards

Building resilience and learning to cope with failure and setbacks is hard. It also takes time. Sometimes girls need to shift their focus to release negative energy before they can actually be able to cope with the problem and work through it. That's okay. A lot of adults rely on distractions to divert negativity before tackling a difficult problem. That's what we refer to as an adaptive coping strategy.

Help your daughter create a personalized pack of coping cards to use when challenges are particularly overwhelming. She can draw or write one strategy per card. They can be fancy or plain, use collage or markers. Let your daughter lead the way.

Coping cards should include strategies that your daughter can access independently and that will help reduce her negative emotions in the moment. Again, your daughter needs to create cards that work for her (and that she will actually use), but some examples might include:

- Take a bike ride.
- Call/text a friend or relative.
- Listen to music.
- Read a joke book.
- Take a bubble bath.

- Journal it.
- Get creative.
- Visit a neighbor.
- Walk the dog.
- Make tea.
- Do a puzzle.

Girls can build resilience and learn to sit with and overcome failure. Setbacks don't have to feel like the end of the world, and girls don't have to feel the pressure to get everything exactly right the first time around. When we give girls permission to celebrate their failures and teach them how to practice the growth mind-set, we set them up for a lifetime of not only accepting but also embracing new challenges and bigger obstacles. In doing that, we empower them to work for their goals no matter how many bumps they encounter along the way.

CHAPTER 11

Growing Great Leaders

Power is not given to you. You have to take it.
—*Beyoncé Knowles*

The boys are always so loud after recess and they take the attention and it's impossible to focus when that happens.
—*A fourth-grade girl*

The boys in the fourth-grade classroom were perfectly comfortable with taking up space. In fairness, 20 minutes of recess isn't much time to get your wiggles out when you've been sitting all day, and it's tough to transition back to quiet mode from a rowdy recess period in an instant. When pressed, Zoe admitted that "maybe some" of the girls do that, "but definitely not me."

You wouldn't call Zoe shy. She was quiet and respectful in the classroom but talkative and engaging out of it. She always had a group of girls around her, and she seemed to be one of the leaders. She was the good kind of leader—the kind who kept the group together. But she was raised to sit quietly in the presence of adults. And she struggled with anxiety. The combination left her quiet in the classroom and on the playing field, even if she had a lot to add. We spent a lot of time discussing the concept of "taking up space." How could Zoe make her presence known? How could she find a happy middle ground between super polite, and rowdy and distracting? It was quite some time before Zoe was comfortable letting her personality shine.

"Don't punish boys for their inability to sit still" is one of the latest battle cries in education, and rightfully so. There's a lot of sitting still—for boys and girls—these days, and it isn't good for either gender. An interesting study showed one small wrinkle that was largely glossed over in the press, though. Research into gender disparities in the classroom found that boys who match the scores of girls but are able to sit still and show a positive attitude are more likely to receive a "behavior bonus."[1] Just to clarify—same scores, same behavior . . . higher grade. While girls are expected to behave, boys are secretly and/or unintentionally rewarded for good behavior. It's a head scratcher, I know.

While we probably shouldn't encourage girls to be more distracting in the classroom in an effort to earn a bonus when they do sit still, we can encourage them to take up more space. We can empower them to showcase their personalities and their knowledge while adhering to classroom expectations. Girls can become classroom leaders, even if they have to overcome a gender bias to get there.

Is Gender Bias Still a Thing in School?

In a word, yes. While girls certainly feel like they have opportunity in the palm of their hands these days, it's not quite that simple. Sure, girls do outperform boys in the classroom. An analysis of research spanning from 1914 through 2011, published by the American Psychological Association, including more than 30 countries, found that girls generally outperform their male counterparts in school, and that this isn't a new phenomenon.[2] That's the good news. Girls, who tend to prioritize mastery over performance, are making the grade. Where girls lag, however, is in leadership skills.

In 2015, the Making Caring Common Project (MCC) at Harvard's Graduate School of Education, led by Richard Weissbourd, released a research report titled "Leaning Out: Teen Girls and Leadership Biases." Results of their survey of nearly 20,000 teens from 59 middle and high schools were eye-opening. The long and short of it is that girls face gender bias from a number of sources, including their own bias and that of many moms. I know, let that sink in for a moment. Check out some of these findings:

- Forty percent of boys and 23 percent of girls prefer male political leaders.
- Both boys and girls prefer (by a large margin) females in traditionally female professions, such as childcare directors and art program directors.
- Students were least likely to support giving more power to the student council when it was led by white girls and most likely to support giving power when it was led by white boys.
- White girls tended to not support giving power to white girls.
- On average, mothers expressed more support for student councils led by boys than girls.[3]

The MCC research team did evaluate the findings to determine why girls are so reluctant to support leadership in other girls and found a number of reasons for this particular bias, including highly competitive feelings among girls (no shock there), girls lacking confidence and self-esteem, and girls being viewed as "dramatic."[4] These are common themes that continue to affect girls, and they certainly aren't anything new or surprising. In fact, a different study found that use of the concept of "drama" helps distance teen girls from practices that adults would refer to as "bullying" or "relational aggression," and it reinforces conventional gendered norms of high school.[5] By referring to acts of relational aggression as "drama" among girls, the behavior goes unchecked and continues. Girls, it seems, can be their own worst enemies.

Girls today are growing up in a world of mixed messages: Be assertive, but be kind. Be a leader, but don't be "bossy." Be successful, but don't brag about your achievements because that might upset another girl (refer back to: be kind). It's no wonder girls are turning on one another and hesitate to support other girls in leadership positions!

Prioritize Leadership

The problem with the way we conceptualize "leadership" is that it feels large and all-consuming. Presidents lead. CEOs lead. Directors lead. To help girls feel confident in their abilities to lead, we have to begin by breaking down leadership into girl-size goals.

Parent-Teacher Conference

Alert! The Girl Scouts of the USA researched barriers to leadership among youth, and these issues stand out:

* ❀ Lack of confidence in skills and competence
* ❀ Stress
* ❀ Fear of talking in front of others
* ❀ Fear of embarrassment
* ❀ Fear of appearing bossy
* ❀ Negative peer pressure[6]

"How many of you have ever been leaders?" Twenty blank faces stare back at me. "How many of you have ever been responsible for something or someone?" Twenty hands shoot into the air. "Tell me how—call it out!" One by one they yell out their "leadership" positions: I'm in charge of feeding my dog! I help get my brother ready for pre-school! I hold my baby cousin! I cook Saturday breakfast! They think they're sharing household chores or responsibilities, but the truth is these girls are referring to leadership positions on a girl-size scale.

One girl tells me that the family dog is her responsibility. Now that she's 10, she can walk the dog independently, feed him breakfast and dinner, and clean up after him in the yard. She tells me that these are her chores, but she doesn't mind the work because it's fun. I tell her that she's the "dog leader" of her family. That brings a smile to her face.

Redefining leadership roles, and making those roles manageable, is a great way to inspire confidence in girls. When girls get the message that adults believe in their abilities to lead across a wide spectrum of opportunities, they rise to the occasion. I see this regularly when I work with groups of girls. When I describe a project and ask the girls to help me break it down into steps and form subcommittees to tackle those steps, they are jumping out of their seats to get a chance to lead (or even develop) a committee. Girls want to lead. While there's a safety factor in a girls' group that works on things like self-confidence and leadership, it doesn't take away from the fact that it's always hard to put yourself out there.

"I think it's a good idea?" Gina uses "upspeak" (she turns her assertions into questions so that others will back her up and restore her confidence) often in our sessions. In this particular moment, I challenge her to think of one new way to add at least one more friend to her friendship map so that she doesn't feel isolated when her close friend is absent from school. Gina needs to learn how to be a friendship leader (her friend doesn't want to make the first move, either) in the school setting. I wait her out for a few minutes. "Yes. It's a good idea because I think we will all get along, and then we all have one more friend." Gina plans to invite a girl who appears to eat lunch alone sometimes to join her and her best friend for a park play date that weekend. "Yes, I agree. That's a great way to show her that you want to be her friend."

Gina used "upspeak" in this circumstance because she felt anxious about putting herself out there and inviting a girl she never plays with to join her play date. Beneath the question/statement, Gina had some big worries: What if she says no? What if she says yes but doesn't show? What if she shows but doesn't have fun and never talks to me again? What if something embarrassing happens? Gina's worries are not uncommon for her age.

Making new friends might seem like one of those childhood skills that come naturally to most, but it takes a lot of guts to put yourself out there. You have to prepare for both acceptance and rejection, and rejection is very hard to manage.

In the end, the girl said yes, and that inspired Gina to invite two more girls. Gina brought a new group of girls together and increased her social circle at school because she was willing to take that risk and become a leader.

Parent-Teacher Conference

Quick tip: Resist the urge to meet "upspeak" with a joke or, worse, sarcasm. When girls use this speaking pattern, they communicate that they are uncertain and possibly anxious or upset. Meet "upspeak" with confident clarification: Repeat back what you heard in a clear, confident tone and verify that you heard correctly. This models effective communication to your daughter.

There's a push for success in girl world right now. Girls feel the pressure to excel in all areas of their lives, but rarely are they placed in leadership positions. That's a significant disconnect for girls. Where does achievement get them if they don't know what to do with it once the work is done? In prioritizing leadership opportunities, parents encourage girls to step up and forward. Girls take the skills and knowledge they've worked so hard to master and do something with them. Have a girl who loves to write? Encourage her to start some kind of classroom writing project. Perhaps her class might like to create a weekly newspaper or blog and she can serve as the editor. Have a scientist on your hands? Encourage her to develop a monthly science club outside of school.

Something that comes up a lot in my office is that girls don't feel that they will have the opportunity to follow through with their ideas, so they don't take the risk. Girls in this age group love clubs, and clubs can be a very positive experience (provided they aren't exclusive). One third-grade student came up with a great idea for a monthly art club because there isn't enough art at school, but she didn't get it off the ground because she was sure her mom would say it was too messy or too much work. After I helped her break it down into things she could do independently to start the club—things that require parent support, and ways to simplify the club—she brought her plan to her parents. They talked about rotating the location of the club and chipping in for supplies, as well as the importance of being inclusive. Within the month, the club was up and running, and this little girl emerged as quite a leader.

The mistake we make is to assume that girls need to enroll in preexisting programs to hone their leadership skills. While leadership programs offer wonderful opportunities for girls to practice a wide range of social-emotional skills that contribute to leadership, girls also need the time and space to follow their own passion when working on leadership skills.

Parent-Teacher Conference

Encourage your daughter to take on these fun leadership roles:

✿ Run a lemonade stand or bake sale for charity.

✿ Host a movie night (or day).

✿ Organize a neighborhood LEGO-building challenge.

✿ Start a book drive or book club.

✿ Organize a family holiday gift exchange.

Better yet, ask your daughter what kinds of things she might like to lead, and start from there. I find that girls have very specific goals a lot of the time, but fear the answer will be no.

Address Self-Criticism Early and Often

Monica quits before she falls behind. It's a strategy that almost never fails her, with one small exception: Her peers (and her parents) refer to her as a "quitter." She's not an "I quit" kind of quitter; she's actually an "I'm hurt, I have to stop" kind of quitter. That makes it even worse, because her peers also refer to her as a "faker" sometimes. These labels hurt Monica very deeply, yet she continues the same behavior because if she walks away before she makes a mistake or fails in some way, she isn't actually a failure. That's what she tells me, anyway.

Her inner dialogue tells a much different story. *I'm not good at sports. I can't keep up. I don't want to lose the game for my team. It's always my fault if my team loses. No one wants me on a team.* Those are just the thoughts about recess. Her self-criticism includes everything from her academic abilities to her family relationships ("Everyone likes my brother better") to her ability to play team sports. Monica doesn't try and gives up easily because she's sure that she isn't capable.

Girls engage in self-criticism for a variety of reasons, and it can be a hard cycle to break. Low self-esteem, unrealistic expectations, lack of resiliency, and cultural expectations (girls are conditioned to be empathic, helpful, and kind to others, but not to engage in self-care) all play a role in the development of the harsh inner critic that drags girls down, but we also have to consider their relationships.

One study of adolescent girls found that maternal dissatisfaction and coldness negatively affect attachment, which triggers self-criticism in girls.[7] I know, I know, the whole "blame the mother" thing feels very made for TV. Mother-daughter relationships aren't the only relationships that can trigger self-criticism. Peer criticism can quickly morph into self-criticism, and repeated negative input from poor relationships with fathers, teachers, and other caregivers also triggers self-criticism.

Heidi entered second grade with tons of self-confidence. She had a core group of friends, identified science and art as her favorite subjects, and played soccer in her town league. Within two months of second grade, everything changed. First, two of her friends pressured her to isolate and ridicule another girl. She said no. She stayed away from them. She even told the teacher. It didn't improve. Heidi didn't know where she fit in, and her inner voice told her that she was the problem. She felt like she had ruined her own friendships by standing up to her pals.

Next, the pressure to perform "efficiently" in the classroom kicked in. Heidi always worked hard, sometimes a little too hard. She couldn't rush through her assignments like many of her peers because she couldn't stand to hand in work that she hadn't reviewed carefully. As a fourth-grade teacher once told me, "There's one in every class! The goal is to help them manage their time." Instead of learning time-management strategies, this girl was penalized for failing to complete her classwork each week. Though the work she completed was nearly flawless, she was repeatedly shamed for the work that didn't make it into the "finished" folder. Halfway through the year, she was sure that she wasn't "smart enough" to keep up with her friends. Her inner critic took over, and she started to not want to go to school.

Many parents seem to hear the message that what I refer to as "Suck it up" or "Shake it off" parenting is the way to go when it comes to girls. One mom looked me in the eye and said, "Every girl gets bullied. She just needs to deal with it." The "she" in question was a second-grade girl. Input like "Suck it up" and "Get over it" are rarely useful, as they only increase the shame that girls already feel. Likewise, overcorrections give power to the inner critic. "I wish my mom

Parent-Teacher Conference

It's not your job to toughen up your girl. It's your job to let her know that she already has what it takes to thrive in this world, so it's important to:

* Remain compassionate.
* Talk about rational reactions to mistakes, failures, and constructive criticism.
* Encourage your daughter to "talk back" to her inner critic (not to silence it, but to be honest with it).
* Share your story about your own inner critic (we all have one).
* Remember that listening is a powerful tool. Sometimes all you need to do is listen.

didn't tell me every single thing I do wrong" ranks as one of the top statements made by girls in my office. What girls need is unconditional support.

A mistake that parents unintentionally make when trying to boost their daughters' self-esteem is stamping out or silencing the inner critic. "How can you say that?" "You can't possibly think that!" "Don't let me hear you say those things ever again!" Girls confide in me what they are afraid to tell their parents because they've experienced some version of those reactions when they dared to share their deepest, darkest thoughts about their perceived shortcomings. Here's the problem: Simply shooing the inner critic away doesn't actually work. Girls need to learn how to work through the feelings that give that inner voice so much power. If the inner critic is whispering, "I'm dumb," there are feelings lurking beneath the surface that need to rise to the top. Girls can't wish away their bad feelings and negative experiences; they have to learn to deal with them.

There is good news in all of this "Oh my gosh, please don't let this happen to my daughter" stuff. When parents and girls work together to get the negative emotions and experiences out and learn to cope with obstacles and failures, girls begin to emerge as leaders. Research into the importance of the parent–child (and specifically mother–daughter) relationship backs this up. In a recent survey on what girls say about bravery conducted by Keds and Girls Leadership Institute, 77 percent of girls responded that their mothers help them pursue their goals with bravery, 63 percent identified their mothers as role models, and 48 percent stated that they turn to their mothers for support first.[8]

The mom who initially felt that her daughter just needed to learn to deal with the inevitable bullying that all girls surely face was able to get in touch with her own resistance to connecting with her daughter. She was bullied in high school, and her daughter's experience brought back some very painful memories that she'd worked hard to stuff deep down into the recesses of her memory bank. Once she began to let those feelings rise to the surface, she was able to empathize with her daughter and remain calm and compassionate when her daughter shared her fears and feelings. Together, they got through it, and her daughter went on to serve as a self-appointed "recess helper." If there was a lonely, left-out girl on the recess yard, she jumped in to offer friendship. With the unconditional support of her mom, she transformed from self-critic to leader on the recess yard.

Repackage "Bossy"

I was shopping with my daughter one afternoon when she spied a girl wearing a shirt that said, "I'm not bossy. I'm the boss." We stared at it for a moment before I broke the silence. "You know, sometimes I'm not a huge fan of shirts with messages, but I like that one. It's important to understand that being a leader means speaking up, and speaking up isn't bossy." She agreed, and we spent a good portion of that shopping trip talking about how frustrating it is that girls get called "bossy" when they take the lead, but boys are always just "leaders."

Girls should be able to share ideas, speak up in groups, take the lead on a project or idea, and communicate clearly without living in fear of that "bossy" label, but as we saw from the results of that Girls Scouts of the USA survey, girls are fearful of being perceived as "bossy."

I once asked a 10-year-old girl what it means to be bossy. She rattled off an endless list of scenarios ranging from always being the "know-it-all" in class who never puts her hand down, to orchestrating every game played at recess, to being a self-appointed team captain, to organizing all the social activities. I was stunned by the sheer number of circumstances she listed. I asked her if this is something she talks about with her friends. "Oh, yeah. You have to talk about it because no one wants to be bossy, so you have to know what not to do." Yet when her list was complete, I had a hard time thinking about what girls *can* do and still avoid the dreaded label.

Girls Scouts of the USA got together with Lean In to spearhead a "Ban Bossy" campaign and encourage leadership skills in young girls. I think they're on the right track. With so much pressure to avoid being labeled "bossy," girls are standing silent on the sidelines while their male counterparts continue to emerge as "leaders." It's time to empower our girls to stop thinking about bossy and start thinking about what they can do to fill leadership roles in their schools, their communities, and even their homes.

Promoting Leadership Decreases Mean Girl Behavior

The mistake society has made with this supergirl generation is pushing girls to compete with other girls to emerge as the clear winner. Everywhere you turn, girls are divided. They've learned that to get to the top, they might have to push a few others down. That's not a healthy message for girls and only increases mean girl behavior. If we want to eliminate the mean girl from our culture, we have to promote leadership *among* girls.

When girls get the message that there's room for all to succeed, they build each other up. When they work together and build each other up, they attain leadership positions together. Mutual support is a beautiful concept to teach our girls. They don't have to take each other down to try to win at the game of life; they can hold each other up and reach just a little bit higher as a whole.

Parenting can feel like a giant maze at times, and we all want the best for our girls, but sometimes that quest for success and happiness sends the wrong message. We can flip that message beginning right now. We can work together as parents, coaches, educators, and all other supporters of girls to teach our girls that together they will soar.

Girls Can!

Leadership Checklist

What does it really take to be a leader? Chances are your daughter already has some good ideas on that one. When I ask groups of girls to define "leader," they have tons of answers. Confident! Friendly! Caring! Organized! Good listener! Likes to talk to groups! Girls know what it takes to lead, but knowing what it takes isn't the same as putting those things into practice.

Ask your daughter to create her own personal leadership checklist. Let her come up with the qualities she thinks a leader needs, and talk with her about those qualities as she makes her list. Encourage her to come up with at least five leadership skills. Once the list is complete, hang it on the fridge. Tell your daughter that you want to work on leadership skills with her. The challenge is to use a minimum of one leadership skill each day. Before bed, have a leadership check-in: Talk about which skills you both used and whether or not those skills were effective in the situation.

In doing this, tapping into leadership skills becomes a daily practice. Over time, it simply becomes habit. When girls get in the habit of consciously using their leadership skills, they are better able to access those skills when the need arises.

Game Shows at Home

Sometimes putting yourself out there takes practice. The fact is that girls are socialized to be polite, nurturing, and giving. If they always let people talk over them or cut them in line, it's because they've been taught to be generous and compassionate first (great qualities to have, but sometimes you have to consider your own goals and needs as well).

A little healthy competition at home can inspire a more competitive spirit in the community. Make up your own version of a quiz show with facts about the family as clues, or create a *Family Feud* of your own. When competition is fun and good-natured, it's easier to jump in and put yourself out there. We love to create wacky kids-against-parents obstacle courses around here. It's amazing how much my daughter shines when she's put in a leadership position . . . even if it's only a relay race.

Weekly "State of the Girl" Address

Girls and women are doing great things in this world. From small, grassroots community efforts, to changing school climate, to leading in small business, big business, and even politics, girls and women are changing our world for the better. The problem is that girls are so very busy today that they don't always hear the great stuff being done.

Host a weekly "state of the girl" address in your home to highlight the progress women and girls continue to make each week. Sit with your daughter and research current events involving girls and women. Take a few notes on news stories and compare them to women in history. Practice your best radio voice and sit down with your daughter to share your reports.

Parents often tell me that their girls "move away" from play at around age 10, and I always respond that you have to view play through a different lens as girls grow. This is exactly the kind of playful banter that girls enjoy engaging in with their parents, and they internalize positive messages about the power of girls in the process.

Debate Night

Society is constantly shushing girls. They are told to keep their voices calm, even when they're really upset. They are told to keep their feelings in check, even when they're totally overwhelmed. And they're told to listen when what they really want to do is speak. Yes, girls often feel silenced in this world.

With all of this silencing, they aren't learning the art of respectful disagreement. Girls can disagree. They don't know that because they feel like agreeing is the best way to be "nice," but they need to learn that we all have different opinions, and that's a good thing. Arguing can actually be quite healthy as long as you don't impose your opinions upon others, learn to take no for an answer, and disagree with others in a respectful manner. That's where debate night comes in.

At the beginning of the week, choose an issue (e.g., gummy bears versus chocolate kisses) and announce that family debate night is coming up this weekend. Your daughter has to choose a side on the stated issue, prepare her points (including any research that might help), and be ready to debate another family member at the appointed time. Before the debate, establish some rules. Keep voices confident, not loud. Listen when it's not your turn to talk. Timers will be set for presenting answers and responding. No interrupting.

This family game can be a lot of fun, and it helps girls learn to practice asserting their beliefs and opinions in a healthy way. The more girls do this at home, the more likely they are to do it out in the world.

Flip It!

We all get caught up in our mistakes and what we "should have" done, right? That's a natural response to a misstep. *I should have planned my time more carefully. I should have gone for a run before returning that upsetting phone call.* We can always find solutions after the fact, but focusing on those pesky "should haves" can really drag us down and prevent us from bouncing back. You know what leaders do? Assess. Find the positive. Begin again.

To help your daughter learn to evaluate and bounce back from her mistakes and failures, engage her in a game of "Flip It." Give her a piece of paper folded into six boxes and ask her to sketch out the sequence of events that resulted in the mistake. Resist the urge to offer comments, and allow your daughter to sit with her perceived mistake for a few moments. Tell your daughter that when you say, "Flip it," you want her to turn the paper over and find four positives that she can take away from the experience. It can be any positive reframing, big or small.

When girls practice evaluating their mistakes to find learning opportunities, they don't get stuck in the negative emotions that often accompany failures. Mistakes are "flipped" into challenges to overcome, and girls can certainly find ways to overcome challenges.

Positive reframing is a powerful way to help girls understand that obstacles don't prevent them from growing into leaders. If anything, obstacles actually help girls hone their leadership skills. You can't possibly steer that ship if you're petrified of stormy weather. Instead, you have to learn how to sail through the storm.

Confidence Reminders

It's amazing how quickly we forget about the wonderful things we've done when we feel overwhelmed by our challenges and obstacles of the moment. When life feels hard, we think about the negatives before us. What we should do is remember the moments of confidence that got us here in the first place.

I like to give girls a confidence sheet that they can fill out and keep in their backpacks. It's a simple exercise, but it helps them remember that they are capable, confident, and able to overcome obstacles. It boils down to three important questions:

1. Can you name an experience that left you feeling confident?

2. What did you do that inspired confidence?
3. What did you learn about yourself during that experience?

Some girls describe positive classroom experiences (like presenting reports or leading a class discussion), some recall positive experiences in sports, and some recall family or friendship experiences that helped them feel confident. Whatever the story, remembering it and writing it down helps girls recall the times when they had the confidence to act as leaders or work through difficult obstacles. Girls can pull these out when they need a confidence boost during a challenging day or post them on the wall to look at daily. Either way, confidence reminders help girls focus on their positive moments from the past instead of feeling swallowed up by stressful moments in the present.

Increase Collaborative Experiences

If we want girls to lift each other up as leaders, we have to provide them with plenty of collaborative experiences. Team sports, under the leadership of positive coaching, are one way that girls learn to work together and collaborate for a group goal, but we can't stop there. All too often, team sports become highly competitive and all about the win. If we want girls to work together toward leadership, they need experiences off the field as well.

Girls Scouts and other girls' leadership programs offer ample opportunity for girls to work in groups to achieve goals and learn leadership skills. I have also found that the gift of free time can be a great springboard for collaborative work. I once watched a pair of girls attempt to create a tree swing out of a hula hoop, a reusable grocery bag, and a jump rope. It took the better part of an hour for them to achieve their goal, and they had to redesign and retest the swing several times, but they did, in fact, engineer a functional tree swing using only the items they had on hand. Together, they did it.

It's amazing what kinds of goals girls set and achieve when parents step back and allow them the time and emotional freedom to create and test their theories on all kinds of things. If you want your daughter to be able to work well with others and achieve goals in a group setting, sometimes the best thing you can do is get a group of girls together and challenge them to create their own fun.

Practice Confident Speaking

Leaders know how to speak with confidence. They stand tall, project their voices in an appropriate tone, and make eye contact. They energize their listeners and pause to listen when questions are asked. Leaders tend to be very effective communicators.

This is why we need to help girls step away from "upspeak," fillers, and hedging. Girls spend a lot of time making excuses for the points they intend to make. "I'm not sure, but I think . . ." "My guess is . . ." "I'm pretty sure . . ." Often this circles back to uncertainty and worrying about how other girls will judge them for speaking up and getting involved.

In group settings, I ask girls to buddy up and take turns talking about something they're passionate about. The listener's job is to notice eye contact, fillers, and voice tone. When the speaker is finished, the listener provides two positives and two suggestions. They trade places, and the listener gets a turn to speak. In working together, girls help each other practice speaking with confidence and showcasing leadership qualities.

Some girls appear to be natural-born leaders from the start, while others need time to grow into the role. It always helps to remember that all girls develop different skill sets at different times. You can't force your daughter into a leadership role with the hope that she will simply "rise to the occasion." That's a recipe for anxiety and resentment. What you can do is support your daughter as she builds her self-confidence, learns to assert her needs and opinions, and practices taking up space in this world. I find that I give the following advice to parents of girls often: If you force her, she might shut down, but if you guide her and support her, she will spread her wings and fly.

CHAPTER 12

Raising Socially Responsible Girls

It's possible to climb to the top without stomping on
other people.
—*Taylor Swift*

I coached girls' youth soccer for just long enough to see that by
second grade, parents are already pitting girls against other girls. In fact,
I spent a good portion of the season teaching the girls to lift each other up
and work together instead of rating each other best to worst. It worked,
but it took the full 10 weeks to get that team to gel. I had girls telling me
that their parents told them to avoid passing to other players who weren't
"good." I had girls telling me how their parents ranked the players. I had
girls whispering about who allegedly "lost" the game on behalf of the
team. And yes, we are still talking about eight-year-old girls. What in the
world happened to the concept of teamwork?

There's healthy competition, and then there's girls pushing down
other girls on their way to the perceived top. Unfortunately, our success-
driven culture, combined with our need to raise supergirls, supports the
latter. This is a mistake.

We can, however, change the current narrative of girlhood for the
better. To reduce the dependence on mean girl culture (I know what

you're thinking . . . we don't depend on that!), we must first examine it under a microscope. How did we get here? Why do girls feel the need to build themselves up by putting other girls down? Those are difficult questions to ask, and to get honest answers, we need to reach deep into our own souls and scrutinize our own beliefs and motives.

Believe me, I understand how difficult it is to participate in changing this narrative when all you want to do is protect your own daughter from unnecessary heartache. Not only do I challenge parents of girls to do this in my office, but I also hold myself accountable. I have a daughter. I know that pull to carve out the best future or even to create the best today. I know the pain of an invitation that never came and the disappointment of hard work left unrecognized. I've stared down those moments when it would be easier to blame external factors and make excuses. I keep myself in check because in order to raise a girl who understands the gift of female friendships and the power of a group of strong women, I have to show her how to work through and rise above the moments of adversity that sometimes cause us to turn against, when we should turn toward, one another.

If we want to raise girls who grow into strong, successful women, we have to raise socially responsible girls. We have to raise girls who not only care about their own individual success, but also consider the greater good. We have to teach our girls that they can be talented and kind, leaders and helpers.

On Removing the "Good Girl" Bonus

> I don't know what my strengths are. I just do what I'm supposed to do.
> —*A second-grade girl*

During a workshop with a group of 18 elementary school girls, something shifted. A fun group activity took a negative turn when a simple error was made. We have a firm "celebrate our blunders" rule in these workshops, and we work hard to reduce the burden of the fear of mistakes. This time, it was different. These girls weren't laughing. "Let's go back a few steps and figure out what we can change to get a different outcome." The words had only just left my mouth when three out of five girls immediately pointed fingers and stated, "It was her fault." The activity didn't get the desired result; instead of working together, they turned against each other.

I can always spot the "good girls" in the group because they are the ones who don't do well with errors. It doesn't matter the project or game; they ask for clarification several times because they want to get it "right." These are the girls who rely on praise for "good" behavior and always do exactly what is asked of them. But beneath that good girl exterior lurk layers of worry and uncertainty. In my office, the good girls tell me that they don't want to disappoint their parents, teachers, grandparents, and coaches. When I ask them to tell me their hopes and dreams and passions, they struggle to find them.

The good girls of the world need constant external input to let them know they're on the right path. They also struggle to relate to their peers because they can't cope with those who aren't afraid to step outside the good girl box. They don't want to get caught up in what might not be considered good girl choices, so they reject and tattle on other girls. Not only do they distance themselves from girls who don't follow the good girl script (or at least fake it), but they also make sure the adults in their lives view them as "good" and others as "problematic." I see it play out in groups, but I've also seen both sides of this story in my practice.

Take Ashley, for example. Ashley is friendly and curious and generally likes her fifth-grade classroom. She has a nice group of friends, and she enjoys learning. Until midway through fifth grade, when a "cool girl" group seems to emerge out of nowhere. The "cool" group is known for what Ashley describes as "practical jokes," but which actually sounds a lot like public humiliation of kids not in the group. Ashley tells me that they do this because the boys laugh, and she wants in. She's torn between her existing group of friends and the pull toward popularity. And the cool girls dangle carrots. If she helps pull off some of the pranks, she gets partial inclusion in the group. Ashley struggles with this for quite some time. She wants in, but she doesn't want to abandon her friends or get in trouble.

One day, Ashley decides to try to merge the two groups by playing a "prank" in close proximity to her good girl friends. She gets caught and immediately faces classroom consequences for "unkind" behavior. The good girls reject her on the spot. So do the cool girls (they can't be seen with her now that she's been caught). Now Ashley is alone, and her teacher views her in a new (negative) light.

I don't know when girlhood morphed into a quest for perfection, or when trial and error was replaced with right or wrong. What I see in the world of girls right now is that a powerful combination of parenting, society, and peer pressure is forcing girls to grow up quickly in an effort to run through that shiny red ribbon at the finish line, and that pressure contributes to the current negative narrative in girlhood.

"We focus on getting our children on the 'right' track at earlier ages," explains Rosalind Wiseman. "So the things they love to do or show aptitude for ironically become a track for relentless anxiety, egoism, or insecurity."[1] What might happen if we stopped hyperfocusing on the red ribbon and allowed our girls to chase curiosity and passion instead? That's the question we need to ask ourselves in our attempt to rewrite this narrative and put the "mean girl" story to bed once and for all.

Parent-Teacher Conference

Check your motives: Not only do girls face intense pressure to achieve, but so do their parents. Parents measure themselves against other parents, and this triggers a cycle of pushing and shaming. Before you push your daughter to be the next great [insert your dreams for your daughter here], ask yourself these questions:

❀ What do I hope my daughter will get out of this?
❀ Why do I need my daughter to master this particular activity?
❀ What is my biggest fear about my daughter's future?

Parents project their worries about their girls' futures by pushing them toward success and perfection, but this often results in the unintended consequence of burnout and quitting.

The Problem with Social Media Parenting

In a recent tragedy, a teenage girl got behind the wheel of her car, with her best friend in the passenger seat, and hit the "Facebook Live" button. An accident occurred, and the two girls died in the crash. As the story played out in multiple outlets across social media, people were quick to judge and criticize.

How could they be so stupid?
It's arrogance! They are so self-centered!
Why didn't their parents teach them not to do this?

As I scrolled through some of the responses, I couldn't help but feel overwhelmed by the fact that this tragic loss for two families was quickly reduced to "stupidity" and "ignorance," and that there wasn't much chatter about the obvious: Perhaps this incidence of "teen arrogance" might have something to do with growing up on display.

Even if you don't fall into the trap of obsessive timeline photo posting (Jenny lost another tooth!), all kids today are affected by social media parenting. And believe me, I'm not judging you if you are a frequent picture poster. I've been there. When I first joined Facebook, I felt an immediate relief. I no longer had to create and e-mail those time-consuming Shutterfly photo albums (and fight my Wi-Fi to upload more than one photo at a time). With the click of a button, I could share heartwarming parenting moments with faraway family and friends. Genius! But when my work life crept into my personal life, and my kids grew out of the toddler years, I suddenly decided to stop that train.

Parenting in the age of social media is tricky business. On the one hand, parents use social media to get support and connect with other parents, to ask for advice, and to seek help with parenting dilemmas. They also use it to unwind. Recent Pew Research statistics show that 74 percent of parents who use social media get support from friends, and 59 percent of parents using social media have come across useful parenting information.[2] There are clear benefits to connecting with other parents, and emotional support through some of the rocky parenting moments is just a status update away. There are even private groups that serve a wide variety of needs—some with experts on hand to answer questions and offer resources.

On the downside, kids are always on display. When they're babies and toddlers, it feels harmless enough because parents tend to share their highlight reels (you know, the holiday-card-perfect moments?), although some take a different approach and showcase their lows, re-

Parent-Teacher Conference

Use the three-minute rule! I work with a lot of tween and teen girls, and regardless of age, most of them have at least one Instagram account. I give girls the following advice about photo sharing, and I believe parents should follow the same social contract:

☐ Always ask for consent before you post a picture. It's not okay to post without checking with your friend.

☐ Gut-check it: Why that photo? What is your motivation— likes? LOLs? popularity? Will anyone be hurt and/or embarrassed by it? Will anyone wish it wasn't posted?

☐ Edit the photo, craft the witty comment, and prepare to post, but set a timer for three minutes before you hit publish. If, when the timer goes off, this still feels like a good post to share and you're 100 percent sure that no one will be hurt by it, go for it. But always do a gut check first.

Note to parents: This also goes for Facebook and Twitter posts that don't include photos. Social media shouldn't be a dumping ground for your parental frustrations.

packaged as "funny" (the screaming toddlers falling apart in the middle of the mall). As girls grow and begin to understand that many of those must-have pictures are actually being shared with other parents, the dynamic shifts in one of two possible directions: Either they get in on the posing and posting ("How many likes did my video get?") or they attempt to get away from it (they avoid photos as much as possible and might even have a meltdown if that's what it takes).

I find that it's difficult to get through to parents that we all need to be more careful about what and how much we post about our kids. What seems cute or funny to us might actually be downright embarrassing to our girls, and you can't account for what other parents will do. For example, one girl was positively furious because her mom shared a story about her on Facebook. It was a perfectly harmless story, but two other mothers shared the story with their daughters, and by the time she returned to school the following Monday, they were retelling the story to two other girls. A harmless story about silly family antics morphed into public humiliation for a sixth-grade girl because her mother couldn't resist looking for a laugh on social media. It doesn't seem fair, does it? And what kind of an example does that set?

A recent study of 249 pairs of parents and their children (between the ages of 10 and 17) showed that twice as many children as parents wanted rules on what parents can share online.[3] Kids communicated that they feel like over-sharing (particularly on Facebook) is embarrassing, and they're frustrated that parents won't stop.

It's difficult to find balance when it comes to parenting in the age

Parent-Teacher Conference

Think twice! Over-sharing, especially without talking to our children about it, has negative repercussions:

✿ Negatively affects the parent-child relationship.

✿ Creates distrust and resentment.

✿ Sets an example of over-sharing and failing to respect the boundaries of others.

of social media. When parents bury their heads in the sand and completely ignore it, their girls outpace them and don't get the guidance they need, but when parents put girlhood on display, girls can suffer negative (unintended) consequences. What my work with girls teaches me over and over again is that we have to keep trying until we figure this out. The landscape of technology is always changing, and it isn't going anywhere. It's up to us to listen to our girls and do our best to stay one step ahead so that we can guide them. It's hard enough to be a girl in the age of social media; the last thing our daughters need is Mom or Dad making it worse for them by engaging in accidental (or not) public humiliation. They need boundaries and values across all domains, including social media.

Values in Action

Do you ever use the word "values" with your kids? Of course, you *have* values and you *teach* values, but do you really break it down so that your daughter understands the core values of your family? It took me a while to realize that using that word in my own home is actually really important.

My daughter often attends my girls' empowerment groups. In one group, I asked the girls to think about their family values and come up with one to share with the group. They stared back at me, seemingly waiting for further clarification. Nine times out of 10, my daughter's hand is in the air before I can even finish a question because, well, she has to live with me so she hears this stuff on a regular basis. But even she sat in silence in that moment, hesitating to speak up. I tried a different tack. "Our family's core values are the beliefs of our family that help us make positive choices. All families are different, but all families have values." All hands in the air.

Later that day, I realized that while I talk about our core values a lot and do my best to model those values as much as humanly possible, I don't always use the words "core values." While labeling them as such doesn't change the fact that we teach them with our words and actions, it does help kids understand what it means to have and practice values. Ultimately, what we want is not simply for our kids to rattle off a bunch of rules that they've been told multiple times (Stealing is wrong! Be kind to others!), but for kids to have a deep understanding of values *and* for those values to hold a place in their identities (as in, I don't steal because I don't hurt others).

Research shows us that adolescent girls place a higher value on prosocial values than their male counterparts.[4] Where boys are more likely to consider values related to justice and fairness, girls focus on the "caring" values. They feel, think, and act in the interest of others, themselves, and their communities. That's a lovely definition, but what does it actually *mean*?

Suzy couldn't stand the thought of homelessness. Her parents were divorced, and in her travels between her parents' homes, she always passed by a small group of tents on the side of the freeway. She asked a lot of questions about those tents and the people living in them. Truth be told, she wanted to open her own home to all of the people living in tents because she felt strongly that when you have more, you help someone who has less. That was one of the core values she learned from her parents. In this case, it wasn't practical. She asked her father to help her think of a plan to make a difference. They made care packs with socks, toothpaste, toothbrushes, dental floss, and granola bars. They kept a few of them in the car and handed them out when they encountered people in need. Her internalized care value (help others in need) propelled her to take action.

Suzy is an example of a girl who engaged in social good, but I see prosocial values in girls who care for their younger siblings, help a friend struggling with peer issues, spend time with a lonely grandparent or neighbor, or take on more responsibility in the home because they know they can.

Values act as a set of internalized guidelines that girls access when they're out in the world, away from home. Values will help prepare your daughter to handle difficult moral dilemmas (tell on the friend who teased the other kid or remain loyal to the friend—honesty versus loyalty), cope with and stand up to peer pressure, and buffer her against some of the negative messages she will encounter in the media and on social media (all girls get there eventually).

It's not for me to tell you which values to focus on in your home. Values are deeply personal, and all families have their own unique value systems. What I can tell you is this: An important component of raising socially responsible girls involves teaching compassion, integrity, responsibility, respect, and empathy. I know we all mean to teach these things, and many of us even believe that we *are* highlighting the importance of these values, but kids today are hearing a much different message.

Parent-Teacher Conference

Girls with a strong value system engage in many positive behaviors:

- ❑ Are better decision makers
- ❑ Show mutual respect to others
- ❑ Are better collaborators
- ❑ Understand the importance of ethics versus simply following a list of rules
- ❑ Appreciate and embrace differences
- ❑ Are positive thinkers

The Making Caring Common team from Harvard University surveyed more than 10,000 middle and high school students in 33 schools (in various regions of the country) to determine what they value more: achievement, happiness, or caring for others. Eighty percent chose achievement or happiness over caring for others. What's more, 54 percent reported achievement and 27 percent reported happiness as their parents' top priority.[5] Achievement pressure, it appears, supersedes moral values when it comes to raising kids in a success-driven culture.

The irony, of course, is that chasing success rarely increases happiness, and achievement tends to feel good in the moment but not necessarily in the long term. Happiness is closely linked to empathy, gratitude, and helping others. While societal pressure might trigger parents to focus on achievement and success for girls, the best course of action is to work on raising socially responsible girls.

Start with Accountability

One of the biggest complaints I hear from parents of school-age girls is that their daughters lack responsibility and refuse to complete chores. When I ask parents how they instill accountability in their girls, many parents admit that with their busy schedules, they don't have the time or the energy to follow through on making their daughters accountable for their responsibilities. They want their daughters to do things like household chores, homework, and caring for pets, but they don't want to have to check up on them.

Reality check: All kids push boundaries and sometimes chores feel like punishments. Sometimes chores even *become* punishments. The best thing parents can do is set clear boundaries and expectations. But you do have to follow through and make sure your daughter is completing her responsibilities.

One mother-daughter duo fought constantly about chores. To hear

> ## Parent-Teacher Conference
>
> Give girls choices and guide them to remove the negative stig-
> ma attached to "chores" or "jobs."
>
> ✿ Alternate chores weekly or give choices.
> ✿ Show, don't tell.
> ✿ Don't nag when results aren't "perfect."

Mom tell it, her daughter wasn't doing any chores. To hear her daughter
tell it, nothing she did was good enough. In dissecting the problem with
the two of them, we uncovered the truth: Mom's standards were very
high for the abilities of an eight-year-old, and her daughter's way of
dealing with the constant criticism was to dig in her heels and avoid the
chores. We reviewed reasonable expectations, cut the chore list in half,
and Mom demonstrated how to do certain tasks (like loading the dishwasher). This relieved stress on both ends, and the daughter began completing her daily chores.

When girls take pride in responsibility, they are more likely to
help out both at home and out in the world. Instead of focusing on
what you think they aren't doing enough of, look at what they are
doing and build from there.

Self-Respect Is Important

Girls hear a lot about being respectful to adults, but they don't hear
enough about self-respect. To raise girls who have a healthy respect
for other people, parents need to talk about what it means to have self-
respect. Girls need to understand, from a very young age, that they

can set boundaries (both physical and emotional), use their voices, and say no (even to an adult).

Self-respect is closely tied to self-esteem and self-confidence, and when girls have respect for themselves, they are more likely to respect other people. This can be a hard concept to teach, but you can talk to your daughter about these things to help her develop self-respect:

- Encourage her to speak up for her own needs.
- Talk about taking pride in one's efforts.
- Do things that matter to her (this circles back to internalized values).
- Trust her to make independent choices.
- Take an interest in her hobbies and passions.

The best thing you can do to help your daughter develop self-respect is to show her that you respect her by taking an interest in her. When we attempt to engineer the lives of girls, we make them feel squashed. When we listen to and support our girls, we empower them to create their own futures.

Empower Socially Responsible Thinking

Girls love to act as helpers, and many families focus on community service projects, particularly around the holidays. That is a wonderful way to teach girls how to think about the common good, and how to put that thought into action. Whether they clean up a park or serve meals to families in need, helping the larger community connects girls to the world around them and encourages empathy on a societal level.

We also have to zoom in on the day-to-day issues of social responsibility that girls face. Girls encounter any number of moral dilemmas and complicated issues while at school or out in the community. Social responsibility might involve speaking up to a friend who litters in the park or dealing with relational aggression on the playground. Girls are inundated with situations that don't have clear answers. They have to figure out how to make socially responsible decisions within their value systems and without turning against their friends.

Mindy knew that her friend was cheating in math. Every time the teacher turned her back, Mindy's friend pulled out an answer sheet to finish her timed test without errors. Mindy struggled with this situation because she didn't want to get her friend in trouble or to lose her friend over it. "Let's try to think about why your friend is cheating in math. Is she having a hard time in school? Is the math too hard? Is she under pressure to get better grades?" We talked about the hidden problems kids face that behaviors don't always show. Then we came up with two possible solutions: Mindy could talk to her friend directly and ask her if she needs help, or she could talk to the teacher about how to help a friend who might be having a hard time at school. In the end, Mindy talked to her friend, and they went to the teacher together.

Ending Mean Girl Culture

The good girl narrative conditions girls to look for what other girls are doing wrong, and that can cause girls to turn against each other. It actually contributes to mean girl culture. When we teach girls to examine the possible clues beneath the surface, we cue them to tune in to empathy and act as helpers instead of keepers of the rules. That, right there, is a simple step all parents can take to help extinguish mean girl culture.

If we all agree to go "blame-free," to help a friend in need, and to remember that there's room for more than one at the top, we can empower young girls to grow into kind, courageous, and resilient young women—together. One thing we have to remember about the back-story of mean girl culture is that although a mean girl might be hurting another girl with her words or actions, that mean girl is also hurting inside. To put an end to this narrative, to give all girls the opportunity to succeed together, we have to stop and help all the girls who hurt, not just the ones in our own homes. We have to reach out, uplift, and work through the hard stuff as a society.

Together we can change the narrative of girlhood, but to do that we all have to enter a social contract to raise socially responsible girls. It has to begin with us.

Girls Can!

Change Agents

When my clients talk to me about problems with other girls, I always remind them of a simple choice they face each time trouble arises: They can be quiet observers or change agents. They can sit back and hope things work out, or they can find ways to create change. As simple as that might sound, it can be very hard to put into practice.

You can start by asking your daughter to define "change agent." What does it mean to be an agent of change within your peer group, your classroom, or your team? Next, ask your daughter to identify scenarios that leave her feeling stuck. Brainstorm what it would take to be a change agent. In the case of one girl feeling left out of a group, for example, your daughter can break off from the group and forge a new friendship, invite the outsider in, or encourage the whole group to extend the invitation. Role-play these scenarios together so that your daughter can find the words she might need in the moment and work through any emotions that might emerge in the process.

Community Service with Heart

Parents have a tendency to micromanage the lives of their children these days. I get it. Sometimes it's easier to make the plans and tell the kids later. The problem is that girls don't feel like they have a lot of control over their own lives. Why would they possibly strive to become leaders if they can't even choose how they want to spend their time?

Volunteering is great for girls of all ages, but it holds more meaning when the girls choose the activity. From therapy dogs and animal shelters to soup kitchens and green projects, the opportunities for getting involved with community service are endless these days. And it's never too soon to begin. Ask your daughter how she wants to contribute to making the world a better place. You might be surprised by her answer. And families that volunteer together are more connected and spend more quality time together. So get out there and support your daughter's call to action!

Separate Allowance from Chores

It's tempting to add a little incentive to household chores by merging allowance with chores, but this can backfire. The truth is that external rewards actually lower intrinsic motivation. To help girls learn the value of responsibility, they have to learn to take pride in their chores and understand that helping around the house is closely tied to "caring values." When we help each other out, we take care of one another.

If you believe your daughter needs an allowance, make it a monthly or weekly stipend that isn't tied to the daily responsibilities you expect from her. Some parents find that odd jobs around the house (or for a grandparent or neighbor) are a great motivator for allowance, and they also increase independence and competence.

Focus on Age-Appropriate Responsibilities

School-age and tween girls are very capable girls. They can manage a wide variety of responsibilities, but that doesn't mean parents should overwhelm them with household chores. Try to limit chores to a manageable load. You know what your daughter can handle, but these examples are a great place to start:

- Personal care (including hair and choosing her own clothing)
- Clearing the table
- Loading and unloading the dishwasher
- Backpack check each night
- Making snacks
- Helping with dinner preparation
- Setting the table
- Sorting and folding laundry
- Sweeping, dusting, and cleaning counters
- Caring for pets

Draw an Island of Integrity

Values and social responsibility can be difficult for younger girls to conceptualize, but I find that creating a visual to accompany discussion about these topics helps. "Integrity" is a big word that people use a lot but don't always stop to define for young children. In essence, integrity is about doing the right thing, even if you don't get acknowledged for it. But what does that mean for girls?

Have your daughter outline and color her own island while you describe what it means to have integrity. Explain that often in life you are faced with making difficult decisions and you have to make the right choice—the choice that is right for the situation, not just the choice that is right or convenient for you.

Help your daughter fill her island with prosocial behaviors that will help her visualize what it means to have integrity. Perhaps she wants to add an honesty tree, a forgiveness river, an apology hut, a helping bridge, a kindness corner, a wall of respect, and a responsibility rock. Help her understand the actions that add up to integrity by labeling her own personal integrity island. Explain that when she's faced with a dilemma and she's not sure what to do, she can look to her island for guidance and ideas.

Practice Caring

Girls need plenty of opportunities to put caring into action. It's wonderful to talk about being a caring person, but nothing beats getting out there and practicing caring.

The first step is to slow down the success train and carve out time for caring. Girls are overscheduled and overtired, and that makes it difficult to practice caring for others. The second step is to formulate some caring plans. I find that girls have excellent ideas when it comes to showing they care for others, so definitely ask your daughter to help you generate a list of caring activities. Not sure where to begin? Try a few of these:

- Be a homework helper.
- Read out loud to a toddler.
- Be a mother's helper to someone in your neighborhood.
- Deliver groceries to a neighbor.
- Bake something for someone in need of a smile.
- Pet or hold animals at a local shelter.
- Help a friend with her chores.
- Visit with an elderly neighbor or grandparent.

Organize Mother-Daughter Adventures

A great way to promote friendly competition and fun among girls is to organize monthly mother-daughter group outings. While group play is fun for girls, it also helps when girls see groups of women having fun together. When moms model healthy friendships, creating connections and building up other women, girls learn to do the same.

Bowling, go-carts, miniature golf, and kickball games are all fun group activities that get everyone moving together, but also consider creative outings like museum trips, pottery painting, and book readings (many independent bookstores have wonderful events for kids of all ages). Be sure to include others and allow the group to grow to show your daughter that friendships aren't limited and that inviting new people makes the adventure more exciting.

Pro tip: Father-daughter groups are also great fun! Let Dad get in on the bonding.

Create a Core Values Scrapbook

Talking about values can be a bit dry and repetitive, and sometimes girls tune out just when we need them to tune in. Adding a little fun and creativity to the discussion creates both a safe emotional distance from the topic (girls tell me that when parents "lecture" about values, they worry that they've done something wrong) and a fun project they can revisit later on.

As always, doing a project *with* your daughter holds more value than sitting there lecturing while she engages in the project, so roll up your sleeves and fire up the hot glue gun for this one. Ask your daughter to think about the values your family believes in (examples might include helping, caring, respecting, etc.). Start her off with an example, such as "helping someone when they fall." Ask your daughter to help you create a scrapbook of values that the whole family can use by creating a page for each value you two can come up with. Ask her for input on how to make the book engaging so that people will want to look through it. Take her ideas and run with them.

A book like this makes a great coffee table piece. Kids and parents can flip through it together or separately and be reminded of the values that are important to the family. It's a nice way to provide reminders without the constant lectures.

Social Media Checklist

It doesn't matter that your daughter isn't allowed to use social media; you still need to address it. If you use it, she's exposed to it. If she goes to school or plays on a team or engages in just about any extracurricular activity, she's exposed to it. Social media is everywhere, and the more we front-load our girls with information about it and how to use it in a socially responsible way, the better prepared for it they are when they actually encounter it. The best part is that social media can actually be very positive for girls. When they know how to use it in a socially responsible way, girls can increase their peer networks and learn new things by engaging with others online.

Come up with a checklist of socially responsible social media behavior. It might look something like this:

- ☐ I will always ask before I post about a friend.
- ☐ I won't use photos or updates to hurt or embarrass others.
- ☐ If I notice other girls doing this, I will speak up with kind words or ask for help.
- ☐ I will use social media to promote kindness and positive thoughts.
- ☐ I will think about how other people feel before I post.

Young girls will face adversity as they grow. Mean girl culture might be starting younger and younger, but it certainly isn't a new thing. Step into the past for a moment and you'll find that, for girls, the struggle to relate—to lift each other up instead of stepping all over each other—has been there a long time (Pink Ladies, anyone?). As long as we stand silent and allow this behavior to continue, girls will continue to struggle. Self-esteem will plummet, labels will continue to define our girls, and bullying will stay the course.

We can raise a generation of girls who flip the script on girlhood, though. When we take the time to connect with our girls, to *teach* them what we know about friendship, to encourage them to work together, and to support them through the ups and downs they encounter, we show them that they have the power to make positive change. When we empower them to take big risks, fail out loud, and chase their own dreams, we send a very powerful message of trust and respect. Our girls have the opportunity to put an end to mean girl culture and change the narrative of girlhood for the better, but they need us to guide them along the way.

I've seen so-called mean girls transform into kind and compassionate friends. I've seen groups of girls learn that isolating others hurts, but making room at the table benefits everyone. I've seen "quiet" girls find their voices and "bossy" girls hone their leadership skills. In nearly two decades of working with girls, I've seen a lot of positive change.

One thing I've seen over and over again, however, is that girls can't do it alone. They will confront confusing and often negative messages in the media. They will experience friendship fails that need to be addressed. They will endure great times, okay times, and downright upsetting times, but if they have the support and guidance they need, they will emerge better for it.

Go ahead and take that supporting role in the life of your girl. Lift her up when she needs lifting, and listen when she needs to talk. Encourage her to take on new challenges, and be there for her when she falls down. Model the power of friendship and unconditional support. Show your girl that she can be part of the change. Communicate that she has what it takes to make a difference.

Today's girls have what they need to change the course of girlhood for generations to come. They can be the generation of girls that finally stands together as one and shouts, "Together, girls can!"

Acknowledgments

Looking back on my youth, I realize that I was fortunate to experience friendships that stood the test of time. That's not to say we didn't have our moments back then. We certainly did. We experienced the range of emotions that girls face to this very day. Jealousy and competition among girls are not new concepts, but how girls cope with these big feelings continues to change shape. An argument between BFFs in 1984 didn't play out on Instagram or Snapchat or any other social platform. It had a beginning and an end. It probably involved some tears, yelling, and advice from Mom, but the end was always in sight. Though I weathered my fair share of storms growing up, it wasn't until I entered college that I truly understood the meaning of the term "mean girls." I'd had a good run.

Today girls are dealing with things like relational aggression and cyberbullying at much younger ages, and the fallout can affect them for years to come. They are up against a constantly changing landscape of stressors, and it's difficult for parents and schools to keep up. I put my heart and soul into this book because I am a firm believer in the power of female friendships. I know how wonderful life can be when girls and women lift each other up and stick together. I hope that this book helps some of you help your girls change the narrative of girlhood for the better.

Behind every book is a tireless group of people working together to make it the best it can possibly be. I am grateful to the many people behind the scenes who understood my vision and shaped it along the way.

To Lauren Galit, fantastic literary agent turned dear friend, thank you for your unwavering support, every e-mail and text at all hours of the day (and night), and for believing in *No More Mean Girls* from minute one. We did this together and I appreciate your guidance and friendship more than you know.

To my lovely editor, Joanna Ng, thank you for jumping at the chance to edit this book, for making me a better writer, and for keeping me grounded throughout the process.

Thank you to Sara Carder for taking me on and giving me a place in the Penguin Random House family.

Thanks to Linet Huaman for the positively beautiful cover design. It captures the soul of the book and inspires a feeling of hope for this generation of girls.

To Patricia Fogarty, my copy editor, thank you for finding every little thing and shaping my words for the better.

To Keely Platte, publicist and anxiety reducer, thank you for everything you do. You are appreciated.

I'm grateful for the early readers and supporters of this book, including: Jessica Alexander, Lisa Damour, Rebecca Eanes, Eileen Kennedy-Moore, Jessica Lahey, Jennifer Lehr, Amy McCready, Idina Menzel, Emily Roberts, Sue Scheff, Robyn Silverman, Rick Weissbourd, and Rosalind Wiseman. Special thanks to Rachel Stafford for the added encouragement and friendship along this journey.

To my dear friend and head cheerleader, Michele Borba—what can I say? Your support of this book is greatly appreciated, but your friendship means the world to me. Thank you for being you.

It's been said that strong women raise strong women. Thanks, Mom. You've been a pillar of strength since I can remember. You've pushed when I needed a push and hugged when I needed a hug. You've laughed, cried, listened, and cheered me on every step of the way. I'm grateful for your love and support.

Thank you to my big sister, Kara Corwin, for cheering me on, supporting my dreams, and countless hours of conversation about everything. No matter where life takes us, you are always a lighthouse on a foggy night.

Thank you to my little sister, Bridgid Weeks, who is always only a text away and knows exactly when to crack a joke, when to send words of support, and when to insert the perfect emoji.

Girl power isn't just for girls. No one understands this more than my brother, John Godbout. Thank you for walking by my side for the last forty-something years.

I consider myself lucky in friendship. From the sandbox to adulthood, I have always been surrounded by strong, supportive, uplifting girlfriends. Special thanks to Sarah Tonetti, the greatest friend I have ever known. There's something magical about a friend who has seen you through the best and worst and loved you just the same every step of the way. My friends on both coasts fill my heart with gratitude and I appreciate every single one of you. Thanks to Sondra Abrams, Hillary Atteridge, Emily Dolan, Cheryl Eskin, Jenny Feldon, Stacey Foster, Andrea Frickman, Nicole Greenblatt, Caitlin Heck, Stacey Kelly, Mary Elise Klug, Claire Maxwell, Tricia Murgio, Courtney Platt, Edenn Perez, Yvonne Portillo, Kirstin Strickland, and the countless other women (from all stages of my life) who lift me up. You know who you are.

Thank you to my friends at Kingswood–Oxford School and Boston College for your continued support. I hit the jackpot with my education, and I am grateful to those who shaped me along the way, and those who continue to play a role in my life.

My two little miracles, Riley Ann and Liam James, play a part in everything I do. I'm proud of you beyond words and honored to be your mom. Few things bring me as much joy and wonder in this life as watching you two grow. I love you to the moon and back (and then some).

The best things in life are a team effort. One million thanks to my husband and lifelong teammate, Sean Hurley. We can, without a doubt, reach all of our dreams . . . side by side and hand in hand.

To Brown Riley, Red Riley, Addy, Dorrit, Hannah, Violet, Ella, Mia, Sydney, and Mallory—the best advice I can pass along is this: When you lift others up, you all reach a little bit higher. When you stand up for others, you all grow a little bit stronger. And when you share your dreams with others, you all dream a little bit bigger. You each have the opportunity to make a difference in this world. All you have to do is work together.

Notes

Foreword

1   P. Paul, "The Playground Gets Even Tougher," *The New York Times*, October 8, 2010.

Introduction

1   Dove Self-Esteem Fund, *Real Girls, Real Pressure: A National Report on the State of Self-Esteem* (Englewood Cliffs, NJ: Dove Self-Esteem Fund, 2008).

2   Girls, Inc., *The Supergirl Dilemma: Girls Grapple with the Mounting Pressure of Expectations* (New York: Girls, Inc., 2006).

3   Dove Self-Esteem Fund, *Real Girls, Real Pressure.*

Chapter 1

1   L. M. Alcott, *Little Women* (New York: Random House, 1987).

2   The Ophelia Project, *Relational Aggression Overview* (Erie, PA: The Ophelia Project, 2012).

3   The Ophelia Project, *Relational Aggression Overview.*

4   S. M. Coyne, J. Archer, and M. Eslea, "'We're Not Friends Anymore! Unless . . .': The Frequency and Harmfulness of Indirect, Relational, and Social Aggression," *Aggressive Behavior* 32(4) (2006): 294–307.

5   M. Anthony and R. Lindert, *Little Girls Can Be So Mean: Four Steps to Bully-Proof Girls in the Early Grades* (New York: St. Martin's Griffin, 2010).

6   "Gossip," in Merriam-Webster's Online Dictionary (*Merriam-Webster's Learner's Dictionary*), retrieved from http://www.merriam-webster.com/dictionary/gossip.

7   "Rumor," in Merriam-Webster's Online Dictionary (*Merriam-Webster's Learner's Dictionary*), retrieved from http://www.merriam-webster.com/dictionary/rumor.

8   "Sarcasm," in Merriam-Webster's Online Dictionary (*Merriam-Webster's Learner's Dictionary*), retrieved from http://www.merriam-webster.com/dictionary/sarcasm.

9   S. K. Murnen, C. Greenfield, A. Younger, et al., "Boys Act and Girls Disappear: A Content Analysis of Gender Stereotypes Associated with Characters in Children's Popular Culture," *Sex Roles* 74 (2016): 78–91.

10 M. Tiggeman and A. Slater, "Contemporary Girlhood: Maternal Reports on Sexualized Behaviour and Appearance Concerns in 4–10 Year-Old Girls," *Body Image* 11(4) (Sept. 2014): 396–403.

11 E. Stone, C. Brown, and J. Jewell, "The Sexualized Girl: A

Within-Gender Stereotype Among Elementary School Children," *Child Development* 86(5) (Sept./Oct. 2015): 1604–22.

12 A. Durlak, R. Weissberg, et al., "The Impact of Enhancing Students' Social and Emotional Learning: A Meta-Analysis of School-Based Universal Interventions," *Child Development* 82(1) (Jan. 2011): 405–32.

13 S. Paruthi, L. J. Brooks, et al., "Recommended Amount of Sleep for Pediatric Populations: A Consensus Statement of the American Academy of Sleep Medicine," *Journal of Clinical Sleep Medicine* 12(6) (2016): 785–86.

14 *Stress in America Survey,* (Washington, DC: American Psychological Association, 2014), retrieved from http://www.apa.org/news /press/releases/stress/2013/stress-report.pdf.

15 K. Gregson, K. Tu, S. Erath, and G. Pettit, "Parental Social Coaching Promotes Adolescent Peer Acceptance Across the Middle School Transition," *Journal of Family Psychology* (March 20, 2017).

Chapter 2

1 *Girls' Attitudes Survey* (London: Girlguiding, 2016), retrieved from https://www.girlguiding.org.uk/globalassets/docs-and -resources/research-and-campaigns/girls-attitudes-survey -2016.pdf.

2 Dove Self-Esteem Project, *The Dove Global Beauty and Confidence Report* (2016).

Chapter 3

1   E. Pomerantz and K. Rudolph, "What Ensues from Emotional Distress? Implications for Competence Estimation," *Child Development* 74(2) (March 2003): 329–45.

2   E. M. Cummings, A. C. Schermerhorn, et al., "Interparental Discord and Child Adjustment: Prospective Investigations of Emotional Security as an Explanatory Mechanism," *Child Development* 77(1) (Jan.–Feb. 2006): 132–52.

3   D. Finkelhor, H. Turner, et al., *National Survey of Children's Exposure to Violence* (Washington, DC: Office of Juvenile Justice and Delinquency Prevention, CDC, 2009), retrieved from https://www.ncjrs.gov/pdffiles1/ojjdp/227744.pdf.

4   D. Munson, *Enemy Pie* (San Francisco: Chronicle Books, 2000).

Chapter 4

1   *Children, Teens, Media, and Body Image* (San Francisco: Common Sense Media, 2015).

2   D. Rosen, The Committee on Adolescence, "Clinical Report: Identification and Management of Eating Disorders in Children and Adolescents," *Pediatrics* 126(6) (Dec. 2010): 1240–52.

3   R. Spencer, J. Walsh, et al., "Having It All? A Qualitative Examination of Affluent Adolescent Girls' Perceptions of Stress and Their Quests for Success," *Journal of Adolescent Research* (Sept. 29, 2016).

4   P. Hewitt, C. Caelian, et al., "Perfectionism in Children:
     Associations with Depression, Anxiety, and Anger," *Personality and
     Individual Differences* 32 (2002): 1049–61.

5   D. Hibbard and G. Walton, "Exploring the Development of
     Perfectionism: The Influence of Parenting Style and Gender,"
     Social Behavior and Personality 42(2) (2014): 269–78.

6   J. Moser, J. Slane, B. Alexandra, and K. Klump, "Etiologic
     Relationships Between Anxiety and Dimensions of Maladaptive
     Perfectionism in Young Adult Female Twins," *Depression and
     Anxiety* 29(1) (Jan. 2012): 47–53.

Chapter 5

1   J. Morehead, "Stanford University's Carol Dweck on the
     Growth Mindset and Education," OneDublin.org, June 19,
     2012, retrieved from https://onedublin.org/2012/06/19
     /stanford-universitys-carol-dweck-on-the-growth-mindset-and
     -education/.

2   M. Borba, *Unselfie: Why Empathetic Kids Succeed in Our All-
     About-Me World* (New York: Touchstone, 2016).

3   R. Wiseman, *Queen Bees and Wannabees: Helping Your Daughter
     Survive Cliques, Gossip, Boys, and the New Realities of Girl World*
     (New York: Harmony Books, 2016).

Chapter 6

1   M. Killen, A. Rutland, et al., "Development of Intra-
     and Intergroup Judgments in the Context of Moral and

Social-Conventional Norms," *Child Development* 84(3) (May/June 2013): 1063–80.

2 V. Ornaghi, J. Brockmeier, and I. Grazzani, "Enhancing Social Cognition by Training Children in Emotion Understanding: A Primary School Study," *Journal of Experimental Child Psychology* 119 (March 2014): 26–39.

Chapter 7

1 Junior Achievement and Deloitte, commissioned by Harris Interactive, *Teen Ethics Poll* (2006).

2 J. L. Hamilton, J. P. Stange, L. Y. Abramson, and L. B. Alloy, "Stress and the Development of Cognitive Vulnerabilities to Depression Explain Sex Differences in Depressive Symptoms During Adolescence," *Clinical Psychological Science* 3(5) (Sept. 2015): 702–14.

3 *WebMD Stress in Children Consumer Survey* (July 2015), retrieved from http://www.webmd.com/news/breaking-news/kids-and -stress/20150827/stress-survey.

4 N. Crick, J. Ostrov, et al., "A Longitudinal Study of Relational and Physical Aggression in Preschool," *Journal of Applied Developmental Psychology* 27(3) (May–June 2006): 254–68.

5 S. Luthar, L. Ciciolla, A. Curlee, and J. Karageorge, "When Mothers and Fathers Are Seen as Disproportionately Valuing Achievements: Implications for Adjustment Among Upper Middle Class Youths," *Journal of Youth and Adolescence* 46(5) (May 2017): 1057–75.

6   C. Wang, Y. Xia, et al., "Parenting Behaviors, Adolescent
     Depressive Symptoms, and Problem Behavior: The Role
     of Self-Esteem and School Adjustment Difficulties Among
     Chinese Adolescents," *Journal of Family Issues* 37(4)
     (March 2016): 520–42.

7   S. Curtin, M. Warner, and M. Hedegaard, "Increase in
     Suicide in the United States: 1999–2014," *NCHS Data
     Brief No. 241* (Hyattsville, MD: National Center for Health
     Statistics, 2016).

8   D. Levinson, J. Smallwood, and R. Davidson, "The
     Persistence of Thought: Evidence for a Role of Working
     Memory in the Maintenance of Task-Unrelated
     Thinking," *Psychological Science* 23(4) (April 2012):
     375–80.

Chapter 8

1   C. Leaper and T. Smith, "A Meta-Analytic Review of Gender
     Stereotypes in Children's Language Use: Talkativeness, Affiliative
     Speech, and Assertive Speech," *Developmental Psychology* 4(6) (Nov.
     2004): 993–1027.

2   M. Sadker and D. Sadker, *Failing at Fairness: How Our Schools Cheat
     Girls* (New York: Scribner, 1995).

3   Netmums, "Sugar and Spice and Nothing Nice? Mums Are More
     Critical of their Daughters" (2007), retrieved from https://www
     .netmums.com/coffeehouse/general-coffeehouse-chat-514/news
     -current-affairs-12/479453-sugar-spice-nothing-nice-mums
     -more-critical-their-daughters.html.

Chapter 9

1 O. Lungu, S. Potvin, A. Tikasz, and A. Mendrek, "Sex Differences in Effective Fronto-limbic Connectivity During Negative Emotion Processing," *Psychoneuroendrocrinology* 62 (Dec. 2015): 180–88.

2 J. Lehr, *Parent Speak: What's Wrong with How We Talk to Our Children—and What to Say Instead* (New York: Workman, 2017).

3 M. D. Lieberman, "Social Cognitive Neuroscience: A Review of Core Processes," *Annual Review of Psychology* 58 (2007): 259–89.

4 P. A. Wyman, W. Cross, et al., "Intervention to Strengthen Emotional Self-Regulation in Children with Emerging Mental Health Problems: Proximal Impact on School Behavior," *Journal of Abnormal Child Psychology* 38(5) (July 2010): 707–20.

Chapter 10

1 J. Lahey, *The Gift of Failure: How the Best Parents Learn to Let Go So Their Children Can Succeed* (New York: Harper, 2015).

2 Center on the Developing Child at Harvard University, *Supportive Relationships and Active Skill-Building Strengthen the Foundations of Resilience: Working Paper No. 13* (Cambridge: Center on the Developing Child at Harvard University, 2015), retrieved from http://developingchild.harvard.edu/wp-content/uploads/2015/05/The-Science-of-Resilience.pdf.

3   Child Trends, *Parental Relationship Quality and Outcomes Across Subgroups*, Publication #2011–13 (Washington, DC: Child Trends, 2011).

4   R. Simmons, *The Curse of the Good Girl: Raising Authentic Girls with Courage and Confidence* (New York: Penguin Books, 2009).

5   "Dr. Dweck's Discovery of Fixed and Growth Mindsets Have Shaped Our Understanding of Learning," retrieved from https://www.mindsetworks.com/science/.

6   S. Blackwell, C. Dweck, and K. Trzesniewski, "Implicit Theories of Intelligence Predict Achievement Across an Adolescent Transition: A Longitudinal Study and an Intervention," *Child Development* 78(1) (Jan./Feb. 2007): 246–63.

Chapter 11

1   C. Cornwell, D. Mustard, and J. Van Parys, "Noncognitive Skills and the Gender Disparities in Test Scores and Teacher Assessments: Evidence from Primary School," *Journal of Human Resources* 48(1) (Winter 2013): 236–64.

2   D. Voyer and S. D. Voyer, "Gender Differences in Scholastic Achievement: A Meta-Analysis," *Psychological Bulletin* 140(4) (July 2014): 1174–1204.

3   R. Weissbourd and Making Caring Common, *Leaning Out: Teen Girls and Leadership Biases* (Cambridge: Harvard Graduate School of Education, 2015).

4   R. Weissbourd and Making Caring Common, *Leaning Out*.

5   A. Marwick and D. Boyd, "It's Just Drama: Teen Perspectives on Conflict and Aggression in a Networked Era," *Journal of Youth Studies* 17(9) (2014): 1187–1204.

6   *Change It Up: What Girls Say About Redefining Leadership* (New York: Girl Scout Research Institute, 2008).

7   R. Thompson and D. C. Zuroff, "Development of Self-Criticism in Adolescent Girls: Roles of Maternal Dissatisfaction, Maternal Coldness, and Insecure Attachment," *Journal of Youth and Adolescence* 28(2) (1999): 197–210.

8   Keds and Girls Leadership Institute, *Dare to Dream, Dare to Act: What Girls Say About Bravery*, Report of Research Findings (New York: Girls Leadership Institute, 2014).

Chapter 12

1   Wiseman, *Queen Bees and Wannabees*.

2   Pew Research Center, *Parents and Social Media Report (2015)*, retrieved from http://www.pewinternet.org/2015/07/16/parents -and-social-media/.

3   A. Hiniker, S. Schoenebeck, and J. Kientz, "Not at the Dinner Table: Parents' and Children's Perspectives on Family Technology Rules," paper presented at the Association for Computing Machinery Conference, San Francisco, CA, Feb.27– March 2, 2016.

4   A. M. Beutel and M. Kirkpatrick Johnson, "Gender and Prosocial Values During Adolescence: A Research Note," *Sociological Quarterly* 45(2) (Spring 2004): 379–93.

5   Making Caring Common Project, *The Children We Mean to Raise* (Cambridge: Harvard Graduate School of Education, 2014).

Index

About the Author

Katie Hurley, LCSW, is a child and adolescent psychotherapist, parenting expert, and writer. She is the founder of "Girls Can!" empowerment groups for girls between the ages of five and 11. Hurley is the author of *The Happy Kid Handbook*, and her work can be found in *The Washington Post*, PBS Parents, and *U.S. News & World Report*, among other places. She serves as a mental health expert for PsyCom, a Web site dedicated to mental health advocacy.

Hurley practices psychotherapy in the South Bay area of Los Angeles, where she specializes in learning disabilities, anxiety disorders, and self-esteem. She worked for The Help Group, a large nonprofit in Los Angeles, for seven years—first as a school-based therapist and later as the clinical director of Summit View School. Hurley earned her BA in psychology and women's studies from Boston College and her MSW from the University of Pennsylvania. She splits her time between Los Angeles and coastal Connecticut with her husband and two children.

Also by Katie Hurley, LCSW

"This practical and highly workable handbook details a broad selection of delightfully creative strategies for helping kids learn from play, manage strong emotions constructively, learn to forgive and empathize, build assertiveness, and accept difference in themselves and others. . . . Highly recommended for people who seek a parenting orientation rather than a method but still want a substantial toolbox of specific activities to use in understanding and connecting with their children."
—*Publishers Weekly*

"A clear and thoughtful approach to parenting your individual child. In a world full of stresses on parents and children, what a relief to read about parenting strategies that focus on my unique child, and on raising an empathetic, happy, and confident person. I would highly recommend this book for all the individual parents and their one-of-a-kind kids!"
—Idina Menzel, Tony Award–winning actress and singer